Supporting the Learner in Open and Distance Learning

CHICHESTER INST
HIGHER EDUCATIC

AUTHOR

—

TITLE

SUPPORTING

CLASS No.

371.3944

D0299992

JAN97   CIEM

Open Learning Titles from Pitman Publishing

Evaluating Open and Distance Learning by Mary Thorpe

Open Learning in Industry by Hilary Temple

Open Learning in the Mainstream edited by Mary Thorpe and David Grugeon

Key Issues in Open Learning edited by Alan Tait

Supporting the Learner in Open and Distance Learning

Edited by

Roger Mills and Alan Tait

London • Hong Kong • Johannesburg • Melbourne • Singapore • Washington DC

PITMAN PUBLISHING
128 Long Acre, London WC2E 9AN
Tel: +44 (0) 171 447 2000
Fax: +44 (0) 171 240 5771

A division of Pearson Professional Limited

First published in Great Britain 1996

© Pearson Professional Limited, 1996

British Library Cataloguing in Publication Data
A CIP catalogue record for this book can be obtained from the British Library.

ISBN 0 273 62316 8

All rights reserved; no part of this publication may be reproduced, stored
in a retrieval system, or transmitted in any form or by any means, electronic,
mechanical, photocopying, recording, or otherwise without either the prior
written permission of the Publishers or a licence permitting restricted copying
in the United Kingdom issued by the Copyright Licensing Agency Ltd,
90 Tottenham Court Road, London W1P 9HE. This book may not be lent,
resold, hired out or otherwise disposed of by way of trade in any form
of binding or cover other than that in which it is published, without the
prior consent of the Publishers.

10 9 8 7 6 5 4 3 2 1

Typeset by Phoenix Photosetting, Chatham, Kent
Printed and bound in Great Britain by Redwood Books, Trowbridge, Wiltshire.

The Publishers' policy is to use paper manufactured from sustainable forests.

Contents

Foreword

This book has been put together with the aim of providing both researchers and practitioners in open and distance learning (ODL) with accounts of the most important contemporary issues in the field of student or learner support. The book does not aim to be comprehensive, nor to offer for those new to the field any kind of starter or 'how to do it' volume. The contribution from leading experts in their field have been constructed with a view, firstly, to addressing issues which are at the cusp of change in the practice of supporting learners in ODL, and, secondly, where in our view there have been omissions in the now extensive literature.

The book opens with four major perspectives from international figures in the field. Opening the volume is a chapter by Alan Mandell and Lee Herman of Empire State College, State University of New York. The chapter refers to dimensions of openness which bridge social distance but not directly to distance education. The chapter stands at the crossroads of education in the late-modern world with its examination of the mentoring role, which represents the evolution of the teaching/learning relationship to an exploratory role for both teacher and learner in making sense in a world constructed out of distance, rupture, new insights and old oppressions.

The second contribution also registers the place of ODL in a world of social and political change, in fact one of the most momentous changes for a whole continent in a decade of momentous change in a global context: namely the demise of apartheid and ensuing reconstruction in South Africa. Reconstruction is taking place through, amongst other things, the remaking of educational structures. It is fascinating to note in Jennifer Glennie's account, from the South African Institute for Distance Education (SAIDE), that student services stand at the heart of the rebuilding of ODL in South Africa, moving away from a system which has been widely condemned for its cruel failure to provide opportunity for education in any real way—an opportunity which so many South Africans had demonstrably demanded.

The third chapter relates to the role of new technologies in ODL. Gary Miller of the Pennsylvania State University examines, from the American perspective within which the adoption of new technologies has been so dominant, what the implications are for the learner. He sees a world where learning is revolutionised and where, with careful structuring and management, the learner will have an enhanced role of enquiry within a media-rich environment. The learner's control over that environment will determine the ways in which technologies are used rather than the other way round. Miller thus sees the role of the learner and the social purpose of education as central; although technology permits change, and indeed heavily influences change, it does not in Miller's view simply impose change.

Finally, in this opening section, Ross Paul and Jane Brindley reflect on what all universities of the future may learn from the experience of distance teaching institutions. They suggest that rather than the use of new technologies, as might be expected, it is the 'softer' side of ODL that merits most attention and is likely to be of most help as campus-based universities face the overwhelming demands of the twenty-first century.

Arising out of these broad international perspectives, we have constructed three further thematic parts which, while referring to a wide range of systems and countries, are written from within the Open University (OU) UK and demonstrate the ways in which these issues are being addressed from that institution. The first of these parts, *Student support, technology and the learner*, has four contributors, and we have included our own chapters here. Alan Tait's chapter engages initially with the processes and values associated with the terms *conversation* and *community*. In a world increasingly dominated by large complex institutions within which bureaucracy and managerialism are paramount, it is argued that it is essential to support the role student services have in ODL in building and maintaining a people-friendly environment, where conversation can take place and community be created. New interactive technologies mediated by computer are seen as offering opportunities to facilitate these, in counterbalance to more formal learning structures.

Roger Mills examines the role of study centres, a facility in so many ODL systems for student meetings with tutors. Initially undertaking a comparative review of study centres, Mills goes on to ask, in the context of new technology providing more and more services through the personal computer in the workplace or in the home, what future functions the study centre can have, dependent as it is on the notion of students physically coming together.

Tony Nixon and Gilly Salmon examine in a very concrete way the working of computer conferencing with students in the OU's Business School, and posit five stages of computer-mediated communication (CMC) usage for students: namely *Access, Induction and socialisation, Seeking information and finding new pathways, Interaction,* and *Boundary shifting.* The mentoring or facilitating role is fleshed out in the CMC context, where interaction and conversation are central learning activities.

Finally in this part, CMC in Initial Teacher Training , represented by the OU's Postgraduate Certificate in Education (PGCE), is described and analysed by Jenny Leach. The chapter locates CMC within a theoretical environment influenced by social constructivism: a set of ideas which asserts the importance of contexts of shared learning and the construction of knowledge in social situations. Leach offers an account of mentoring as being central to the model of reflection on professional practice which stands at the heart of the PGCE. CMC has provided a mechanism for such activity for teachers in training who are distributed through their communities across the regions of the OU rather than gathered together within an institution in the conventional way. In contrast, Leach also provides a brief case study of teacher development in Albania, a country in a process of fundamental social change, and concludes that 'student support would seem to be a process through which understanding is both created and transformed, rather than a "provision" to be "managed"'.

The third part of this book, entitled *Recognising and supporting difference*, provides a number of issues which must be addressed in educational systems which term themselves open, and which arise naturally in the societies of the UK, South Africa, the USA, and across Europe from West to East, to name some of the regions of the world which are discussed in this book. First in this section, Diane Bailey, Gill Kirkup and Lee Taylor address, from a broad perspective, the ways in which ODL may and may not support equal opportunities, taking a critical though not unappreciative perspective on its democratising potential on an international basis.

In her own chapter, Gill Kirkup addresses the issue of gender, reviewing its use as a term in education this century. In particular she notes that ODL was thought of as particularly appropriate for women, who were more constrained in opportunity, especially from the point of view of time and place, than men. However, later research has demonstrated that women's needs have not been addressed either at the institutional level or at home (the place of study in ODL). Kirkup moves on to examine the place women need to create for themselves within the new information and communication technologies, and adopts the term 'cyborg', a being who lives and works in relation to a machine. The cyborg represents, suggests Kirkup, a potentially liberating way to avoid the dualism presented by the terms 'women' and 'men'.

Barbara Bilston and Vincent Worth offer case studies of groups of students who have been under-represented in discussions of learners in ODL. Bilston has studied older learners on a European basis. Such learners have not retired from society, although they may have done from the workplace, and form a small but significant group. They are not marked by sharp differences from other students but do have their own characteristics which merit attention. Worth examines students in prison, a small and largely overlooked group of OU learners who have had dedicated support since 1972. Worth identifies different frameworks for motivation and time within the closed environment that exists with many long-term sentences, and offers a conceptual model for understanding the background of the inmate-learner. The practice of student support within prisons is examined and, despite the difficulties, Worth is able to write of the rewards of supporting 'intellectual as well as emotional development'.

The last part is entitled *Quality, evaluation and student progress*. It is opened by Tim O'Shea, Sandra Bearman and Anne Downes, who provide a comprehensive account of the impact of the new Higher Education Quality Assurance procedures which have been introduced on a national basis, and in particular examine the ways in which a distance teaching university has engaged with QA designed principally for conventional systems. However, one of their conclusions is that distance teaching universities are in many ways better placed to operate QA procedures than conventional universities.

Judith Fage and Rosemary Mayes address the critical question of how to monitor and support student progress. This issue represents a continuity of concern as, from the beginning, the OU UK set itself the task of honouring the commitment to open access with a concomitant commitment to student success. Setting its face from the start against any complacency about drop-out which had plagued earlier models of correspondence education, the OU UK is now examining the potential which a large-scale redevelopment of computer systems will provide for monitoring and initiating supportive intervention.

The final chapter by Mary Thorpe addresses the topic of evaluation in the context of Quality Assurance. Thorpe identifies a number of ways that the external QA procedures have a negative impact on evaluation, but Thorpe also believes the renewed commitment to the collection of feedback will have some beneficial effects on institutional and practitioner research.

We would like to conclude by saying that the book arises on our part out of a shared commitment of over more than 20 years to student support, during which period the profile of the services needed to support learners in the form of advice, tutoring and counselling, decentralisation of services, the management of study centres, and IT systems to support the monitoring of student progress, has risen considerably both within the UK, within Europe, and indeed on a global basis. Working for the Open University UK as we do, we have had the advantage of being located in an institution of which it can with justice be said that it established student support in ODL on a modern basis with the start of teaching in 1971. The practice and study on an international basis has been assisted, we would like to believe, by the Cambridge International Conferences on Student Support in ODL, of which the seventh is to take place in 1997. Certainly our awareness of international developments has been substantially enhanced at these meetings, as well as on working visits to other institutions around the world. Our own identification of themes and issues of concern owes much to the colleagues we have worked with in those forums, and whose experience and wisdom we would like to acknowledge here.

Roger Mills
Alan Tait

Cambridge, 1996

About the authors

Diane Bailey

Diane Bailey is currently Director of the Open University's Equal Opportunities Unit, having worked for several years as a Senior Counsellor in the OU's East Anglian Region. After research in nineteenth-century literature, she taught extensively in higher education, including teaching on schemes for women returners and students from non-traditional backgrounds. She has also worked as both a practitioner and a researcher in educational guidance for adults, particularly in relation to open and distance learning, including three years on the UK's Open Tech Programme. She has contributed to distance courses on adult guidance and has published work on career counselling, women's learning and open learning and guidance.

Sandra Bearman

Sandra Bearman has a degree in Education from the University of London and joined the Open University as an administrator in 1978, working initially in the University's Residential Schools Office. Other posts she has held have been in the Office for Students with Disabilities and the Arts Faculty. She joined the Quality Assurance team as Assistant Secretary (Quality Assessment) in June 1993.

Barbara Bilston

Barbara Bilston was a lecturer in gerontology before joining the Open University. She is currently Regional Education and Training Manager in the School of Health and Social Welfare. She spent some time as a social worker in the field of gerontology and has been an active member of both the Open University Older Students Research and the European Older Students Research Group.

Jane Brindley

Jane Brindley is an experienced distance educator having played a leading role in the development of counselling services for students at Athabasca University in Alberta, Canada. She was Director of the Edmonton office of

Athabasca University and has undertaken work in the East Anglian Region of the Open University of the United Kingdom. She is currently a doctoral student at the University of Ottawa, Canada.

Anne Downes

Anne Downes has a degree in English from the University of Leeds, and joined the Open University as an administrator in 1975, working initially in the University's north-west Regional Centre based in Manchester, where she was involved in the provision of services to students and tutorial staff. In 1985 she moved to the University's headquarters in Milton Keynes, where she has held a number of administrative posts. She joined the Quality Assurance team as Secretary for Quality Assurance in February 1995.

Judith Fage

Judith Fage joined the Open University of the UK in 1977 after working as a BBC producer on further education and OU programmes. She began as a tutor-counsellor on the Arts foundation course before becoming a Senior Counsellor in the London Region in 1982, since when she has also completed a four-year secondment as Assistant Director in the OU UK's Regional Academic Services. She is particularly interested in policy and systems development in the areas of student support and guidance, having been a member of Information Systems strategy and development teams, as well as key policy working groups on admissions services and on the development of counselling policy. She has also conducted practitioner research into provision for preparation for study and for vocational guidance, including an international survey of distance education. She was for five years the OU's academic consultant for its Open Advice TV programmes. Her work has been influenced by study trips to Canada, the United States and Australia. Her most recent project has been involvement in the production of a CD-ROM programme describing student support in the UK OU, which was presented at the ICDE conference in July 1995.

Jennifer Glennie

Jennifer Glennie was born and raised in Gauteng Province, South Africa. She worked for 15 years for the SACHED Trust, a prominent anti-apartheid education organisation which pioneered a range of educational programmes (including several distance education programmes) for black adults. As head of department, deputy and acting director, she played a central role in resisting the numerous attacks made on the organisation by the apartheid state, and in developing it to become the largest and most influential in the country. In 1995, she became the first executive director of the South African Institute for Distance Education (SAIDE). As a small, non-government organisation committed to an open learning approach, SAIDE works with existing and new distance education programmes to strive for democratic access to quality learning opportunities. Jennifer holds an honours degree in Mathematics from the University of the Witwatersrand, and a master's from the University of London.

Lee Herman

Lee Herman is mentor/co-ordinator at the Auburn, New York location of Empire State College and co-founder of the ESC Mentoring Institute. He has worked with adult students for the past twenty years, and has tried during that time to understand and practise the ideas presented in his chapter. For many years, Lee Herman and Alan Mandell have collaborated on developing the meanings of student-centred education, through conversation, teaching, presentation and writing.

Gill Kirkup

Gill Kirkup is a Senior Lecturer in Educational Technology in the Institute of Educational Technology at the Open University UK. She is involved in course development and evaluation and sometimes as a materials author. Her particular interests are: the relationship between gender and technology, the role of women in distance education, and the use of information and communication technologies in distance education. She has published extensively in these three areas, in both books and academic journals. She plans to do more international comparative work with colleagues across the world. When she isn't trying to work out where the 'ON' button is on the latest computer she's struggling with, she is learning ballroom dancing.

Jenny Leach

Jenny Leach taught in secondary schools in East Africa, Scotland and London before becoming an advisory teacher in London. She has worked extensively with teachers on a range of professional development issues, both in Britain and abroad, and with students in initial teacher education. Three years ago she joined the Open University's School of Education, where she has been working as staff tutor for the East Anglian Region and more recently as academic co-ordinator for English with the OU's new Postgraduate Certificate in Education course team.

Alan Mandell

Alan Mandell is Associate Dean and Director of the Metropolitan Center of State University of New York/Empire State College. He has been an administrator and mentor for more than twenty years, and has published reviews and essays on adult learning including *Portfolio Development and Adult Learning* (with Elana Michelson) published by the Council for Adult and Experiential Learning.

Rosemary Mayes

Rosemary Mayes worked for the UK's Council for National Academic Awards from 1981 until 1992. During that time she had a number of roles but a common emphasis in all of them was, as a user, on the design and implementation of computer systems which would not only improve mass record-keeping but also the quality and flexibility of outputs and especially management information. Since joining the Open University of the UK in 1992, she has become involved in the major redevelopment of the University's computer systems and served as Project Manager from 1994 to 1995 for that part of the redevelopment related to the provision of study support. In her current role as Assistant Secretary of Student Services in the London Region of the Open University, she has overall responsibility for the provision of all services to enquirers, applicants and students and an important aspect of this role is to ensure that mechanisms for monitoring student progress are set up and regularly reassessed to ensure continuing effectiveness.

Gary Miller

Dr Gary Miller is Assistant Vice President for Distance Education at the Pennsylvania State University, where he heads one of the nation's largest distance education programmes. Dr Miller holds a Doctor of Education degree in Higher Education from Pennsylvania State. He is the author of *The Meaning of General Education: The Emergence of a Curriculum Paradigm* (Teachers College Press, 1988) and contributed a chapter to *Contemporary Issues in American Distance Education* (Pergamon Press, 1990). He has presented numerous papers on undergraduate curriculum, continuing education, and distance education issues at national and international conferences. He serves on the editorial board of *The American Journal of Distance Education* and the Program Committee of the Standing Council of Presidents for the International Council for Distance Education. He recently chaired the Commission on Principles of Good Practice in Continuing Education for the National University Continuing Education Association. Prior to his current position, Dr Miller served as Associate Vice

President for Program Development at the University of Maryland University College and as Executive Director of the International University Consortium.

Roger Mills

Roger Mills is Director of the East Anglian Region of the Open University with responsibilities for over 14 000 students and 800 teaching and counselling staff. He is supported in the East Anglian Regional Centre in Cambridge by 96 academic, administrative and support staff. He has particular interests in the field of student support, staff development and management in open and distance education. He has undertaken consultancies in India, South Africa, Australia and most recently Slovenia. With Alan Tait, he was the founder of the Cambridge conferences which have taken place biennially since 1983.

Tony Nixon

Dr Tony Nixon currently works for the Open University as a Technology Staff Tutor in the East Anglian Region. He has developed a continuing interest in Computer Mediated Learning through his experience as a Staff Tutor and Course Tutor for the Open University. The Technology Faculty has several courses which utilise this medium. He did his first degree and doctorate in Physics at the University of York and has recently been involved in developing a new approach to the teaching of algebra, which has now been developed into a piece of teaching software.

Tim O'Shea

Professor Tim O'Shea has a BSc in Mathematics and Experimental Psychology from the University of Sussex and a PhD in Computer Science from the University of Leeds. He has carried out research on the educational applications of computers at the universities of Texas at Austin and Edinburgh. He joined the Open University in 1978 where he founded the Computer Assisted Learning Research Group and worked on a range of educational technology research and development projects. His best known publication is *Learning and Teaching with Computers*, co-authored with John Self, which has been translated into various languages including Japanese and German. His other publications include eight books, more than a hundred articles and the six-part BBC series 'The Learning Machine'. He is past Chair of AISB, the Artificial Intelligence Society, and past President of the Psychology section of the British Association for the Advancement of Science. His current research projects include work on portable computing in education, the use of very large electronic whiteboards in group decision-making (with the Rank Xerox Cambridge Research Centre), making formal methods more accessible (with Richard Bornat of Queen Mary Westfield College), ordering effects in human learning and the design of interactive learning environments for hard mathematical and scientific concepts. The Open University awarded him a Personal Chair in Information Technology and Education in 1987 and in 1994 appointed him Pro-Vice-Chancellor for Quality Assurance and Research.

Ross Paul

Dr Ross Paul is President of Laurentian University, Ontario, Canada, a middle-sized university serving north-eastern Ontario, with a strong distance education programme. He has published many papers in the field of open and distance education and is the author of *Open Learning and Open Management*. He is the International Council for Distance Education (ICDE) Vice-President for North America and a member of the planning team for the 1997 world conference at Pennsylvania State University.

Gilly Salmon

Gilly Salmon is a Senior Lecturer with the Open University's School of Management. She works as Group Regional Manager from the OU's Regional Centre in Cambridge with responsibility for tutoring and student support on the MBA. She has been a user, student and more recently teacher of Computer Mediated Conferencing since the mid-1980s. Her research interests include the use of computerised Cognitive Mapping. She is currently undertaking doctoral research in the area of Computer Mediated Learning with the Division of Education at Sheffield, England. Her teaching areas include Creative Management, Managing Change and the issues in Europe surrounding the opportunities and constraints for women managers.

Alan Tait

Alan Tait has worked for the Open University UK since 1974 in a variety of roles in the field of student support, at the University's headquarters in Milton Keynes and as Senior Counsellor in the Cambridge Regional Centre, and has worked widely in Europe. He was Planning Executive of the Budapest Platform (the forerunner of the European Distance Education Network) and Head of European Student Services Development from 1990 to 1993. With Roger Mills, he has jointly organised the Cambridge international conferences on open and distance learning. His main interests are in the study and practice of open and distance learning, particularly on an international basis, and he has carried out policy studies and acted as a consultant in a range of contexts. Since 1989 he has been Editor of the international journal *Open Learning* and he has recently joined the OU School of Education as Staff Tutor in the Cambridge Regional Centre.

Lee Taylor

Lee Taylor is a senior manager at the Open University. As Director of Equal Opportunities at the OU, she led the planning project and initial implementation of the OU's EO action plan from 1989 to 1994. She was founder Chair of the UK Equal Opportunities Higher Education Network, and is a member of the national Commission on Career Opportunities. In 1992 she held a Fulbright Fellowship to research comparative practice on EO in higher education in the US. She writes and speaks widely on EO issues, and is particularly interested in EO and culture change.

Mary Thorpe

Mary Thorpe has over 20 years' teaching and research experience in distance education at the Open University. She has published extensively in areas of adult learning, evaluation, approaches to reflection and course development. She is Director of the Institute of Educational Technology at the OU UK.

Vincent Worth

Vincent Worth joined the Open University in 1973 as a Staff Tutor in Social Science. During that period, as well as his full-time faculty and regional work, he maintained his interest in teaching by tutoring a range of courses. In the 1970s and 1980s he spent more than three years helping to develop the Centre for Distance Learning, Empire State College, New York, directing the Centre for some of that time. He began prison tutoring and counselling work in the late 1980s and presently continues these roles. Since early retirement in 1990 he has also acted as a prison liaison person in the London Region of the Open University, a role that entails working with education departments in eight London prisons that participate in the Home Office/Open University Scheme, advising staff and students, briefing tutors and undertaking administrative tasks. He has had a long-term interest in criminology and the place of education, especially higher education, in the prison world. Since early retirement he has himself enrolled as an Open University student and taken courses in computing and in the arts.

Part 1

Perspectives on change

1

From teachers to mentors: Acknowledging openings in the faculty role

Alan Mandell and Lee Herman

As the demand that people learn more grows, the time they have for learning lessens. As the demand for learning grows, what constitutes important, reliable knowledge becomes more doubtful. And as the amount, diversity, and availability of information increases, the ability of people to assimilate it is taxed if not overwhelmed. These problems, in turn, pose both practical and normative problems for students and faculty.

What does it mean to be a student when one may not have time to attend university in the traditional way, but nonetheless needs a university education and credentials in order to succeed? What does it mean to become educated when the very definition of important knowledge is shifting and contended, and when the sheer amount of seemingly important knowledge is too great to comprehend?

A set of parallel questions increasingly confronts university faculty, who find themselves dealing with issues for which their expertise never prepared them. How and how far, for example, should faculty accommodate students whose attention and time are not primarily focused on school? In our uncertainty about the constitution of a meaningful education, how can we counsel students who are asking us what they need to learn? What should be our expertise in a world in which the dependence on specialised knowledge is a practical necessity, but in which the aspiration for stable general knowledge is equally important? And how can we search for coherence and for a role that guides people towards achieving this sense of the whole, acknowledging that the search itself is both precious and quixotic?

In this chapter we seek to describe this search in terms of the discovery of three 'openings' in the definition of the faculty role. These openings are about faculty learning to acknowledge that there is intellectual authority in what their students say about gaining access to the university, finding comfort there, and about designing a meaningful curriculum. We call them openings because each requires an unfolding of usual faculty responsibilities. Each also tends to open historically closed institutions of higher learning to more and more diverse students. And, as one moves through these openings, it becomes clear that students are increasingly being understood as collaborators in the design and implementation of their own learning. In other words, open learning as we present it in this chapter can be seen as both an exercise in and an agitation for participatory and egalitarian democracy.

This progression—from faculty as teacher-scholars to faculty as counsellors, to faculty as what we call mentors—is neither simple nor historically literal. Indeed, with the move through each opening, there is tension, conflict and real uncertainty about the legitimate needs of students, the authority of faculty and the proper functions of the university. At each stage there is potential for loss as well as for gain. Also, in explicating these openings, we are attempting to evoke a set of role images that emerge in different ways, at different times, and in different institutions. We believe these images can also serve as a critical template through which to judge what we do and to open ourselves to imagining new ways of both teaching and learning.

1 Access: Faculty as teachers

University students are not only older, they are also more likely to work as wage-earners, spouses and parents (Kegan, 1994). Moreover, the time (at least in the US) that they devote to these duties has actually increased on average over the past twenty years across gender and class (Schor, 1991). Yet these very activities, especially those in workplaces outside the home, demand more learning and credentials than ever before (Sheckley *et al.*, 1993; Collins, 1991). Universities have responded to this market (particularly since their traditional pool of 18–22-year-old students has decreased) by seeking to respond to the needs of adult learners. For example, courses and lectures are scheduled more conveniently; there are more opportunities for independent distance learning; curricular materials are more 'user-friendly' and self-guiding; and, in an increasing number of institutions, learning acquired outside of the university is identified and academically legitimated (Fugate and Chapman, 1992).

For many institutions, providing access for these students has become central to their mission. And for thousands and thousands of students in North America, Europe, and increasingly around the world, such access is an invaluable means of acquiring qualifications they use and learning they cherish (Daloz, 1986; Lamdin, 1989).

Faculty members, who traditionally regard themselves as conservators of valued learning and creators of new knowledge, may well ask themselves if their responsibilities ought to change and, if so, how, in this unstable and demanding educational environment. These questions can be distracting for a professor who sees that the time which was once devoted to lectures and research is now consumed by services to people whose purposes are more pragmatic than intellectual and whose academic preparation might not suit traditional assumptions. To these doubts may be added a cynical yet reasonable suspicion that the university is not seeking to serve these students with intellectual care or to promote the promise of democracy, but is largely eager to position itself favourably within an increasingly entrepreneurial and competitive market.

Ironically, on the other side, students may be asking themselves comparable questions. Provided with more accessible options, students might justifiably wonder whether their learning activities are truly alternative or merely second rate. To what extent do 'user-friendly' study guides, for example, genuinely enable students to be serious, self-directed learners? Or, do those study materials pander to the pragmatism of having to gain an academic qualification expeditiously? Is the pride and excitement in having earned a university degree shadowed by a thought that the achievement of the adult student is viewed by the academy with some condescension? Indeed, wouldn't even these new learners, if given the opportunity, choose to have the traditional university experience?

These are all credible doubts. But, in response to both sets of questions, we believe that opening access to higher education does not dilute its substance or richness. Opening higher education to a larger, older and more diverse student population has two distinct purposes. First, access serves the practical goals of a more productive workforce and an expanded market for university services and qualifications (Sheckley *et al.*, 1993). Second, we should agree that a more learned and thoughtful citizenry, including faculty as well as students, becoming informed of its own diversity, is the best hope all of us have for creating a more civil, just, and democratic society in a tumultuous, stratified and confusing world (Bellah *et al.*, 1991; Barber, 1992).

Indeed, this hope for an informed and thinking body politic must be the heart of higher education, even if historically the practices of the university rest on a profound elitism. The authentic and essential ends of learning—a life that is examined, fair, meaningful and also sensitive to beauty—require sharing. This learning is inherently communicative; it requires common enquiry and unlimited propagation. Far from being elitist, this notion of learning rests simply on the assertion that, as Aristotle said, all human beings by nature desire to know, and the more Socratic view that no-one finally knows and that the very possibility of knowing expands with a community of enquirers. It is thus entirely consistent with the highest aspirations of the mind to seek to open educational access and to expect that the truly difficult problems that enterprise poses can be solved. In fact, the ideals of educational institutions can be practised through our very struggle to reform those institutions to make them more accessible. By serving both the practical idea of access as the means to success and the noble idea of access as the sharing of knowledge, the university contributes to the expectation of a democracy whose citizens are both informed and prosperous.

Such a shift, however, calls for change in the assumptions we make about the faculty role and its support system. Questions like these then arise: What would faculty have to learn in order to make the university more accessible? What new institutional procedures, policies and systems should be created and accepted?

At its core, a more accessible university means changing the traditional ways of delivering the curriculum. For example, staff have strong assumptions (enforced by university and sometimes legal mandates) about attending lectures, fulfilling 'contact hour' quotas per course, and finishing assignments by the end of term. Yet we too easily conflate these requirements, which have often become comfortable arrangements for us, with standards of academic substance and intellectual quality (Coulter and Herman, 1992). In doing so, we neglect to question our assumptions or change the practices built upon them. We believe that making the university more accessible means challenging those routines which we equate with true learning and with our roles as teachers and scholars. In a new system, accommodating students who can't attend on-campus lectures or be enrolled regularly or full-time could mean teaching at night or at weekends, using electronic conferencing and video/satellite transmissions, or supporting an individual student's independent learning. It also means changing our habits of thought and perceptions of student needs and commitment to learning. Opening access need not be a poor substitute for what we customarily think of as authentic higher education. Rather, it is an invitation to think critically about our dependence on internalised rules, protocols and forms of academic work and to create new models of studying and learning that we can imaginatively and responsibly offer to our students. In order to create this practical and psychological opening, we must also look at our assumptions about our own authority. We must consider the tensions which arise between accommodating student access claims and our traditional prerogatives, including the leisure we need to pursue the very scholarship from which our students seek to benefit.

One of the most important attributes of the faculty's professional identity is to control the time and place of curriculum delivery. By and large, we expect students to come to us—our offices, our classrooms, our laboratories—at times we establish. Significantly increasing access means extending to students choices about these matters, which in all likelihood will affect our guild-like liberty. For example, some students may choose to take a course in the evening; others, at the weekend. Someone must offer that course in the evening; another, at the weekend. Some students may choose to learn without being physically present on campus at all, via electronic mail, for example. Some faculty members must learn to teach in the peculiar epistolary style of that form of communication, including learning new habits of timely and pertinent response. Some students may choose to carry out their research without physically searching the library shelves. Someone must arrange for and teach facility in electronic searching (Lanham, 1993). Indeed, many students taking the same subject may not even be on the same timetable. For one student a 'course' might begin and end at different dates than for others; some might proceed faster, others more slowly; and some might have substantial interruptions along the way. For all these options, staff must make themselves variously available. Certainly, all of these possibilities change the image and routines of 'the professor' as an august presence to whom students are expected to defer.

Do these means of access require a surrender of appropriate faculty authority? To some degree, in this 'opening', we do invite students to participate in deciding the pace and setting of their learning, and to begin to become collaborators. In this way, there is a first instance of faculty, not so much surrendering their authority, but learning to share it. In our usual patterns of work, students may have already asked us to teach a course at a distance, to extend it beyond the time normally scheduled, to respond helpfully and in a timely manner to questions they pose via electronic mail. But we have probably understood such requests only as exceptions to our routines. That is, they are opportunities we occasionally allow students when, on an individual basis, they can make a case for them. Opening access requires that we adopt a different assumption: that students have as much right to choose the time and place of their learning as the university does. Thus, effectively matching student learning and faculty teaching becomes something of a negotiation, and academic authority becomes more pluralistic as the organisation of learning now becomes determined by both students and faculty.

In this first opening of the faculty role, through access, students no longer have to adapt so entirely to the university. They can expect that it will also adapt to them. This requires yet another new assumption: that we learn to expand our ability to communicate and to listen carefully to student expectations. It is exactly these expansions of the faculty role that involve us in becoming aware of and re-examining what we have assumed to be the very conditions of our being serious scholars and our students being serious learners. Practising our new understanding creates a momentum that turns our attention to our students' need for meaningful academic supports and moves us towards dialogue with them about their interests, their goals and their learning. Simple access is just a first opening to yet further elaboration of the faculty role, and another occasion for the critical enquiry which is the hallmark of the life of the mind.

2 Friendly assimilation: Faculty as counsellors

The principle that the university should adapt to students as well as the other way around extends to areas of academic life beyond 'access'. If faculty make the time, place and modes of curriculum delivery more accessible, they are simultaneously opening the university to new kinds of students. They will be opening themselves to listen to students in new ways. It is logical, if not inevitable, that our range of professional interactions with them will also increase. Such conversations involve us in paying attention to aspects of students' lives which we have probably been accustomed to think of as being peripheral to our expertise and professional engagement. These include how students feel about being in school, their attitudes and assumptions about learning, the links and interferences between studying and working, the tensions between their identities as accomplished family and community members and their inexperience as students, and the gap between worldly competences and unfamiliar academic skills. For a faculty member to converse as a matter of professional habit with students about these matters is at once intimate and academic. Just as the first opening allows the faculty to accommodate the demand and need for access to what we already do, friendly assimilation means expanding our repertoire by imaginatively integrating the seemingly diverse realms of teaching and counselling into a new faculty role.

If we agree that the university should become more open at its thresholds, shouldn't we also agree to provide more help to students once they are inside? More students will be arriving who are 'non-traditional'. Not only will their other commitments and priorities prevent them from dwelling on campus and partaking of traditional modes of teaching; other traditions of academic life may well be unfamiliar to them: reading with intensity and exclusive concentration, writing in the expository academic style, doing library research, or absorbing oneself in concepts and information which may be only directly or remotely connected to one's immediate interests. These and associated ways of acting comprise the traditions of academic 'culture'. A 'non-traditional' student is one to whom that culture is unfamiliar, alien or even frightening. Its customs

8

may not be harmonious with the traditions, histories and ways of learning the student brings to his/her new study experiences.

There is a continuum of labels, from 'non-traditional' through 'special', 'underprepared' and 'unprepared', used to roughly categorise these students. All are heavily value-laden and reflect a range of academic attitudes to new and/or newly acknowledged populations of students. It is important to be cautious about drawing neat generalisations about these students. However, it is a fact that opening the university both honours the interest of some students in having the university more comfortably suit their complex lives, and brings into the university other students who would previously have been altogether excluded by such factors as age, race, and/or class. These claims of accommodation are in themselves diverse and complex, but in response to their collective presence, universities have sometimes devised specialised services and programmes: counselling, learning skills centres, remedial tutoring, non-credit-bearing developmental courses, and peer support groups, among others. And a whole range of professionals and paraprofessionals have evolved to deliver these services: tutors, advisers, counsellors, and learning specialists. Following the normal academic hierarchy, these services are usually delivered by people accorded a lower status than faculty. Even more important, although the services they provide may well be essential for academic success, the actual delivery of those services is typically not integrated into what is still judged as 'real' academic work (Maxwell, 1981). Professors of literature and linguistics are not normally expected to teach 'developmental expository writing'. Professors of social research are not expected to teach basic library skills. Professors of psychology, sociology or cultural studies are not normally expected to help their students learn to assimilate the habits of academic life or to become effective advocates for their particular needs. Clearly, while new layers are added, the hierarchical division of academic labour remains largely intact.

There are some good reasons for such segregation. Perhaps understanding and teaching the skills of assimilation is sufficiently complex and demanding as to require separate specialists. And it is at least plausible to argue that the time and energy we take to teach students 'developmental' skills and to adjust to the emotional, social and intellectual demands of academic life drain the attention we can give to enhancing our own scholarly expertise and presenting it to our more 'prepared' students. These claims cannot be ignored, especially if we are to insist that the students within this opened university shall have the benefit of the same academic riches as their once more privileged predecessors.

But what if 'special' students are no longer special? What if the non-traditional student population becomes the demographic norm (or at least close enough to it that the attentions the university must provide to retain them must be central rather than peripheral)? Or, from a more idealistically intellectual perspective, what if the same commitment to the life of the mind that promotes increased access also requires that the scholarly faculty look at dimensions of student experience we had never carefully considered, and that we integrate those aspects into our understanding of what it means to teach, and into our basic identity as faculty members?

Thus, the tradition of stratifying academic labour is an impediment to meaningfully responding to student needs. Yet the solution is by no means self-evident. Faculty members who take on this more complexly responsive identity are not freed from discomfiting questions about priorities for distributing their attention, for sustaining their scholarship and for maintaining academic standards.

An institutional parallel could be instructive. Some American corporations seeking a more diverse workforce (whether for legal, political, demographic and/or economic reasons) have encountered a similar issue and have responded with so-called 'mentoring programmes'. Personnel achieving entry-level professional and managerial positions through increased access often find themselves unfamiliar with 'corporate culture'. So that they might succeed, once inside, they are assigned a 'mentor': a senior member of the organisation intended to be a role model, to teach all the skills, manners and expectations necessary for success but rarely covered by the job description, one's prior training or academic preparation. It becomes part of the mentor's or counsellor's duties, in addition to or sometimes partially in lieu of his/her normal managerial or professional responsibilities, to listen to the individual and personal concerns of a 'protégé' and to impart to him/her the organisational culture. Some universities are also engaging senior professors to be counsellors to new, untenured staff, especially those from populations not traditionally well represented among academic professionals (see *Proceedings of the International Mentoring Association Conference*, 1994).

In this second opening of friendly assimilation, we are envisioning an expansion of the faculty role to include this kind of non-traditional teaching. Of course many teachers genuinely interested in their students already serve as more than presenters of the curriculum and strictly academic advisers. They listen, empathise, and counsel. They craft assignments with their students' strengths and limitations in mind. They spend more time with individuals or small groups outside of scheduled class hours. They add to their repertoire an ability to respond to questions, concerns, stories and ideas that have typically been viewed as interruptions and not been heard in the official world of academia (Rose, 1988). They do their best to help sometimes confused, uncomfortable but otherwise promising students find a place in university life.

We are suggesting, however, that this work can become a part of the normal faculty function and, moreover, that it should be available not simply to exceptional students or to those we might select from time to time based on our subjective responses to them, but that faculty should learn as a matter of course, not just as discretionary on-the-job development, to respond to and comprehend the aspects of their students' lives and the particularities of their experiences and needs, which pertain to their becoming successful learners (Astin, 1992). This means that to some degree the skills of counselling become integrated into those of teaching. If we as teachers can imagine our own hesitancies, fears and distances from new and demanding situations, we can actively see the world from the perspective of our students. This is, in part, a matter of respect for them (Kegan, 1994). Such respect also extends the scholarly enterprise of understanding the human experience, specifically how we learn and how we judge what is important to learn.

How do faculty responsibilities change when we pay attention to students in this way? Certainly this enriched role can be experienced as an 'add-on' or as a distraction from the duties of normal scholarship, curriculum preparation and academic teaching. Faculty might also worry that they are being asked, as well, to act like therapists for the problems their students experience adapting to academic life. Instead, the second opening offers a new moment of collaboration which extends the experience of students and faculty sharing authority in matters of the pace and schedule of learning. More than increasing the accessibility of the university, we and our students now reveal through this second opening new intellectual opportunities.

In fact, the very impediments to learning that students experience can be translated into starting points for new academic work. The commitments in our everyday roles as parents, workers and citizens, which are often experienced as interferences to study, can become topics of enquiry. What was felt as a blockage to learning becomes an occasion to redefine and expand it. For example, students concerned about having insufficient time for study (even in a more flexible academic schedule) could take their problem as an object of study. They could learn about time management skills. They could enquire why some contemporary cultures, devoted, as they advertise themselves, to recreation, in fact provide so little leisure for their members (Schor, 1991). Or, they could explore how other cultures have created different rhythms of work, learning and play. So too, students frustrated that the normal means of acquiring and demonstrating academic learning seem to obscure rather than reveal their abilities and insights might, with faculty help, transform this experience into a topic for study. Thus, the meaning of effective learning becomes not ancillary to but an essential part of the learning enterprise itself. For example, students can learn that there is a range of learning modes, and can explore topics such as cognitive research about multiple intelligences (Gardiner, 1993), ways of knowing (Belenky *et al.*, 1986) and learning styles (Anderson, 1988; Kolb, 1976). Both faculty and students can become more attentive to the variety of materials and techniques which play to strengths but look after weaknesses.

Even deeply troubling issues in students' experiences and in the entire university community, such as racial and gender intolerance, can become a focus of learning. Students and faculty can examine together the origins and power of their own prejudices. They can learn theories and practices of conflict resolution. They can apprehend and learn to work with the tension between celebrating diversity and practising pluralism. And they can strengthen such academic skills as research, expository writing, and critical reading by exercising them upon the concerns of their daily lives which affect their studies. The faculty person as counsellor thus helps students tease out the assumptions behind their feelings and opinions, thus transforming them into important matters of enquiry. In this way students gain important practice by working with ideas, struggling with problems and questions which they have previously avoided or kept to themselves and which faculty have deemed 'merely' personal. Both students and faculty thereby discover that these experiences normally beneath the notice of the academic disciplines are really locations of significant learning.

In all of these situations, the faculty role is to devise learning opportunities hospitable to students' experiences rather than to expect that students will entirely adapt their intellectual expectations and academic habits to institutional policies and procedures. By listening to students in this way, faculty members open themselves to new collaborative possibilities. They counsel students about transforming discomfort, anger, and fear into mutually resonant and academically rich questions. Simple 'listening to' becomes collaboration when we seek not only to hear sympathetically our students' concerns, but to understand them as constituting new points to study and explore together (Forester, 1989). Student experiences thus become not merely relevant to supporting learning but central to provoking the very process and content of academic work.

3 Student-centred education: Faculty as mentors

Faculty members who do become counsellors and sustain the scholarly intensity which probably impelled them to become academics in the first place will, in all likelihood, find themselves confronting fundamental questions about the meaning of higher learning. That is, as we listen to our students in these new ways and learn to apprehend new objects of academic attention, we will begin to think beyond the customary structuring of knowledge. Faculty will, for example, often recognise that students are compellingly articulating their own questions: ones which do not necessarily fit well within our established courses or the existing curriculum. For such students, the omnipresent listing of required studies has little intrinsic interest and less meaning, except as external structures whose demands must be met before a needed degree is granted.

There is a polite, effective, and quite common way for us to handle the differences between student interests and faculty expectations while maintaining our authority. We ask students to wait. We explain that while their questions are 'interesting', they, as beginning students, for lack of the proper foundation, are not yet ready to pursue them. Though this is a condescending response, it is entirely consistent with the belief that a clearly demarcated progression of skill, knowledge and wisdom is necessary for proficiency. One must know how to use certain tools to build a table, know the law before one can argue a case, or be mature before one should be a parent; that is, we must have learned certain bodies of knowledge to pose and pursue informed, intelligent questions. Indeed, this basic assumption legitimates the value and authority of the expertise—the scholarly contents, methods and orderings within each discipline—that we cherish.

But the actual work of sincerely entering into dialogue with our students suggests that this traditional response does not precisely fit the questions they ask, nor does it adequately capture the spirit of their curiosity. Students rarely want immediately to study what is obviously beyond their current preparation: be it the style of Flaubert without knowing French, nuclear energy without physics, adolescent behavior without theories of human development, or the AIDS pandemic without research methods. Rather, students are eager for the chance to make a curriculum out of their everyday experiences, and it is the role of faculty as mentor in this third 'opening' to guide them in this project of curricular invention: to help them academically articulate and frame the concerns animating their desire to learn. Moreover, the third opening means that in taking students' curiosity seriously, we are also opening ourselves, as the dialogue develops, to our own questions and perplexities. We find ourselves wondering, along with our students, about shared topics and problems. In fact, a reciprocity of interests emerges, as we discover that we have more to learn about the very questions our students are trying to answer.

The patterns and possibilities of mentoring include an unlimited number of ways to build a curriculum from what students want to learn: from the questions they ask, their perceptions of things, and from their attempts to make sense of the world. For example, when a mentor attends to and wonders about students who want to make their learning address their struggles to prosper and achieve intimacy, that mentor, reminded of similar discomforts, might propose to them a reading of *Madame Bovary*. Similarly, a mentor hearing students express concern for the costs and environmental consequences of various energy sources might work with them to design a study of nuclear and alternative energy. Or, students fascinated, perhaps troubled, by the prospects of their teenage children might ask a mentor to help them create and work through a study of adolescent behaviour: one that is enriched by both mentor and students reflecting on their experiences as parents. And as students and mentors proceed with their enquiries, they may encounter statistics on the accelerating spread of AIDS and other sexually transmitted diseases among adolescents. With the help of a mentor, who in turn may seek advice and direction from colleagues, further in-depth enquiry on epidemiology and effective approaches to prevention could be added to the original study plan.

In each of these instances of building curricula the mentor is prepared to improvise. Gaining skill in the necessarily ambiguous domain of improvisation means learning to play with and create connections. The mentor provokes, prods, invokes and points to possibilities, thereby aiding students in structuring meaningful learning whose direction and goals cannot be known from the start (Bateson, 1994). The mentor and student can engage in this process of improvisation at three levels. It can occur extemporaneously within a prescribed course. It can occur as the design of an entire course (which may well cross several disciplines) for an individual or group of students. Or, as mentor and student move from the construction of imaginatively responsive individual courses to building clusters of learning, they can invent whole curricula. It is in this experience of looking at an education as a whole that the fullest expression of mentoring can be realised. And it is in appreciating this experience that the aesthetic dimension of learning becomes palpable (Orr, 1992). In the play, the improvisation, the design, the imagining—in the wonder—learning, for both faculty and students, is not only cognitively and ethically significant, but also becomes an enjoyment of the beautiful.

Mentors acknowledge both the richness and the risks in exploring this third opening. We are willing to trust the legitimacy of their students' enquiries and their own abilities to reshape the structures and contents of what we know in the service of mutual reflection and new learning. In so doing, we try to adopt an attitude in keeping with the discourse ethics of reciprocity required by what Jürgen Habermas calls 'communicative action' (Habermas, 1993). Thus, mentors are faculty members who not only try to suit the schedule and the community of learning to student needs (they are indeed master teachers of access and assimilation), but they also help students reflect on and construct curricula to suit their curiosity and to bring to bear their own and their colleagues' scholarly resources to respect, attend to and support that curiosity.

However, just as in the first and second openings, there are critical questions, both conceptual and practical, to be asked about the mentor role. Among them are claims that a mentoring culture would neglect scholarship and diminish the role of the teacher as expert. Another is that, if carried out to its fullest, mentored studies would promote idiosyncratic learning at the expense of the community of learning and knowledge for which the university has always stood.

These issues provoke important questions. In a mentoring culture, wouldn't faculty lack the expert knowledge necessary to responsibly arrange and guide their students' learning? Indeed, in a mentoring culture, wouldn't specialised scholarship literally diminish? It is true that mentors will need to plan and enter into investigations with their students which are not fitted to the outlines of their expertise. But it is also true that the culture of expertise, to which many of us are accustomed, undercuts its own aspirations. The explosion of highly-specialised scholarship has produced, in addition to extraordinarily valuable discoveries and whole new areas of exploration, an aggregation of knowledge, even within any single discipline, which is too large and varied for any expert to comprehend. Moreover, as new discoveries and controversies appear with accelerating frequency, the certainty which we seek from experts and upon which their authority rests, becomes that much more unreliable. Thus, instead of enhancing our general understanding and appreciation of our complex world, which after all must be one of the most significant goals of higher education, the culture of expertise often generates confusion. So, the university, instead of thriving as a community of scholars and students, becomes a world of small territories and dominations. We learn to grow comfortable and attached to our own small plots of academic industry, and try to protect them with rituals of exclusion rather than caring for them with the practice of honest, open and critical enquiry. In this way, the ideal of an engaged democratic community becomes that much more distant from what students and even scholars experience. Thus, the experience of expert discourse as competition and exclusion means that the values of democracy are neither enacted within the university nor, in turn, nourished in the larger society.

In such a problematic academic context, which so many of us encounter today, there is an important place for generalists—people who are in fact willing to reach beyond their expert knowledge to try to reconnect the fragments. Such practitioners, far from disparaging academic work, are devoted to it. Indeed, this shift of intellectual priorities to 'integrate ideas [and] connect thought to action' should be recognised as an important form of scholarship (Boyer, 1990, p. 77). Mentors epitomise a new kind of expert: one who tries to help students make connections between their possibly idiosyncratic interests and more general ideas, themes and areas of enquiry. In so doing, they also serve as a medium between student interests and faculty knowledge. They help reform what was thought to be private, personal and esoteric into that which is public and accessible to conversation and critique (Roth, 1995). Just as important, mentors, by learning to work with the diversity of students and student interests, also begin to comprehend the diversity of the

15

world. Thus, the mentor serves to re-open the promise of expertise, drawing the natural insularity of the scholar into a democratic public sphere (Fischer, 1990).

Like Odysseus himself, a man of 'many ways', who sought out the original Mentor as teacher for his son, the mentor faculty role we have described contains many parts. As an advocate of access who tries to open academic institutions to students, as a counsellor who makes the opened university both stimulating and hospitably responsive to student experiences, and as a particular kind of teacher, the mentor helps students create courses and curricula from their curiosity. We sponsor our students' intellectual journeys, as Mentor served Telemachus, and seek to guide them to the many and unpredictable ways of their enquiries.

But just as the mentor seeks to promote a pluralistic student community, the faculty community, of which mentors are members, should be pluralistic as well. It is neither necessary nor appropriate that every professor should become a mentor, nor even that every faculty member supportive of openness and student-centred education should become skilled in all the advocacy, counselling and teaching aspects of mentoring. Indeed, as we have tried to show, successful passage into each of the openings we have described in the faculty role depends upon a thriving community of scholars and teachers. Central to this is the principle that an accessible university must offer a valuable education to those who obtain entry. That environment must be flexible and bountiful enough in intellectual resources—in teachers, courses and materials—to have made students' adaptive efforts worthwhile. And precisely because mentors will often be inventing enquiries and curricula which will take them beyond their home disciplines and across many fields of expertise, they will need the advice and participation of scholars sustaining and discovering knowledge within their subject areas. Indeed, just as a culture of mentoring seeks a closer community between teachers and students, so does it depend upon and promote a truly interconnected community of diverse scholars and academic disciplines (Lord, 1994).

What, finally, brings this pluralistic community together? What does this indefinitely diverse conglomeration of students, scholars, counsellors, advocates and mentors have in common? Other motives aside, what brings them all to the university is the desire to know. In every student, we believe, in every scholar, teacher and every other kind of academic, there is a wonder, an honest, discomfiting but delighted acknowledgement of 'not knowing' and the consequent curiosity, the desire to learn, to savour and enquire into the object of one's wonder. This is the originating principle of the innumerable lives of the mind. It animates the most unsophisticated questions of new students and the most esoteric questions of distinguished scholars. And indeed, as we have tried to show throughout our discussion, discovering and developing each of the 'openings' in the faculty role emerges from encountering and acknowledging signs that there are important questions to be asked and more to learn about putting our knowledge and skills at the service of students. The mentor, in this view, is a scholar who enhances our understanding of the faculty role by directing wonder and the art of 'not knowing' upon the meanings of learning itself. As an image and form of practice, mentoring pushes us to critically evaluate what we take for granted and to remould what we do, by expanding the community of enquirers and thus honouring enquiry itself.

REFERENCES

Anderson, J. (1988) Cognitive styles and multicultural populations, *Journal of Teacher Education*, Jan/Feb, pp. 2–9.

Astin, A. (1992) *What matters in college?: Four critical years revisited* (San Francisco, Jossey-Bass).

Barber, B. (1992) *An aristocracy of everyone: The politics of education and the future of America* (New York, Ballantine Books).

Bateson, M. (1994) *Peripheral visions: Learning along the way* (New York, HarperCollins).

Belenky, M. *et al.* (1986) *Women's ways of knowing: The development of self, voice and mind* (New York, Basic).

Bellah, R. *et al.* (1991) *The good society* (New York, Alfred A. Knopf).

Boud, D., Cohen, R. & Walker, D. (Eds.) (1993) *Using experience for learning* (Buckingham, Open University Press).

Boyer, E. (1990) *Scholarship reconsidered: Priorities of the professoriate* (Princeton, The Carnegie Foundation for the Advancement of Teaching).

Brookfield, S. (1988) *Developing critical thinkers: Challenging adults to explore alternative ways of thinking and acting* (San Francisco, Jossey-Bass).

Burbules, N. (1993) *Dialogue in teaching: Theory and practice* (New York, Teachers College Press).

Coles, R. (1989) *The call of stories: Teaching and the moral imagination* (Boston, Houghton Mifflin).

Collins, M. (1991) *Adult education as vocation: A critical role for the adult educator* (London, Routledge).

Collins, R. (1979) *The credential society* (New York, Academic Press).

Coulter, X. & Herman, L. (1992) Timeliness and the organisation of learning. Paper delivered at the Conference of the American Association of Adult and Continuing Education, Salt Lake City, Utah.

Daloz, L. (1986) *Effective teaching and mentoring: Realising the transformational power of adult learning experiences* (San Francisco, Jossey-Bass).

Evans, T. & Juler, P. (1992) *Research in distance education 2* (Geelong, Victoria, Australia, Deakin University Press).

Fischer, F. (1990) *Technocracy and the politics of expertise* (Newbury Park, California, Sage).

Forester, J. (1989) Listening: The social policy of everyday life. In Forester, J., *Planning in the face of power* (Berkeley, University of California Press), pp. 107–118.

Fugate, M. & Chapman, R. (1992) *Prior learning assessment: Results of a nationwide institutional survey* (Chicago, The Council for Adult and Experiential Learning).

Gardiner, H. (1993) *Frames of mind: The theory of multiple intelligences* (New York, Basic).

Habermas, J. (1993) Discourse ethics: Notes on a program of philosophical justification. In Habermas, J., *Moral consciousness and communicative action*, trans. Lenhardt, C. & Nicholsen, S. (Cambridge, MA, MIT Press), pp. 43–115.

Hall, J. (1991) *Access through innovation: New colleges for new students* (New York, Macmillan).

Hall, J. (1993) Convocation and convergence: Restructuring the university through technology. Paper delivered at the International Conference of the American Association of University Administrators, Dublin.

Kegan, R. (1994) *In over our heads: The mental demands of modern life* (Cambridge, Harvard University Press).

Knox, A. (1989) *Adult development and learning* (San Francisco, Jossey-Bass).

Kolb, D. (1976) *Learning style inventory technical manual* (Boston, McBer).

Lamdin, L. (Ed.) (1989) *A Festschrift in honour of Morris T. Keeton* (Columbia, MD, The Council for Adult and Experiential Learning).

Lanham, R. (1993) *The electronic word: Democracy, technology and the arts* (Chicago, University of Chicago Press).

Lord, B. (1994) Teachers' professional development: Critical colleagueship and the role of professional communities. In Cobb, N. (Ed.) *The future of education: Perspectives on national standards in America* (New York, College Entrance Examination Board), pp. 175–204.

Maxwell, M. (1981) *Improving student learning skills* (San Francisco, Jossey-Bass).

Mezirow, J. (1991) *Transformative dimensions of adult learning* (San Francisco, Jossey-Bass).

Orr, D. (1992) *Ecological literacy: Education and the transition to a post-modern world* (Albany, NY, State University of New York Press).

Rose, M. (1988) *Lives on the boundary* (New York, Penguin).

Roth, M. (1995) On a certain blindness in teaching, *Higher Education Exchange*, pp. 8–17.

Schon, D. (1991) *The reflective turn: Case studies in and on educational practice* (New York, Teachers College Press).

Schor, J. (1991) *The overworked American: The unexpected decline of leisure* (New York, Basic).

Sheckley, B., Lamdin, L. & Keeton, M. (1993) *Employability in a high performance economy* (Chicago, The Council for Adult and Experiential Learning).

ACKNOWLEDGEMENT

We thank Joy W. Shortell, Professor of Student Development at Cayuga Community College, Auburn, NY, for her helpful suggestions and questions about this chapter.

2

Towards learner-centred distance education in the changing South African context

Jennifer Glennie

The two social orders, for which education is preparing white and black, are not identical and will for a long time to come remain essentially different. . . . The education of the white child prepares him for life in a dominant society and the education of the black child for a subordinate society. (Welsh Commission, 1936)

There is no place for [the African] in the European community above the level of certain forms of labour. Within his own community, however, all doors are open. For that reason it is of no avail for him to receive a training which has as its aim absorption in the European community. (Verwoerd, 1954)

Education and training are basic human rights. The state has an obligation to protect and advance these rights, so that all citizens, irrespective of race, class, gender, creed or age, have the opportunity to develop their capacities and potential, and make their full contribution to the society. (Department of Education, 1995)

South Africa in transformation: New goals, values and principles

With the adoption of the interim constitution in 1993, South Africa ushered in a commitment to a just, democratic society based on a culture of human rights. In almost every respect, this constitution is in direct antithesis to the colonial and apartheid regimes which the majority of South Africans endured for so long. The African National Congress (ANC) made many compromises in the process of negotiations. Not least of these was its agreement to a Government of National Unity, in which cabinet seats are allocated according to the proportion of votes a party receives. So, for example, in education, the deputy minister is a key member of the National Party, the party which gave birth to and nurtured apartheid for over 45 years. Furthermore, in the negotiations, the National Party and the Inkatha Freedom Party achieved extraordinary powers for the provinces, on the confident expectation that they would win at least one of the nine provinces each.

Nevertheless, this Government of National Unity has adopted a vision for transformation of our country: the Reconstruction and Development Programme (RDP). The programme recognises that the legacy of colonialism and apartheid has resulted in South Africa being one of the most unequal societies in the world, with lavish wealth co-existing with abject poverty. It seeks to mobilise all our people and our country's resources towards the final eradication of the results of apartheid, and the building of a democratic, non-racial, and non-sexist future (ANC, 1994, p. 4), and 'to meet the objectives of freedom and an improved quality of life for all South Africans' (GNU, 1994, p. 4). Central to the programme is that it should be a 'people-driven process'; in other words it should focus on people's immediate needs and rely in turn on their energies, 'so that together the people of South Africa can shape their own future' (*ibid.*, p. 6).

One of the prerequisites of the RDP is the transformation of our education system (ANC, 1995). On the 25th of June, 1955, at Kliptown, the Freedom Charter demanded 'that the doors of learning and culture shall be open'. Thirty-nine years later, and for the first time in the history of our country, the government has the mandate to plan the development of the education and training system for the benefit of the country as a whole and for all of its people. So, at long last, South Africa has an education white paper which states that:

> education and training are basic human rights and ... the state has an obligation to protect and advance these rights, so that all citizens, irrespective of race, class, gender, creed or age, have the opportunity to develop their capacities and potential, and make their full contribution to society. (Department of Education, 1995, p. 25)

The white paper, which includes a comprehensive set of educational goals, values, and principles, states that:

> the over-arching goal of policy must be to enable all individuals to value, have access to and succeed in **lifelong education and training of good quality**. Education and management processes must therefore put the **learners first, recognising and building** on **their**

knowledge and experience, and responding to their needs. An integrated approach to education and training will increase access, mobility and quality in the national system. . . . [That system] must provide an increasing range of learning possibilities, offering learners greater flexibility in choosing what, where, when, how and at what pace they learn. (ibid., p. 21)

The white paper goes on to commit itself to the redress of education inequalities, the deployment of resources according to the principle of equity, and the encouragement of *independent critical thought.*

The emphasis in the previous paragraph is mine, and serves to underline the way in which our new government has committed itself vigorously to the various aspects of a learner-centred approach as outlined by, for example, Lewis and Spencer (1986), Hodgson (1993), and Knowles (1990). This is no surprise: anti-apartheid popular education movements and thousands of non-governmental organisations have struggled for these ideals over the last forty years. Their influence in the white paper is apparent.

In the organisation for which I work, The South African Institute for Distance Education (SAIDE), we view learner-centredness as a key principle of any open learning approach. We emphasise the notion of the learner as an active participant in an interactive process which builds on learners' own experiences, and meets their needs, while developing independent and critical thinking and problem-solving skills (Butcher, 1994). For us, independent learning is about learners taking responsibility for what and how they learn, rather than an emphasis on individual students working by themselves, 'banking' the content handed down to them by the teaching institution.

But what chances are there of putting these ideals into practice? The South African education department faces enormous and diverse challenges. Nowhere has the effect of colonialism and apartheid been more devastating than in the field of education. Five key features are pertinent.

First, the system was fragmented along racial and ethnic lines, producing what was euphemistically called 'The Decentralised Education Structure in Southern Africa'. This consisted of no less than fifteen racially- and ethnically-based departments of education, with the authority for white education being further divided into four provincial departments. Second, vast disparities existed between black and white provision. South Africa has spent a sizeable proportion of its budget on education (in 1994, 22.5 per cent of budget and 7 per cent of GDP). This has resulted in a substantial, well-resourced sector designed for, and still primarily used by, white people. Simultaneously, millions of black South African adults are functionally illiterate, millions of African children and youth are learning under devastating conditions, and, in 1994, no less than 1.8 million African children aged between 6 and 18 were not enrolled at school. Third, the curriculum was saturated with racial ideology and the educational doctrines of apartheid. Fourth, the undemocratic nature of educational governance excluded teachers, parents, workers, and students from decision-making processes. Fifth, and finally, apartheid education and its aftermath of resistance destroyed the culture of learning in large sections of our communities.

The white paper outlines a number of strategies to create a unified education system, to rectify past inequalities, to develop appropriate curricula, and to introduce democratic participation. These include the introduction of a national qualification framework, a major curriculum development exercise, compulsory schooling for 6-year-olds from 1995, particular attention to a comprehensive reform and redirection of in-service education for teachers, and a student recovery programme in science and mathematics.

The white paper also commits itself to open learning:

> The dimensions of South Africa's learning deficit are so vast in relation to the needs of the people, the constitutional guarantee of the right to basic education, and the severe financial constraints on infrastructural development on a large scale, that a completely fresh approach is required to the provision of learning opportunities.

The Ministry suggests that open learning is such an approach, and proposes to establish a National Open Learning Agency as a flexible and responsive agency whose task would be to promote open learning principles and assist institutions to translate these principles into practice (Department of Education, 1995, p. 28).

The white paper has also identified distance education as an essential mechanism for achieving its goals. However, it does not envisage distance education methods as being used exclusively by dedicated distance education institutions. Rather, it sees these methods being adopted by a very wide range of institutions and organisations, and having particular relevance in at least four areas: teacher education, further education, adult basic education and resource-based learning at schools.

What can current distance education provision offer?

Size

The distance education sector in South Africa is already considerable. In 1995, its overall budget was well over one billion rand, in a country where the education department's budget was about thirty billion rand. It includes the University of South Africa (UNISA) which, with its registration of over 130 000 students, rates as one of the ten largest distance education institutions in the world. There are other significant players. Technikon SA (TSA) has approximately 85 000 students studying towards various vocational certificates and diplomas at the post-secondary level. VISTA university, created in 1980 as a university for African students in so-called 'white South Africa', has an enrolment of over 20 000 teachers in distance education programmes. Another 80 000 teachers are improving their professional qualifications using distance education methods at a range of colleges and universities. This means that approximately one-third of the national teaching corps are involved in distance education programmes. A distance education technical college, Technisa, enrols some 8000 students. In 1992, the commercial correspondence colleges had an enrolment of 50 000 for secondary qualifications and of 101 000 in courses leading to professional qualifications.

The considerable growth seen in this sector can largely be attributed to the increase in African students. For example, UNISA's enrolment of African students increased from 4943 in 1975 to 50 292 in 1992: nearly a tenfold increase. Technikon SA's African enrolment increased from 4253 in 1989 to 31 203 in 1993, while VISTA's distance education enrolment (all African students) has increased rapidly from its inception in 1981 to its current numbers of about 20 000 students. We thus find that distance education students made up some 47 per cent of all African students enrolled in universities in 1993 and 38 per cent of all African students enrolled in Technikons. Furthermore, a growing number of students at these institutions are studying on a full-time basis. At UNISA and TSA, this category constituted over 30 000 students in 1995. Clearly, distance education institutions are becoming a very significant part of higher education provision, not only for working students but also for those wishing to study on a full-time basis who are unable to find places as on-campus students. This trend is likely to grow. A recent student demonstration at a college of education, which had closed its doors to hundreds of disappointed applicants, was quietened by the arrival of registration tables from distance education institutions.

While distance education institutions can certainly claim to be opening up educational opportunities, particularly to African students, they cannot claim to have provided great opportunities for success. Of course they can boast an extraordinary array of graduates, including President Nelson Mandela, Prime Minister Robert Mugabe of Zimbabwe, and the Chairperson of the Constitutional Assembly, Mr Cyril Ramaphosa. Such students, one would suspect, fall into Ross Paul's category of 'students [who] would succeed in any university, given the opportunity, and they sometimes succeed despite the university!' (Paul, 1989). But for the ordinary mortal, the situation looks much less rosy.

Quality

A recent international commission into distance education, commissioned by the African National Congress (ANC), organised by SAIDE, and chaired by Professor Ghanaraj Dhanarajan, demonstrated appalling completion rates for all students, but particularly for African and Coloured students. In the main, only 10 per cent of African students who enrol in a degree programme at UNISA can be expected to graduate over a nine-year period. An analysis of Technikon SA results produced slightly higher throughput rates of approximately 17 per cent. On the basis of these figures, visits to the institution, and an analysis of documents, the commission declared that:

> *the new government will have to consider the cost efficiency of its investment in human resources development, and serious questions must be asked of institutional policies that give access, but fail to provide forms of education that enable students to capitalise on their opportunity.* (International Commission into Distance Education, 1995, p. xxii)

This is indeed a serious consideration for the newly established National Commission into Higher Education because, at university and technikon level, distance education is well-resourced. Distance education institutions receive two-thirds of the subsidy which contact institutions receive for an equivalent full-time student. Indeed, in the case of VISTA, there are strong indications that the subsidies for the distance education students act as the 'cash cow' for highly cost-ineffective decentralised campus provision on seven sites, none of which has more than 2500 students.

The international commission further points out that the quality of current provision is *comprehensively deficient*, based as it is on an *outmoded and very limited conception of what distance education is and how it should be managed, and provided* (*ibid.*, p. xxi). The commission concluded that:

> *taken as a whole, distance education's contribution to the priorities for education and training in the [ANC] Policy Framework is variously marginal, inefficient, and, in the values sought for democratic South Africa, dysfunctional.* (*ibid.*, p. xxii)

Some of the key reasons for their conclusions relate to the near-complete absence of learner-centredness in the design of the teaching and learning system. This absence is considered under three headings: the system and learners' needs; learning resources and learners' experience and needs; and the promotion of rote learning and thinking.

The system and learners' needs

The kind of students most likely to benefit from distance education at the post-compulsory stage in South Africa are those over the age of 18 who may not have completed formal schooling. The majority of these students cannot afford residential study for reasons of cost or time, come from working-class houses where self-paced study may be difficult for social or material reasons, and rely on public transportation systems which may be deficient. The vast majority are black, and at least half are women, a fact that is generally ignored. School-leavers who have had inadequate schooling are particularly likely to need some form of distance education either to get them into the job market or into post-secondary education. Some may be released from employment for distance education study. In some regions (for example, KwaZulu-Natal), the majority live in semi-rural or rural areas. It is not unusual for a dozen people to share four rooms. The average student will not necessarily share all of these characteristics or limitations but a high proportion of them will.

Many learners undertaking distance education programmes at secondary and tertiary level do so on the basis of very negative experiences of education. Their schools have operated sporadically, their teachers have often been alienated, unmotivated, and authoritarian, and rote learning will have been the norm. The prospective learners are likely to lack many essential learning skills, and, in general, are underprepared.

To compensate for this degree of disadvantage, distance education institutions would have to provide multi-faceted learning environments sensitive to the particular needs of the students. However, the international commission found that, in the vast majority of cases, public distance education provision is no more than correspondence education; perhaps with occasional personal touches, such as brief visits by a lecturer to outlying centres (sometimes to give a lecture to two or three hundred students at a time). In such a context, study materials become all-important. Yet, in South Africa, comparatively little time is given to their preparation. Typically, the task is undertaken by a single author, sometimes with the help of an editor. The result is usually dull, impersonal, authoritarian, and uninspiring.

With regard to tutoring, the general impression of the commission of the public provision was of a service 'that was completely fragmented, unco-ordinated, unplanned, *ad hoc*, insensitive and, but for a few exceptions, largely useless'. It is provided by the centrally-based academic who carries out the task by one or more methods: telephone tutoring; a 'travelling lecturer' scheme where the central academic visits selected sites to deliver a few hours of lectures; and student appointments with the academic.

> *When one tries to think of how this might operate in a UNISA course with several thousand registered students, it is difficult to avoid the conclusion that the arrangement is a charade, even when the academics concerned see themselves as spending a great deal of time in the process.* (Dhanarajan, 1994, p. 4)

Telephone tutoring is a hollow option for most African students, who often have access only to public telephones, especially where it is suggested that calls be made between 8 a.m. and 12 noon on weekdays. Assignment marking is poorly monitored and its quality uneven. In courses with low enrolment, 'lecturers' may take care to mark assignments carefully and quickly, giving constructive comments; but in large courses, the turn-around time is often as long as three to four months in the public institutions, and the remarks are dismissive and demotivating. Scant attention is given to counselling. For example, one institution has no formal provision, another has a half-time person responsible for 20 000 students, and a third has only 12 counsellors for 125 000 students.

On the basis of this picture, the commission found that publicly-funded distance education systems were certainly not designed with the needs of learners in South Africa in mind.

Learning resources and learners' experience and needs

The commission found many examples of distance education courses whose developers clearly had no desire to know or understand their learners, or to respect their life experiences. In a ludicrous, but actual, example one course asserted that 'non-white people tend to be impulsive and to have a more impetuous temperament which, in many cases, cannot be restrained', whereas 'whites lead dignified, quiet and calm lives, have self-discipline and self-control and are highly developed and intelligent people'.

Even where racist stereotyping is not involved, well-meaning course developers demonstrate little desire to learn of and respond to learners' needs. For example, SAIDE is in the process of conducting a national audit of teacher education through distance education and it has reviewed a sample of courses from 19 institutions. Preliminary findings demonstrate that there is frequently no reference made or account taken of the context in which the learners (in this case, practising teachers) find themselves: second language usage, classes containing 80 pupils, an absence of learning culture in the school, etc. The audit also indicates a general lack of interest as to whether the courses are indeed meeting the learners' needs. For example, few mechanisms appear to be in place for course-evaluation by students. This is particularly surprising considering that the students themselves are teachers.

Promotion of rote learning

A key aspect of learner-centredness is the promotion of independent and critical learning skills. In South Africa, across almost the entire primary and secondary education systems and some sections of the tertiary system, the exact opposite, rote learning, is the norm. This tendency does, of course, exist in all countries, but in South Africa it is grossly exaggerated, largely on account of the approach of Christian National Education (CNE). Central to CNE policy is the notion that:

> *through the Fall, sin has penetrated by means of heredity to later generations, and the child as the object of teaching and education is therefore a sinful and not a sinless being.* (FAK, 1948, Article 4)

The policy purported to be a policy for white Afrikaans-speaking children, but it had far-reaching consequences for the education of all children in South Africa since it paid special attention to African education which it saw as the responsibility of 'the Boer nation as the senior white trustee of the native', who is in a state of 'cultural infancy' (*ibid.*, Article 15).

The results of this approach are still very much with us. One of the course reviewers in the teacher education audit notes:

> *The style is impersonal and the tone prescriptive. The course writers are the authorities and the students must do as they are told. In courses, assignments and examinations have been designed to check whether students have 'absorbed' the course content. There are no opportunities for students to develop a critical perspective on the subject matter.* (Reed, 1995, p. 2)

Creating learner-centred distance education in South Africa

As distance education moves from the margins into the mainstream in South Africa, progressive distance educators have a heavy responsibility to bear. Although many of us have advocated, with near missionary zeal (Tait, 1994, p. 1), the advantages of distance education methods, we have been acutely aware of the less savoury social-control functions which distance education has so easily served: political indoctrination, production of docile and uncritical graduates, and the appearance of opening access without providing conditions necessary for success. How then do we try to ensure that distance education serves the emancipatory, empowering and developmental functions to which we have committed ourselves? In particular, as a crucial aspect of

27

these goals, how can we encourage learner-centred distance education in South Africa?

An open learning approach

At SAIDE, we have committed ourselves to developing distance education within a framework of open learning. The concept 'open learning' has often been used in service of distance education, with the unfortunate consequence that the two terms have tended to become conflated. This we believe is not very useful, particularly because there is nothing innate in distance education methods of provision which automatically equates with openness in approach (Rumble, 1989). We see open learning as an approach to all education, the principles of which can continually inform educational practices in order to improve them. In South Africa, these principles should suffuse the education and training system as a whole in order to ensure its effective transformation. Only then can that system begin to cater for the diverse educational needs of all people in the country while meeting the needs of a developing economy. For us, open learning describes an approach which seeks to transform the nature of educational opportunity and to remove all unnecessary barriers to learning, so that as many people as possible are able to take advantage of meaningful learning opportunities throughout their lives. Education should therefore cease to be something that only occurs within the walls of a school, conducted by the talking teacher and aimed principally at young people. The focus should move instead to the learner and the outcomes of learning. Learning should take place in a number of contexts, in a multiplicity of sites, through a variety of mechanisms, and for people of all ages. We have highlighted the following as key principles around which the concept of open learning is built:

- The learning process should **centre on the learners,** build on their experience, and encourage independent and critical thinking.

- Learning opportunity should be **lifelong** and should encompass both education and training.

- Learning provision should be **flexible**, so that learners can increasingly choose where, when, what, and how they learn, as well as the pace at which they will learn.

- **Prior learning, prior experience, and demonstrated competences** should be recognised so that learners are not unnecessarily barred from educational opportunities by lack of appropriate qualifications.

- Learners should be able to **accumulate credits** from different learning contexts.

- Providers should create the conditions for a **fair chance of learner success**, inter alia by ensuring support throughout the learning process.

- Learning should be of the **highest quality**.

Well-functioning distance education

Within this framework of open learning, we have begun to develop the notion of the well-functioning distance education provider in South Africa. Such a provider's main task is, as we see it, 'to design and manage successful learning', while understanding that its product is 'service to the learner' (Swift, 1994, p. 2). In designing the learning environment, we encourage education providers to choose appropriate combinations of methods for particular learning contexts. For this reason, we see the sharp distinction between face-to-face and distance teaching as unhelpful. Some key features of our notion of the well-functioning distance education provider include well-designed courses, integrated learner support, counselling, and a commitment to the self-improving organisation.

We plan to assist in the development of a network of such providers who will design and offer a very wide range of education programmes aimed at meeting the diverse needs of learners. Mechanisms will need to be established to encourage collaboration, so that enough resources are available for quality course development, and so that institutions who have operated so separately in the past can begin to work together in a spirit of collegiality. Such programmes would fall within the soon-to-be-established National Qualifications Framework. This will ensure that learners can accumulate credits for their learning outcomes towards nationally-recognised levels of learning and agreed pathways of progression.

Network of community learning centres

Such providers would, in South Africa, need to be supported by a network of community learning centres. In brief, community learning centres provide a place where people can meet, attend classes and discussion groups, study, pick up books and other materials for learning, and, where possible, make use of computer facilities, workshops, and laboratories (Davids, 1994). Some of the most exciting recent developments in South African education and training already revolve around such centres of learning. Community learning centres could be established at a range of physical structures which already exist, and could make use of facilities during afternoons, evenings, and weekends. These could include local schools, local libraries, community buildings, places of worship, places of work, technical colleges, colleges of education, and residential institutions of higher education working co-operatively with distance providers. Learning centres would be used by distance education learners as well as by a range of other learners, especially in adult basic education and training (Ngengebule *et al.*, 1992).

Of paramount importance, however, is that the development of such a network should not take away from institutions' responsibility for their learners. Rather, the network is an aspect of the necessary social infrastructure, which distance education institutions would use in much the same way as they use (and pay for) the postal service. The institutions must, however, ensure that they develop, implement, and continually evaluate and adjust the services offered to learners.

Progress thus far

SAIDE's task is to promote and develop this vision of a national network of providers and learning centres, and to assist in the establishment of innovative initiatives which give it practical expression. We do this through advocacy, information sharing, networking, research, professional development, and assistance in planning.

Already there is a range of exciting developments. In the Free State, a consortium of the local university, technikon, and technical and other colleges, together with the national dedicated distance education institutions, are working on the collaborative provision of programmes for lifelong learning from basic to advanced level. Essential to their scheme is the establishment and maintenance of a network of learning centres by the province.

In KwaZulu-Natal, the Regional Institutional Co-operation Programme (RICP) brings together all the universities and technikons in the province in an effort to meet the province's higher education needs by rationalising and co-ordinating efforts. In particular, the RICP is committed to increasing access to first-year study by offering 'foundation courses' using distance education methods. This will involve the creation of a provincial higher education course development unit.

SAIDE is supporting both these efforts, while simultaneously preparing a submission to the National Higher Education Commission on how, in general, to develop and fund mechanisms to facilitate the use by traditionally face-to-face institutions of distance education methods.

In teacher education, the distance education aspect of the national audit is developing a vision of a future teacher education system, dedicated to South

Africa's newly articulated development goals, and operating according to open learning principles. Currently, there are 19 distance education programmes separately producing in-service courses for the quarter of the teaching force that is un- or under-qualified, and for the countless others requiring professional development. Collaboration amongst these institutions, and the use of the approximately one hundred colleges of education, as well as the approximately two hundred teacher centres, as learning centres, make such a vision realisable. The Eastern Cape is already exploring such a scheme.

Meanwhile, the dedicated distance education institutions are responding to change. Technikon SA has adopted an Integrated Learner-Centred Distance Education (ILCDE) approach, and has recently voted the necessary finance from its existing resources to implement the approach (Technikon, 1995). The implementation of these objectives requires huge organisational change, and is fraught with difficulty as these changes are resisted by sections of staff and council.

At VISTA, the university as a whole is in a state of turmoil, and at the time of writing has been without permanent senior management for over six months. The distance education section is valiantly developing new course development procedures, against the background of great uncertainty.

At UNISA, a more piecemeal approach has thus far been adopted. An encouraging step was the adoption by UNISA of the learner support system which was run independently by SACHED Trust for over 20 years (Nonyongo, 1993). Unfortunately, the integration of this support system has not yet taken place. Very recently, UNISA began a strategic planning process. The following objectives were put forward at its initial planning workshop as essential components of its new mission:

- Establish a legitimate, democratic governance structure that continually and creatively shapes the university's future.

- Develop a devolved management system and style that is inclusive, transparent and efficient.

- Provide conditions favourable to maintaining a well-qualified and highly-motivated staff that reflects the demographics of South African society as far as possible.

- Operate a student-centred tuition system characterised by flexibility, access and the delivery of study material that is quality assured and contextually relevant.

- Formulate a language policy which strives for maximum communication and recognition of cultural values and respect for human dignity.

31

■ Foster an open, tolerant and reconciliatory South African society with a spirit free from all discrimination and prejudice. (UNISA, 1995, p. 7)

However, implementation strategies have yet to be developed to achieve these objectives.

Conclusion

As we seek to develop these promising beginnings into our grand plans, the key challenge will be to try to ensure that the design of learning programmes is not dictated primarily by the needs, traditions, and vested interests of the institutions and their staff, but rather by the needs of the learners. As the international commission notes:

> *Whereas in the past, universities, technikons, colleges and schools have determined the conditions under which they will teach, they must now think of themselves as facilitators of other people's learning.* (International Commission into Distance Education in South Africa, 1995, p. 48)

At the heart of this goal is, as Tait (1995, p. 1) points out, knowing who your students are and what their needs are. In a country as deeply divided as ours has been—where many staff, especially in essentially correspondence institutions, have had no contact with major student groupings and where some, at least, would prefer to keep it that way—this is a major challenge. We must consciously and actively:

> *develop and maintain approaches which enable students to have their voices heard, and for open and distance educators and their institutions to be able to listen to and understand the practical implications of what is being said.* (Evans, 1994, p. 128)

REFERENCES

African National Congress (1994) *The Reconstruction and Development Programme* (Johannesburg, Umanyano Publications).

African National Congress (1995) *A policy framework for education and training* (Manzini, Macmillan Boleswa).

Butcher, N. (1994) Challenges to open learning. A workshop paper.

Davids, S. (1994) Learner support services: The role of distance education support in community learning centres. A SAIDE workshop paper.

Department of Education (1995) *Government Gazette*, White Paper on Education and Training, 357 (16312), Notice no. 196 of 1995 (Pretoria, Government Printer).

Dhanarajan, R. (1994) Student support services: The first challenge for distance education. An unpublished contribution to the International Commission into Distance Education in South Africa.

Evans, T. (1994) *Understanding learners in open and distance education* (London, Kogan Page).

Federasie van Afrikaanse Kulteervereenigings (1948) *Christian National Education Policy* (Johannesburg, Instituut vir Christelike-Nationale Onderwys, Beleid).

Government of National Unity (1994) *Reconstruction and Development Programme*, White Paper Discussion Document (Pretoria, Government Printer).

Hodgson, B. (1993) *Key terms and issues in open and distance learning* (London, Kogan Page).

International Commission into Distance Education in South Africa (1995) *Open learning and distance education* (Manzini, Macmillan Boleswa).

Knowles, M. (1990) *The adult learner: A neglected species* (4th ed.) (Houston, Gulf Publishing).

Lewis, R. & Spencer, D. (1986) *What is open learning?* Open Learning Guides, no. 4 (London, Council for Education Technology).

Ngengebule, T., Glennie, J., & Perold, H. (1992) Distance education: How can it contribute to adult education for a democratic South Africa? Presented at the inaugural conference of the SAIDE, Johannesburg, 7–9 September 1992.

Nonyongo, E.P. (1993) Student support programmes for distance learning. A paper presented at the University of South Africa on distance teaching.

Paul, R.H. (1989) Do Open Universities do a better job of developing independent learners? In Tait, A., *Interaction and independence: Student support in distance education and open learning. Conference papers* (Cambridge, Open University).

Reed, Y. (1995) English courses: issues, trends and general observations. Unpublished paper.

Rumble, G. (1989) 'Open learning', 'distance learning', and the misuse of language, *Open Learning*, 4(2), pp. 28–36.

Swift, D. (1994) A well-functioning distance education institution. A SAIDE workshop paper.

Tait, A. (1994) The end of innocence: Critical approaches to open and distance learning, *Open Learning*, 9(3).

Tait, A. (1995) Addressing the principles of student support in open and distance learning. In Lockwood, F. (Ed.) *Open and distance learning today* (London, Routledge).

Technikon of South Africa & South African Institute for Distance Education (June 1995) Funding the development of policies and strategies for integrated learner-centred distance education at Technikon SA. Johannesburg, an unpublished document.

University of South Africa (May 1995) Project: The future role of UNISA. Discussion document emanating from a planning workshop. An unpublished paper.

Verwoerd, H.F. (1954) Speech delivered in the Senate.

Welsh Commission (1936) Report of the interdepartmental committee on native education.

3

Technology, the curriculum and the learner: Opportunities for open and distance education

Gary Miller

When Gertrude Stein was on her deathbed, she looked up at her companion, Alice B. Toklas, and asked, 'What is the answer?' When she got no reply, she nodded and asked, 'In that case, what is the question?' The story is relevant to the theme of this chapter for several reasons. First, of course, Gertrude Stein was a native-born Pennsylvanian and we like to promote our local heroes. But more important, we are now living in a time when there are few quick answers and when we must constantly challenge and clarify our assumptions—ask ourselves, 'What is the question?'—before we draw conclusions.

This is certainly the case when we look at technology and the curriculum. Typically, people want answers about how technology will affect the curriculum, but is that really the question? Perhaps, the real issue is not the impact of technology on the curriculum or on the learner, but the emerging *relationships* among technology, the curriculum, and the learner and the impact of those relationships on higher education. Those are the questions we in open and distance education need to ask ourselves. We are no longer alone in asking them, as these are the questions facing higher education generally, as we explore the transformation of our universities from teaching institutions to learning institutions.

My thesis in this chapter is fairly straightforward. By itself, technology has only an incremental impact on education. However, if you consider how to use technology in light of the changing social need for education, for a different kind of curriculum and a different relationship with the learner—needs that are not themselves technological needs—then technology can be seen as a tool that can help us orchestrate broad curricular and institutional change. The key is that several factors have to be in place at the same time. The first question, then, is whether those factors are currently present and, if they are, what do we want to do about them? To get an answer we have to take a fresh look at some long-held assumptions.

Some history

Many of us are the product of an educational paradigm that has remained fairly well intact for a millennium: the Western model of a university. In medieval times, higher education was directed to the children of landed aristocrats spread across the agrarian countryside. It was a small, thinly spread population: well-suited, perhaps, to the economics of distance education. However, there were other factors. First, there was a limited, well-defined canon or body of knowledge; the goal of education was simply to transfer this canon to the students. Second, that knowledge was in the hands of a very few scholars. Third, communications technology was in a sad shape. There were few decent roads, no real postal service, and, importantly, not enough books to go around. In short, there were few media for presentation of information and no real way to achieve interaction at a distance.

Given the social and technological situation and the educational goals, the most practical response was to capture the students when they were young, bring them together during the off-season for agriculture, put them into groups to learn from the scholars, and give them what you could before they returned home to pursue the responsibilities of the elite. Out of this basic accommodation to the environment came organising principles that we now take for granted: the organisation of knowledge into disciplines and into units of knowledge that we call courses, the concept of academic time as a way of pacing groups of students through the curriculum, the central authority of the faculty over the teaching/learning process, and the essentially passive role of the learner as the receiver of knowledge. Thus, the university evolved as a teaching institution.

It has proved to be a robust paradigm. Over the years, we have added many new technologies to the basic classroom. We have added blackboards and whiteboards, overhead projectors, slides and, more recently, computer-based presentations. These technologies have greatly enriched the teaching environment, but they have done little to alter the basic assumptions on which the institution and the curriculum are based.

Film, which Thomas Edison said would revolutionise education, simply provided tutors with a new way to illustrate lectures. Television provided a way to distribute the lecture to more students, but did not change the basic relationship between the student and instructor. In the United States, the telecourse helped move education off-campus, but again had little impact on the curriculum itself; in fact, many community college-level telecourses initially mimicked the classroom by matching one television programme for every traditional lecture.

Today, we are using two-way interactive video to expand our outreach to students nationally and internationally; however, even this advanced technology has done little to change the basic assumptions about the role of knowledge, the primacy of the instructor, the iron rule of institution-defined academic calendar, etc. In fact, the way most institutions use interactive video reinforces our traditional assumptions about teaching. Even the mass-produced book, with all the changes that it wrought on society, did little to change the basic assumptions and organising principles of the curriculum.

The same has turned out to be true of open and distance education. In the United States, correspondence study was first developed around the nine-teenth century's version of a national information infrastructure. Called Rural Free Delivery this was a national postal service that guaranteed delivery of mail directly to your home no matter where you lived. It was a truly transforming 'technology' for Americans. Individualised distance education— one of the progenitors of open education—took full advantage of this new access to the home. For the first time, a university system was created that assumed that the learner should control the time, place, and pace of study. This level of access and control was a significant achievement, but it ended there, at the level of access and control over the time and pace of learning. Although an educational system based on materials offered new opportunities for multi-disciplinarity, education continued to be organised around discipline-based canons (even inter-disciplinarity assumes the primacy of disciplines), the scope and sequence of which were organised and controlled by faculty and presented to students.

Individualised distance education has also proved to be a robust technology. For the past century, almost every attempt to introduce new technologies has served only to limit student access without dramatically improving the learning environment. The most obvious example was the addition of broadcast and cable television to the media mix of individualised distance education. Although it added new and sometimes effective ways of conveying information, it also required that the students be within range of the television channel broadcast area and be available at a particular time. The teaching advantages were offset by a reduction in the learners' control over their environment.

This suggests that technology, in itself, does not *necessarily* have an impact on the curriculum. Nor does technology itself lead us to a learner-centred curriculum. As long as technology is being used within the existing paradigm, its effects are incremental at best. Ultimately, it is not the technology that matters, but how we choose to design learning through that technology. Dramatic change comes when we use the technology to respond to other factors that force us to challenge our basic, underlying assumptions. These factors might include changes in the characteristics or situation of the learner, changes in the social context or goals of education, or changes in the nature of the content and process of learning.

The important questions facing open and distance education today as we consider the curriculum are not, initially, questions about technology. They are issues of social purpose, of the role and goals of the learner, and the nature of knowledge in an information culture.

The nature of change

'In that case,' as Gertrude Stein said, 'what is the question?' What are the changes that are affecting our assumptions about the curriculum, and about the role of technology, today? Are they paradigm-breaking changes? That is, are they significant enough to force us to rethink the basic assumptions that underlie the traditional university model?

Here, it might be possible to say that technology is having a direct effect on the curriculum, because many of the changes that we are seeing today in society are a direct result of technological change. Let us assume for a moment that we can set the beginning of the Information Age with the publication of Alvin Toffler's *Future Shock* (1970), the book that brought the information revolution to the attention of the general population. That book was published in 1970, a quarter of a century ago, and it is safe to assume that the information revolution was well underway by that time. That means that it can be said that we are now one full generation into the Information Age. The revolution may not be over—certainly, we have not yet felt the full force of the digital transformation—but the changes in our lives have been broad and, largely, irreversible.

The information revolution has resulted in several changes that force us to reconsider our basic ideas about learning and the curriculum. First, of course, it has greatly expanded the amount of information in our lives. This has had several effects. It has, for instance, democratised information: information is no longer the province of the scholar alone. In fact, the main problem that many of us face is how to avoid information overload. 'Selective ignorance' has become a safeguard for the educated professional. At the same time that it has been democratised, information has been devalued by the 'information explosion'. Information in itself does not grant one as much power as it used to. The idea of 'knowledge for its own sake' has lost some of its appeal in the process. Instead, we are beginning to understand that real power rests in our ability to find, analyse, and use information critically to make decisions, solve problems, and respond effectively to new situations. These capacities become the explicit goals or outcomes of education, rather than the implicitly-understood byproducts of having knowledge about something. This is a dramatic change in how we understand the goals of education and the role of information.

Second, the information revolution has turned the ideal of lifelong learning into an everyday necessity. Education is no longer a one-time, or even a two- or three-time, experience that prepares us for the rest of our lives. We are all lifelong learners. We've even begun to see our institutions as 'learning organisations'. One of our corporate colleagues, Jerry Steele, formerly of Ford Motor Company, noted at a Penn State symposium last year that the successful corporation is not necessarily the one that can work cheaper or faster, but the one that can 'out-learn' the competition. Given the rate of social change, the top competitor—be it an individual or an organisation—is the one that can apply critical analysis to new situations.

The philosopher John Dewey had a term for this competency. He called it 'reflective experience'. Reflective experience involves a kind of ongoing experiment, in which the purpose of action is to learn about the relationship of that action to the rest of the environment. It starts when one recognises a problem, envisages a solution and then takes actions directed towards the goal, checking assumptions and adjusting course at each step. The goal, ultimately, is to transform one's environment.

It is easy to make the leap from reflective experience to the idea of reflective learning. This new learning environment is inherently non-linear and non-hierarchical. It is highly individualised, placing the learner in an active role and transforming the 'instructor' into a 'mentor' or 'co-learner'. Most important, it is directed towards empowering an individual to transform his or her environment and to solve problems. Knowledge is not the end of the reflective learning process, but the means: the actions that allow the learner to reassess the situation and take fresh aim at the target. It is the process that allows an organisation to 'out-learn' its competition. It is also the process that allows an individual to find his or her way of keeping up with the constantly accelerating rate of social change.

In fact, the argument could be made that reflective learning will be an important element in effective citizenship in societies where change is the only constant. The move, in a single century, from an agrarian to an industrial to an informational society, continues to dislocate our understanding of, and adherence to, social norms. Moreover, in an information-rich society, a citizenry that cannot critically evaluate information runs the great risk of falling victim to demagogues and ideologues. Lifelong learning is no longer for the highly technical professional; it is for everyone. Reflective learning is how we chart our courses, as individuals and as members of society, through these sometimes rough waters of change.

We can begin to see that our assumptions about the needs of learners, about the social need for education, and about the nature of the curriculum, may be changing. Higher education is no longer a one-time preparation for the elite, but a necessary requirement for learning organisations and a learning society. The learner is no longer a passive receptor, but an active shaper of learning. Knowledge is a means to an end, rather than an end in itself. The scholar becomes a guide rather than the owner of knowledge. These are dramatic shifts in our assumptions. However, it remains for we educators to decide whether or not we want to act upon them.

The role of technology

Technology plays a central role in this potential transformation. Clearly, it is a catalyst for the information revolution and, thus, for the social transformation that is underway. Also, newer technologies are part of the toolbox that will allow us to create an educational transformation.

As an educational tool, technology has been associated primarily with transmission or presentation technologies. Film, television, radio, the VCR, satellite, compressed video—the technologies that have come to be associated with distance education over the past couple of decades—are transmission technologies whose primary value rests in providing learners with access to linear instructional messages selected and organised by faculty. The basic activity is well within the traditional paradigm. The newer digital media are different, not only in the technologies used, but in their basic nature. These are inherently non-linear media. Their value lies, not so much in providing access to organised instruction, but in how they allow people access to a wide range of data that can be organised by the learner around his or her own needs and preferences.

However, if we are to get full value from these new tools, we have to understand the broader impact of technology. In his new book *Being Digital* (1995) Nicholas Negroponte, of the Media Lab at the Massachusetts Institute of Technology, makes a couple of points about these new media that have special relevance for open and distance education. Negroponte writes:

Computing is no longer about computers; it is about life.

In other words, the digital environment is one of the forces that is reshaping the entire social fabric. Not only is technology creating a new delivery system for education, it may be creating some new educational needs. Just as the industrial revolution created new disciplines and new ways of structuring the learning environment, the information revolution appears to be creating demands for new kinds of learning and, in the process, new ways to think about the academic venture.

He also notes that, whereas in the past we moved atoms, in the future we will move bits. Negroponte is not talking about distance education, but about society in general; however, the image has a particular relevance for distance education. The notion succinctly describes one element in the changing relationships between technology, the learner, and the curriculum.

For traditional education, the 'atoms' were, and are, those of the students themselves, who physically move to a college campus to gain the wisdom of instructors, who bring their own 'atoms' to campus. By moving the atoms of instructors and students, we make it possible for instruction to take place.

Open and distance education has already changed that somewhat. Whether we are talking about the US tradition of independent study or the UK Open University model, the key change is that, instead of moving the atoms of our students and instructors, we created materials and then moved around the atoms of our set books, course guides, video tapes, audio tapes, and so forth. But we are still moving atoms. To a degree, the new interactive video systems allow us to move bits more efficiently: digitising visual and aural communications among groups. This is limited, though: interactive video is still synchronous in that the community of learners must still gather their atoms in particular places at particular times. On-line computing and CD-ROM technologies, on the other hand, are both digital and asynchronous, as well as non-linear. Here, then, is a match between the new learning environment and technology.

Curriculum, technology, and the learner in the Information Age

In the traditional paradigm of higher education, technology serves two basic purposes. First, it extends the reach of the institution, increasing student access to the instructional process. Second, it offers opportunities to improve the effective presentation of knowledge to students. Within the emerging learning environment, technology *can* play a role that is much more central to the basic assumptions and organising principles of the curriculum itself. As the goals change from teaching to facilitating learning, to empowering students to be reflective learners, then we can begin to consider the role of technology as being to provide four functions.

First, technology continues to increase learner access to other educational resources. However, the nature of that access changes. In the old model, technology provided learners with access to the teacher's ideas, be they in the form of texts, video programmes, audio tapes, etc. Technology helped span the distance between the instructor and the learner. In the new environment, technology is providing access to a somewhat more complex learning system that includes access to presentation materials, but also access to other learners and, perhaps most important, access to a variety of information resources or the raw materials of learning.

Some technologies are especially well-suited to extending access to organised instructional presentations: the printed word, the video programme, the audio tape, some kinds of computer presentations. Presentation of knowledge continues to be an important part of the learning environment.

Other technologies facilitate interaction among students and between students and scholars. Electronic mail, audioconferencing, interactive video systems, etc., remove the isolation of the individual learner and open up new opportunities for the learner to participate in a learning community.

Other technologies—or, more appropriately, other applications such as the World Wide Web, gopher systems, file transfer protocols—give the learner access to information resources, empowering them to select information most relevant to their own goals. Beyond the increasing variety of software, the truly significant aspect of this part of the technology picture is the breadth of information that is available to learners: databases, images, texts, sound records, visual and text archives, museum resources, and an ever-increasing array of original source documents. It is the 'anytime, anywhere' access to information resources that allow us to think seriously about transforming the curriculum.

What is emerging is not a distance education programme or open university programme that is enhanced by technology, but a media-rich learning environment in which different technologies are brought to bear on the goals of the curriculum itself. To fully understand the changing benefit of these technologies, we need to keep several key words in mind. First, the technologies are *integrated*: the educational power of these technologies comes not from how one or the other allows us to achieve some specific goal, but from how we combine them to achieve a new kind of learning community. Second, they must be integrated in a *seamless* way so that learners can easily move from receiving presentations to interacting with other members of the community to searching information. Third, they are *user-driven*: this means that the learner must be able to control his or her use of the technological environment. This integrated, seamless, user-driven multiple-media environment is, most likely, the near future for open and distance education and the long-term future of higher education generally.

In looking at this new learning environment, it is important to remember that the technology does not *cause* the change. Instead, it is probably better to say that the capabilities of the new technologies allow us to facilitate change. In this sense, it is safe to say that John Dewey was a couple of generations ahead of his time as an educational philosopher. Although many have accepted the idea of reflective experience as the hallmark of education, until now we have not had the necessary tools to make this kind of education available to learners on a large scale.

It is also important to keep the technology in perspective. Decisions about technology should not drive our decisions about the curriculum. Instead, open and distance education should be defined by the relationship that it establishes between the learner and the institution and how the curriculum itself directly and explicitly empowers learners and facilitates learning. Technology decisions should flow from these considerations. Technology is an enabler, a collection of tools and, like knowledge, a means to an end.

There is no question that the information age will be as different from the industrial age as the industrial age was from the age of agriculture. We in open and distance education are confronted today with some truly staggering choices with regard to the learner, the curriculum, and technology. The choices we make about the role we give the learner in the teaching/learning process, about the purposes to which we put the curriculum, and about how we design the use of the technologies available to us, will all greatly affect the role that our institutions play in this new era.

REFERENCES

Negroponte, N. (1995) *Being digital* (New York, Alfred A. Knopf).

Toffler, A. (1970) *Future shock* (New York, Random House).

4

Lessons from distance education for the university of the future

Ross Paul and Jane Brindley

Introduction

In the knowledge society, there is increasing recognition among governments of the importance of investment in higher education. In many countries, this coincides with burgeoning fiscal pressures as politicians struggle to cope with mounting deficits and the realisation that the demand for services outstrips their ability to pay for them. In such a climate, government leaders are always on the lookout for panaceas and distance education has emerged as one of the latest.

Superficially, distance education provides a ready response to the twin pressures of greater investment in higher education and fiscal responsibility. Using new communications technologies, distance learning institutions can deliver programmes and services to the learner in his or her own time and place. Through open admissions and recognition of prior learning, they provide greater access and support for previously disadvantaged students and, if the scale is large enough, in a cost-efficient way. It is no wonder that almost every country, rich or poor, is investing heavily in distance education in the 1990s.

There is considerable irony in this development, however. The same distance learning initiatives may perpetuate one-way, industrial modes of teaching or restrict access to those readily able to adapt to new technologies. Distance learning can be very isolating, and inadequate attention to course design, student counselling and support can yield poor completion rates and the worst aspects of one-way knowledge transmission. If this approach to distance education prevails, disillusionment will quickly follow.

Although politicians and some academics dream of utopian 'high tech' solutions, our central argument is that they will be better served by learning the 'softer', less technical lessons from distance education over the past few decades. The challenge, then, is to ensure that the lessons learned are the right ones: those that most directly affect the learning outcomes of students.

Contradictions and challenges in the modern university

There are many daunting contradictions and challenges facing the modern university in most Western countries. This section identifies four of the most current.

1 At a time when the modern university might reasonably be expected to be in the forefront of social and educational change, it is often seen as inflexible and unresponsive to emerging needs.

By all accounts, as the foremost institution in the knowledge business, the university should be thriving in today's society. Yet, many view it as an institution in crisis, too conservative and tradition-bound to adjust to rapid change and ironically less of what Senge (1990) calls a 'learning organisation' than might reasonably be anticipated.

Nonetheless, some resistance to change is a legitimate part of the university tradition, given its roles to promote the understanding and preservation of culture and to serve as social critic, both of which require a certain arm's-length relationship with the primary social and political institutions. The conflicts and tensions between the roles of change agent and guardian of culture or social critic render university management more difficult and yield understandably confused public perceptions of its mandate.

Hence, universities can be portrayed as among the most liberal and conservative of public institutions at the same time! The challenge is to find ways to realise the expectations held for the modern university without sacrificing its academic freedom and integrity.

2 As higher education has been democratised, governments have played an increasing role in university funding. This has led to new challenges to their traditional autonomy in the form of pressures for accountability, performance indicators, and public ranking systems.

Nothing has challenged the autonomy of universities more than the changes in funding patterns since 1960. Small, private institutions which relied mainly on student tuition fees and alumni support have developed into major businesses where up to 80 per cent of the budget is paid by the taxpayer. As public funds get tighter, there are more calls for accountability in the form of performance indicators and more direct intervention by stakeholders in the governance and direction of universities.

It is not enough merely to demonstrate more accountability for fewer funds than in the past. Another factor impinging on the culture of universities is their increasing reliance on other funding sources, notably tuition fees and private sector support.

Rising fees have threatened to reverse recent trends to broaden participation in higher education by reducing access for the less affluent. They have also raised students' expectations and encouraged them to demand better programmes and services.

The stronger private sector role, with its emphasis on results and accountability, has also threatened traditional academic cultures and the autonomy of professors and departments. Many academics worry about the long-term impact of corporate language on the culture of the academy and decry threats to pure research where financial support is increasingly interventionist, directive and commercially oriented.

3 Although research still shows a university education to be a key factor in the employability and earning power of a graduate, there is growing student concern about the value of a university degree, while faculty worry about the impact of preparation for employment on the academic culture of the institution.

Within one of the greatest achievements of the modern university, its relative democratisation, lies a new challenge: that of living up to the expectations it has raised. If universities train leaders and everyone goes to university, can everyone be a leader? If they train for jobs and there are none, will a better education help the individual or simply increase his or her anger and frustration?

Student disillusionment is understandable in economies where more and more graduates are unemployed. This has led to strong pressures on universities to make themselves more relevant to the job market, as students are becoming increasingly apprehensive about investing large sums of money in their own education if there is no guarantee of a payoff at the end.

For the first time in decades in the West, the new generation has lower expectations than its predecessor. The practice of overspending, relative to income levels, has produced massive government debts, the servicing of which has become the single biggest expense for many governments. We can no longer avoid massive cuts in welfare programmes, health care and education. Although necessary, these may discriminate against the younger generation who had nothing to do with the debt accumulation in the first place. The consequent disillusionment and cynicism of youth may emerge as the biggest threat to the future of higher education.

45

The pressure for relevance and preparation for the job market is seen by many faculty members as a direct threat to the academic integrity and autonomy of their institutions. Many worry that the language of business is distorting the role and mission of the university. Pressures for public accountability also place a high premium on measurable outcomes: graduation and publication rates, earning power of graduates, reputational surveys. There is a common fear that a strong emphasis on these will gradually homogenise the university system to the detriment of the missions and mandates of individual institutions.

4 New technologies are often introduced without consideration of their impact on the organisational culture, with detrimental, unintended consequences for the university.

Many believe that the best response to the dilemma of trying to provide universal access to universities, and to respond to the expectations thus raised, rests in the application of new technologies. The development since about 1970 of distance education is one example of how new ways of learning can both extend accessibility and increase efficiency.

Much has been written in glowing terms about the future contributions of communications technologies to higher education. The Internet or electronic highway that is sweeping the world shrinks distances in ways that were not even contemplated a few decades ago. Interactive video, satellite television broadcasts, CD-ROMs, computer conferencing and innovative new software packages are being applied to learning systems all over the world. Academics and students can communicate instantly, at almost no cost, with their peers and colleagues in any country.

However, these same technological innovations are a significant threat to the continuing dominance of the university. Technologies change rapidly and, although costs are coming down quickly, the most sophisticated are often very expensive. This undermines the capacity of the educational system to respond, especially given its inability to meet the associated faculty and staff training requirements.

New technologies also encourage private sector competition for training money and may be associated with a blurring of distinctions between education and entertainment, so as to trivialise learning. The challenge is to find applications of technology that develop interaction rather than isolation, critical thinking over rote learning, and independent learning skills rather than passive dependency on one-way communications.

Although the university must be in the forefront of applying new technologies to research and teaching, a more fundamental concern is that it develop its capacity to understand and to interpret technology, so as to harness its strengths while remaining fully aware of and resistant to its dangers.

The four challenges previously cited illustrate the often contradictory pressures on today's universities in their struggle to adapt to new conditions. What lessons from distance education are most responsive to these concerns, and what is the likelihood that they will be heeded in the development of tomorrow's university?

Learning from the experience of distance education

When it is suggested that traditional universities can learn much from the recent experience of distance teaching institutions, there is a tendency to expect this to be focused on their use of such technologies as television, interactive video or computer-managed learning. Although such learning aids are central to educational change, technology in this narrower sense is not the main issue, and it will not be the major contribution of distance learning to the evolution of the university.

Instead, it is the 'softer' side of open learning and distance education that merits the most attention. Here, then, are several lessons from the experience of distance education that may help campus-based universities adjust to the overwhelming demands of the twenty-first century.

1 Adopting a 'critical' perspective

The early success of open universities owed much to the 'industrial model' (Peters, 1983) with its reliance on behaviourism in instructional design and linear course production systems. Longer-term experience, however, has exposed some of the shortcomings of the industrial approach. Not only have completion rates often been low, but a strong literature has developed criticising the one-way nature of the learning that ensues and urging a more 'critical' perspective (Evans and Nation, 1993; Harris, 1987). If nothing else is learned from recent experience with distance education, mainstream advocates of high technology would be well advised to pay attention to this literature to combat any tendency to perceive distance learning as a panacea for the ills of education today.

Notwithstanding Rumble's (1995) legitimate concerns about the suitability of the label 'Fordist' in describing institutions like the Open University, it is hard to deny that many distance education practices share such industrial characteristics as the division of labour, the deskilling of workers, an assembly line approach to course development, and exposing all students to the same instructional design regardless of their individual differences.

It must be of concern that so many recent converts to distance education

47

view it in Fordist terms as a low-cost, high-volume application of technology to the delivery of knowledge. Whatever the merits of the Fordist debate, it is no accident that experienced practitioners expected to extol the virtues of new technologies are more apt to surprise their audiences by focusing instead on course design, student support and a critical perspective. To do otherwise would be to ignore the lessons of the past three decades of distance education.

2 The management of technology

For all of their experience with innovative delivery systems, distance learning practitioners have contributed surprisingly little to the literature of technology and education (Paul, 1995, p. 132). Although innovative in the organisation of learning, they have relied on simple technologies such as correspondence education supplemented by telephone tutoring or audio or video support. There is little evidence to suggest any change in the tendency for break-throughs in the application of technology to learning to come from outside the distance education sector.

Distance education still offers valuable lessons, however. The work of David Wolfe (1990, p. 63) suggests that an organisation's ability to adapt to new technologies is its greatest determinant of success. The challenge is less the adaptation of a particular technology to learning than the management of the associated organisational change, recognising that technology is:

> not a neutral tool but a value-laden culture that must both be understood and taken into account in any attempt to apply it to change in an organisation. (Paul, 1995, p. 140)

The implication is that changing the way we teach or expect students to learn will require us to change our universities in ways that may not be anticipated.

A key challenge is to learn to harness technology to integrate learners, not to isolate them, and to provide better personal support and motivation to students. The recent history of distance education teaches us to be particularly wary of those who zealously promote a particular technology as the answer to all educational needs and to pay more attention to those, like Bates (1991), who adapt a critical perspective in considering the suitability of a given technology and how it can be integrated into an institution.

3 The importance of developmental student support

Support for distance learners has evolved considerably from the time of correspondence study. When high attrition rates began to be of great concern, one response was to invest resources in such support services as tutoring, advising and counselling.

Such responses tended to reflect the industrial model of distance education, investing only in student support intended to directly facilitate course delivery, starting with enhanced tutoring services, advising and counselling. Introducing new services as 'add-ons' when there is disillusionment with the old models is an expensive and inadequate response. The lesson from open universities in particular is the importance of planning and integrating support services from the outset into the overall design of the institution.

With the evolution of distance education in both theory and practice, institutional research has shifted its focus to better understanding individuals: what and how they learn and how they can be encouraged to develop more independence. As a result, the vision of learners as passive and somewhat invisible receivers of knowledge has given way to one of learners as being much more actively involved in their own learning processes.

Within this dynamic, distance educators have been challenged to reconsider the role and purpose of support systems. There is growing recognition (Brindley, 1995a; Sewart, 1993; Sweet, 1993; Tait, 1988) of the central role of learner services in making distance education more responsive to individual learners. Several of the most important are discussed here.

The importance of context in developing a service model

There is no one set of services appropriate to all distance education settings. Services should be governed by the institutional mission and philosophy adapted to local learner characteristics, geography, resources and types of courses offered. Each service offered should have a clearly-stated purpose and be an integrated part of a contextually-defined service model.

Integration of services

As much as appropriate, services should be integrated so as to appear seamless to the student. This may mean 'flattening the organisation' so that decisions are made closest to the learner or reducing specialisation. Sweet (1993), for example, presents a rationale for integrating tutoring and counselling which does not preclude having specialised experts as designers, developers, trainers, or researchers to guide service providers.

Importance of staff development

Some distance education institutions, through necessity, have become models of learning organisations. In many cases, staff development particular to the needs of distance education was not readily available, and institutions had to develop their own training programmes, such as retraining front-line clerical staff as educational advisers, or producing specialised programmes on using technology in teaching.

Use of technology

It is not easy to offer complex student support services at a distance and, each time a new one is mounted, a particular challenge is ensuring its availability to all students, regardless of their access to technology. Distance education practitioners have a wide experience of delivering such services as academic assessment, new student orientation, career counselling and study skill assistance through both simple (print-based materials) and complex (interactive video) methods. This, one of the most innovative areas of distance education, has received scant attention until recently but, according to Brindley (1995a), is a key to its future success.

Collaboration

Facing complex and expensive needs for service at a distance, support providers have provided models for collaboration with colleagues in other institutions and agencies. They have also looked outside of their own institutions for referral points for services for learners, developing a wealth of information about and relationships with other sources of support for their clientele. Distance learning centres are frequently housed within collaborating agencies and staff may be shared between institutions.

Importance of evaluation

Although much remains to be done in the evaluation of learner services (Brindley, 1995b; Thorpe, 1988), distance educators are increasingly questioning their role and purpose. Continuous evaluation allows support providers to articulate clearly the role which services play in the learning process, to provide a constantly improving and valued service, and to develop a theoretical framework for their practice. Most importantly, continuous evaluation is a way systematically to challenge assumptions, beliefs and values upon which practice is based.

4 The reorganisation of teaching and learning

The rapid expansion of campus-based universities and their increasing reliance on technology has not appreciably changed the way teaching and learning are organised. The highly bureaucratised structure of a large, modern university, together with collective agreements which formalise processes and structures, combine to institutionalise resistance to change.

At the same time, the recent fiscal crises in most Western countries are forcing universities to consider radical reform of teaching and learning if new cost efficiencies are to be realised. Distance education has demonstrated that students can learn at home and in the workplace, that many quite simple technologies can support and enhance learning, and that faculty time can be freed up for research, course writing and tutoring by innovative approaches to the organisation of academic work.

The pressures for change and greater efficiency in universities will inevitably focus on the role of the professor, given the huge investment that faculty salaries represent. There are many ways in which technology can free up faculty time by permitting students to take more responsibility for their own learning. If the response to shrinking resources is merely to increase teaching loads, this will detract further from research and undermine the quality of the institution. It follows that much more innovative approaches are required: ones that model many of the practices in open universities across the world.

5 Collaboration across institutions and agencies

There has been much resistance to notions of system in higher education as universities value their autonomy as the ultimate protection for academic freedom. Recent fiscal pressures have required mainstream universities to narrow their individual mandates, to focus on their strengths, and to look to collaboration with others to maximise their effectiveness.

Moran and Mugridge (1993) offer a useful collection of examples of collaboration in distance education, many of which could be applied to the mainstream university sector. It can be argued that, in the main, such ventures as shared course materials, enhanced transfer credits and national and international consortia have been realised, not at the expense of, but for the benefit of institutional autonomy by strengthening each collaborating institution in the process.

6 Stronger service orientation and the quality movement

It is no accident that open universities and other providers of distance education have been in the forefront of the quality movement in universities (Mills and Paul, 1993). Catering primarily to adult learners on an individualised basis, they have had to adopt more of a 'customer' focus than more traditional universities where students have been expected to adapt to the institution rather than *vice versa*.

The fit of quality and continuous improvement processes to universities has not been without its difficulties, given concerns about the appropriateness of a customer approach for students who are being evaluated and judged at the same time. Again, however, the debate that has taken place within distance education provides some useful lessons for how such initiatives can best be carried out in the university setting.

The outlook: The university of the future

Distance education in itself will not resolve the fundamental difficulties facing universities today, but the case has been presented that it has much to contribute to the university of the future. Although the prevailing outlook here is optimistic, there are countless grounds for pessimism, especially given tendencies to elevate technologies to deistic status. It is useful to contemplate the university of the future from both perspectives.

An optimistic vision for the future

In our optimistic scenario, the university of the future will be a much changed but strongly reaffirmed institution: one that makes little distinction between face-to-face and distance education. It will no longer cater primarily to full-time, campus-based undergraduate students, but will be a lifelong learning institution with a great range and variety of programmes and educational delivery systems that cater to the needs of all citizens.

Computers, interactive video and international databases will be so readily available that formal learning opportunities will be accessible to all. Every member of society will be able to design his or her own learning programmes with strong support from families, businesses, labour unions and formal educational institutions. Learning will increasingly be valued for its own sake and every institution and agency in the community will have a role to play, often in partnership arrangements. National boundaries will be far less significant to learning. An expert in Beijing or New York will be able to 'teach' students in any country through interactive technologies using a multi-mediated approach.

Opportunities for information will be so pervasive that students unequipped to deal with them will be seriously disadvantaged. This emphasises the importance of incorporating basic skills development into teaching to facilitate the ability of students to pursue their own learning needs independently. It involves openness to changes in personal values and attitudes (self-confidence and self-motivation), as well as the development of new skills such as time management, study and research competences, problem conceptualisation and analysis, critical and lateral thinking, and the ability to integrate learning into one's everyday life. A quest never completely fulfilled, it is a process central to our concept of a university.

Taped lectures and computer-assisted learning will free faculty from the traditional knowledge-transfer role and permit them to focus on personal and tutorial support for students and the pursuit of their own research interests. Specialised training will continue, but learning how to learn and how to cope with change will be much more important than any specific technical skill.

Whether in the classroom or via distance education, the development of independent learning does not just happen. University faculty are seldom trained as teachers and it is no mean task to lead students to discover the joys of learning and to develop their own learning skills. It also does not necessarily follow that distance education develops independent learners just because students are on their own. Careful and tailor-made course design, strong student support and library services, and an emphasis on interactive learning are all fundamental to such an approach. Without such care, student drop-out rates are sufficiently high in distance education as to belie its supposed advantages in cost and convenience.

Hence, in this utopian vision, the university degree of the future will be a formal attestation that the graduate has mastered the skills of the independent learner and is an imminently trainable and adaptable citizen, well prepared for a world of constant and dramatic change. He or she will be served by an accountable, lifelong learning institution, very much like the best of our open universities.

The pessimistic side

It is not difficult to take the same sorts of objectives and environmental contexts and envision much more pessimistic scenarios. For example:

■ The pace of change will be so rapid and discontinuous that the relatively cumbersome universities will not be able to keep up. Their functions may or may not be taken up by government or private agencies, but, in any event, the integrity of the autonomous university will be lost.

■ Too many distance education proponents will place the highest premium on technological toys without first determining the learning needs of the students, the challenges of the particular discipline and how a given technology can address these directly. The means to learning will become ends in themselves and some of the most important lessons of distance education will be lost in the rush to use fancy hardware and impressive graphics.

- As has too often been the experience of distance education, technologies such as satellite television can easily be misused for one-way learning and indoctrination. There is tremendous scope for tyranny here (Tait, 1989) through manipulation of the system for corporate or political ends that are contrary to libertarian ideals of education. Hence, learning may become indoctrination, and diversion may increasingly supplant genuine enquiry and debate as technology becomes a form of drug to keep the masses blissfully preoccupied and conformist.

- We will not be able to afford the dream. Spiralling costs and debts will force us to cut back so much and so quickly that we will revert to more elitist times where only the privileged had access to higher learning. This will exacerbate the conflict of generations and lead to major confrontations and even violence within our individual societies.

One could go on at great length. We offer the pessimistic side mainly to emphasise how difficult change is, and how much is at stake. Our purpose is not to overestimate the role of the university as an institution, but to make sure that we don't underestimate the importance of lifelong learning.

Finding the way through

Is there a middle-range view of all this? Without creating Utopia on earth, can we avoid Armageddon? Can a single institution even dream of achieving all of the higher-order goals that we have set out?

It is difficult to preview how our universities will evolve, but their core value systems of openness and the search for truth must be preserved at all costs. Strong leadership is critical, but it must exemplify the very values that universities espouse through what Badaracco and Ellsworth (1989) have termed 'value-driven leadership' (Paul, 1990). The challenges will be great, but the effective new university will be one that has benefited greatly from the recent lessons of distance education and open learning.

REFERENCES

Badaracco, J.L. & Ellsworth, R.R. (1989) *Leadership and the quest for integrity* (Boston: Harvard Business School Press).

Bates, A. (1991) Third generation distance education, *Research in Distance Education*, **3**(2), pp. 10–15.

Brindley, J.E. (1995a) Learners and learner services: The key to the future in open distance learning.

In Roberts, J.M. & Keough, E.M. (Eds.), *Why the information highway? Lessons from open and distance learning* (Toronto, Trifolium Books), pp. 102–125.

Brindley, J.E. (1995b) Measuring quality in learner services: Building towards the future. In Sewart, D. (Ed.), *One world, many voices: Quality in open and distance learning*, Vol. 2, Selected papers from the 17th World Conference of the International Council for Distance Education at Birmingham, UK (Oslo, Norway, International Council for Distance Education; Milton Keynes, UK, The Open University).

Evans, T. & Nation, D. (1993) Educational technologies: Reforming open and distance education. In Evans, T. & Nation, D. (Eds.) *Reforming open and distance education: Critical reflections from practice* (London, Kogan Page), pp. 196–214.

Harris, D. (1987) *Openness and closure in distance education* (London, The Falmer Press).

Mills, R. & Paul, R. (1993) Putting the student first: Management for quality in distance education. In Evans, T. & Nation, D. (Eds.) *Reforming open and distance education: Critical reflections from practice* (London, Kogan Page), pp. 113–129.

Moran, L. & Mugridge, I. (Eds.) (1993) *Collaboration in distance education: International case studies* (London, Routledge).

Paul, R.H. (1990) *Open learning and open management: Leadership and integrity in distance education* (London, Kogan Page).

Paul, R.H. (1995) Virtual realities or fantasies? Technology and the future of distance education. In Roberts, J.M. & Keough, E.M. (Eds.) *Why the information highway? Lessons from open and distance learning* (Toronto, Trifolium Books), pp. 126–145.

Peters, O. (1983) Distance teaching and industrial production. A comparative interpretation in outline. In Sewart, D., Keegan, D. & Holmberg, B. (Eds.) *Theoretical principles of distance education* (London, Routledge), pp. 98–110.

Rumble, G. (1995) How Fordist is distance education? *Open Learning*, **10**(2), pp. 12–28.

Senge, P.M. (1990) *The fifth discipline: The art and practice of the learning organisation* (New York, Doubleday).

Sewart, D. (1993) Student support systems in distance education. In Scriven, B., Lundin, R. & Ryan, Y. (Eds.) *Distance education for the 21st century*, Proceedings of the 16th World Conference at Nonthaburi, Thailand (Brisbane, Australia, International Council for Distance Education and Queensland University of Technology).

Sweet, R. (Ed.) (1993) Perspectives on distance education—student support services: Toward more responsive systems. *Report of a symposium on student support services in distance education*, Delhi (Vancouver, The Commonwealth of Learning).

Tait, A. (1988) Unpublished presentation, International Council for Distance Education World Conference, Oslo.

Tait, A. (1989) Democracy in distance education and the role of tutorial and counselling services, *Journal of Distance Education*, 3(1), pp. 95–99.

Thorpe, M. (1988) *Evaluating open and distance learning* (Harlow, Longman Group UK Ltd).

Wolfe, D. (1990) The management of innovation. In Salter, L. & Wolfe, D. (Eds.) *Managing technology: Social science perspectives* (Toronto: Garamond Press), pp. 89-111.

Part 2

Student support, technology and the learner

5

Conversation and community: Student support in open and distance learning

Alan Tait

The issues which this chapter seeks to address concern the role that learner or student support plays within open and distance learning systems from the affective, value-related and social dimensions. By learner or student support is meant those activities which are individualised or delivered in interactive groups (whether face-to-face, by telephone, electronically or in some other medium), such as tutoring and counselling, in contrast with the learning materials prepared for a mass of users without any actual individual or group in mind. In short, the extent to which open and distance learning reflects and indeed reinforces the atomised and privatised nature of life in developed countries is examined, an issue which has concerned no less an exponent of open and distance learning than Michael Young:

> *Since the birth of the Industrial Revolution, thousands of millions of people have laboured to produce a world populated by strangers, and not all of them are as benign as the absent teacher who is trying to empower the individual rather than dominate him or her for political or commercial reasons.* (Young, 1995, p. 8)

The counter current that has always been asserted by student support in this field, in its insistence that learners interact not only with the learning materials but with each other and with a tutor or facilitator figure, is critically considered. The relationships which are denoted at the micro-level by the term *conversation* and at the macro-level by the term *community* are explored in terms of their explanatory power in relation to student support, and it will be suggested that student support in open and distance learning, beyond the need to deliver teaching on a personalised and/or localised basis, represents ways of meeting fundamental human needs for social interaction in the educational context: a very significant and widely inhabited domain of human development.

The increasing dominance of managerialism in the educational context, driven by a broad socio-political environment which concretely demands 'more for less' in an environment of rapid technological change, is reviewed in terms of its tendency to diminish the potential for student support to embody the processes and values of conversation and community. The counter-tendency of computer-based communication is also examined, and is seen as having the potential to reinforce the processes and values of conversation and community, and to diminish the loneliness and alienation of the learner.

Industrialised learning in an industrialised society

The dominant account of the nature of open and distance learning has been of its industrialised nature, referring to the creation of learning materials for correspondence education which, in the well-known analysis of Peters, moved teaching from a craft to an industrialised base. Although Peters' original analysis appeared in the 1960s, it was not until 1989 that he was able to clarify that his attitude was not necessarily an enthusiastic endorsement of such a shift, but an observation that it was taking place. In his later work Peters makes clear his concerns about:

> the dangers of a technological model of distance study, the over-emphasis on technical devices, the inevitable reduction of possible learning objectives, the fragmentation and compartmentalisation of the learning process, the dominance of technical rationality at the cost of 'critical rationality'. (Peters, 1989, p. 4)

It is interesting to note that, from the beginning, one of the leading academics and practitioners in this field alerted enthusiasts of open and distance learning to some of the characteristics which it shared with industrialisation in general and which offered cause for concern. This has often been overlooked.

However, the development of student services by the Open University UK has represented a significant element in the humanisation of correspondence education and the creation of modern distance education, and in this the OU has enjoyed a remarkable quarter-century of broad continuity from 1971, its first year of teaching. Primary elements are the provision of advice at a pre-study stage, the central role of personalised and individualised correspondence teaching, the individual link to tutor and counsellor, with the opportunity to meet face-to-face on as local a basis as the OU could offer through more than 250 study centres in the UK and later in continental

Europe, and the provision of residential schools. Some organisational reworking of the arrangements, for example joining the tutor and counsellor roles for undergraduates in 1976, has not disrupted that essential continuity. The account of its genesis is given by the man who largely conceived its implementation, the first Director of Regional Tutorial Services, Robert Beevers (Beevers, 1975). His account is tantalisingly brief, but is clear that the services in tuition and counselling, to be provided from a range of study centres, represented continuity of English traditions as well as their radical reworking for the first open entry higher education institution for mature students. The insistence on personal attention and small group teaching derive, it can be suggested, from two traditions: university education in the UK, especially the Oxbridge tradition of micro-group or individual teaching, which enjoyed until the recent period of expansion an effective pastoral element within it, and adult education with its emphasis on group discussion and participation on a democratic footing. Interestingly, Beevers at this early period foresees, in discussion of arguments for greater freedom for students and tutors to develop their own questions for assessment (partly in place of the assignments centrally set by course teams in Milton Keynes), that whatever changes are brought into the tutorial and counselling system, 'the student will need an academic mentor whose work is predicated on him (sic) rather than on the course material' (Beevers, 1975, p. 15). Beevers' own background as an Oxford-educated historian and later a lecturer in adult education has been considered to have contributed to the sort of student support which he was so influential in creating (Ferguson, 1975, p. 46–47). That it stood the test of time over some 25 years is a remarkable testament to a blueprint created without any real precedent or analogous experience to guide him and his close colleagues. The significance of achievement is not limited to the OU UK, as its practices in the field of student support, as well as the creation of courses, have been examined, adapted and adopted in the more than 25 distance teaching universities later established around the world.

Underlying values and processes

This chapter seeks to identify the underlying values and processes which exist in the activities that we expect to take place in the field of student support services. Ideas are initially examined from three major theoretical contributors to this field, namely Holmberg, Moore and Sewart. The early work of Holmberg, with the concept of 'guided didactic conversation', provides an opening to discussion. Holmberg identifies the importance of *the spirit and atmosphere of conversation ... that should—and largely do—characterise educational endeavours'* (Holmberg, 1983, p. 114). Amongst other things, Holmberg refers to *'conversation-like interaction'*, and notes that *'feelings of personal relation between the teacher and learning parties promote study pleasure'* (Holmberg, 1983, p. 116). We can identify from this early work a range of ideas which are important for the thesis developed here, including the centrality of conversation as a metaphor for educational relationships, and the importance of affective factors such as affinity and pleasure.

Moore's theory of transactional distance, that is to say the psychological and communications space that separates the teacher and the learner, includes discussion of 'instructional dialogue' and notes that the term dialogue has a greater degree of purposefulness, being 'valued by each party', than the broader term interaction (Moore, 1993, pp. 23–24). Moore's earlier work had challenged the behaviourist ideas which represented such an influential paradigm in distance education, arguing from the humanistic tradition *'which gave special value to interpersonal, generally open-ended and unstructured dialogue in education as in counselling'* (Moore, 1993, p. 31). Moore's work established that in relationship with structure—that is to say the pre-written learning and assessment materials—central to distance education was a *'relationship [that] was individual and dialogic'* (Moore, 1983, p. 76).

Although the early vision of student support in the OU UK can be largely attributed to Beevers, the analysis of basic principles has been most substantially carried out by his successor in the same post, David Sewart, whose work has been internationally influential. The published work by Sewart has, first, led the study of student support to focus on the mediation role of individualised tuition and counselling:

> *the way in which the student as an individual fits this new knowledge into his (sic) own peculiar pre-existing framework and into his (sic) everyday lifestyle.* (Sewart, 1983, p. 50)

Second, Sewart encourages one to examine the thinking from the perspective of service rather than product-based industry, the latter area having dominated discussion in the open and distance learning field because of the more evident existence of the 'product' in the form of course materials (Sewart, 1982; 1993). Sewart's perception that the mediation role was essential in educational terms, providing the means to assist particular students in their learning, has provided the basis for a wide range of subsequent work, including the relevance of constructivist approaches to teaching and learning, which recognise the contribution made by the active learner (Brindley, 1995a), and *'the responsibility to provide more than mere access to mass-produced knowledge'* (Brindley, 1995b, p. 108). The concern for the abuse of distance education and the potential for indoctrination where such mediation is absent also draws on

Sewart's work on mediation (Tait, 1995a). Sewart's later linking of the managerial dimension with educational ideas has been persuasive. His view is that:

> *the traditional management of universities is inappropriate for distance education. As an industrialised form of teaching and learning it is to industry that it must look for its decision-making structure.* (Sewart, 1993, p. 11)

This view reflects the widespread trend of higher education in the UK moving away from collegiality and towards hierarchical structures. The issue of management and managerialism will, however, be returned to.

Conversation and community

Having examined the pioneering work of the OU UK and three major writers in the field, it is suggested at this stage that, drawing from the sources previously alluded to, two areas can be identified which underlie activities in education at a distance which are especially grounded in student support services. These are conversation and community, and they represent the notions of interaction both in process and values, as well as acknowledging the social dimension of relationships which exist through whatever medium, including learner-learner as well as learner-tutor relationships.

By the term *conversation* is intended, first of all, the notions of interaction and dialogue already referred to, but in addition, a wider context of human communication which exists outside the educational environment which, in terms of actual relationships, is equally important to learners. A framework of interaction amongst equals, irrespective of roles such as student and tutor, is embodied in the term, as is the autonomy of the individuals rather than the management of the institution in the spontaneity and non-instrumental nature of such interaction. Conversation thrives where participants value each other and gain pleasure from the exchange. Mutuality becomes a principal in such an exchange, and gain and profit are perceived as inappropriate objectives. Affinity, i.e. the characteristics in terms of value and process which inform friendship, represents the backdrop against which such conversations optimally take place. The values and characteristics associated with conversation and community can be represented as shown in Fig. 5.1.

Arising out of such conversations we can posit social relationships which can be termed those of community. Barnett has written analogously in the context of higher education more generally that:

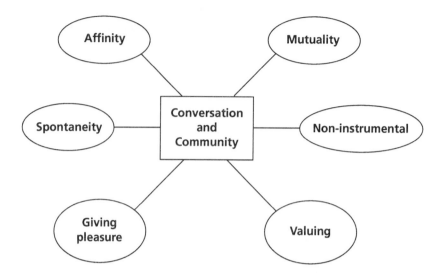

Figure 5.1 Values and characteristics associated with conversation and community

> *The development of communication—both within the academic community and between the academic community and the general public—is connected with the development of a more rational society, characterised by a general conversation.* (Barnett, 1992, p. 83)

The term community is not intended to include the non-voluntary and potentially oppressive social groups which communitarianism has recently sought to re-establish in reaction to perceived social anomie (Etzioni, 1995). Rather, community encompasses the values and processes of conversation in a wider context, including the voluntary joining (and leaving) of the communities which conversation creates. In this, as face-to-face meetings are non-compulsory and attendance partial, the OU UK system is well placed.

It can be readily conceded that students should enjoy their work, and indeed, with adult students, if this enjoyment is not present in any form, they are likely to withdraw. Drawing on the values of humanistic counselling and adult education, which form part of the tradition of ideas in distance education as Moore notes (1993, p. 31), it is commonly held that students should feel valued and should not diminish each other or be diminished by the tutor or institution in order to learn most effectively (although, like other ideas presented here, these assertions are culturally specific). However, at first glance, the notion that spontaneous conversations have an important part to play in distance education—an educational domain which by its nature seems to demand schedules and critical path analyses by both course developers and students—seems far-fetched. Equally, in educational systems where students want qualifications, and stakeholders like governments and institutions want student success, the idea that student support services might be non-instrumental seems as unlikely. As for affinity and mutuality (the latter term meaning the willingness, indeed desire, to assist one another without gain as an objective), can it really be suggested that students should like each other or seek friendship with their tutors, or that tutors would want to contribute without material reward?

What is being delineated here are non-institutionalised interactions within non-hierarchical groupings, which it is suggested form the basis for ideal-type human relationships, such as friendship (Argyle and Henderson, 1990). Such ideals are schematic rather than descriptive. Thus student services within distance education should allow the possibility of or the potential for such relationships, while of course assisting with time management and task completion. Indeed, spontaneity will be irrepressible in certain circumstances, with students forming friendships and pursuing discussion outside the tutorial, or, as is well known at the Open University and other residential schools, until late at night. Equally, while Earwaker warns against the usefulness of friendship as a model of relationship between tutor and student in higher education, insisting on the dimension of the working rather than the social relationship (Earwaker, 1992, p. 55; p. 86), and although the potential for abuse of power in relationships between lecturers and students has rightly received attention, students and tutors will find affinities on a human level that will arise out of conversation and may continue to the level of community, i.e. non-institutional and non-instrumental relationships. Similarly, on the basis of student need or particular interest in a line of thought which a student is exploring, a tutor may give time, beyond the normal time limits, because of mutuality rather than material gain. Indeed all educational systems are happy to allow this, and to some extent the OU UK depends on such commitment. What is being argued is that underneath the structures of courses, assignments, and schedules, which programmes of study must have, and which student support primarily exists to facilitate, lies a range of potential human relationships which will assert themselves whatever managerial structures exist to encompass them in instrumental and rational terms. Feminist analysis has much to offer in this context with Belenky's term *'the passionate knower ... when women find points of connection between their own lives and what they are trying to understand'* (Belenky *et al.* cited in Sweet, 1993, p. 35). It is clear from recent ethnographic studies that this is the reality for many learners in open and distance learning (Evans, 1994; Lunneborg, 1994).

Managerial approaches to student support

Issues such as conversation and community have been marginalised by the increasing dominance of managerial approaches over the last decade. It needs to be said, at the outset, that management is not considered here as an option, but is understood to be a necessity. It is taken as axiomatic that those who do not engage with the consideration of the management of tasks in any organisational setting will be bad managers rather than not be managers. However, according to Ball, management theories in education *'tend to be top-down theories: they contain a view of the organisation looking down from the position of those in control'* (Ball, 1990, p. 165). Furthermore, management has predominantly grown up in education in what can be termed a technocratic or 'value-free' approach, drawing on ideas from the business world, where the social and economic parameters which are so powerfully encompassing are accepted without adequate critical examination (Bottery, 1992, pp. 7–19). This is especially damaging in an institution, particularly, though not exclusively, at a higher education level, which should represent social space in which critical challenges to the social environment, so essential for its well-being, can be conceived.

Work by Paul has provided the most convincing linking of the importance of the learner's role and the management of open and distance learning systems (Paul, 1990). Paul begins from the perspective, not of accepting that educational institutions are as represented in stereotypical (but probably misleading) accounts of business organisations, but of suggesting that universities are and should be environments of 'organised anarchy' (Paul, 1990, p. 67). Paul identifies integrity as an essential element in management in an open learning-based institution, by which he means consistency and constancy in decision-making and a commitment to fundamental values in consonance with the organisation's central mission (Paul, 1990, pp. 68–69). Paul links management strategy with the objective of producing 'independent learners': those students possessing qualities of critical thinking, with an ability to contribute to their learning in the senses intended by the constructivist school (cf. Brindley, 1995a), and in general having the robustness to manage the freedom, demands and choices offered by open and distance learning. A clear outcome of Paul's line of argument is anti-technocratic, i.e. he suggests not that there are no options because of the domination of 'the bottom line', but that it is essential to debate the values and ethics which are central concerns in an educational setting. As Bottery puts it in his discussion of educational management:

> *The notion that dissent is, within limits, a necessary quality ... should become part of the educational agenda.* (Bottery, 1992, p. 68)

The institutional necessity of dissent, within a broad understanding of institutional mission, has also been proposed in the context of quality assurance in open and distance learning (Tait, 1993).

Quality assurance (QA) is now seeking a central place in higher education in the UK as well as internationally. Extended manuals from a body like the Higher Education Quality Council (HEQC) in the field of 'Guidance and Learner Support' are set out in an exhaustive list of over 40 headings of learner expectations, insitutional and learner responsibilities, and ways in which 'indicative evidence' may be sought (HEQC, 1995). They have been adapted for use by the OU UK, acknowledging the necessity of satisfying the HEQC procedures for funding purposes as well as modernising approaches to QA within the OU. It is not an original observation, however, to note that the necessary and welcome introduction of systematic QA procedures does not assure the presence of the hard-to-define 'buzz' of successful learning in all the breadth of term which notions like 'conversation' embody, or the creation of learning through the social dimension around as well as within the curriculum, which is embraced by the term 'community'.

It is necessary to ask whether the drive for increased volumes and more intense use of resources in the OU UK, in common with other universities here and elsewhere, creates the danger that student support services might have to move away from their capacity to offer interaction and towards a bureaucratised and impersonal system. A combination of factors has led to an extensive review in the OU UK of these services in the period 1985 to 1995 (Brindley and Fage, 1992), including the greater complexity of available programmes of study, the volume expansion overall of students within the OU which is taken to represent a qualitative and not just an incremental jump, the continuing demands for efficency gains or 'doing more for less' at government behest, together with the revolution driven by technological developments in the workplace which is still in process. (In considering the pace of change it is salutary to note that the Cambridge Regional Centre of the OU took possession of its first word-processing personal computer in 1986, did not begin to use e-mail on a widespread basis until 1990, and gained its first fax machine in February of the same year.) Changes include the reduction of the possibility for students to enjoy 'continuity of counselling' (some will, but others will be expected to look to a team of advisers in their Regional Centre). The new Student Service Teams, which replace some local counsellors:

> would have a broad proactive student progress monitoring role for all students, irrespective of the course, facilitated by the comprehensive student records database ... This service would be available outside normal office hours and would be staffed by Advisers working from the Regional Centre and/or from their homes using developments in new technology. (Lewis, 1994, p. 3)

67

The individual and personalised relationship that is represented in course tutoring remains in place, and has additional responsibilities placed on it in terms of monitoring student progress. However, it is to be feared that the reform of counselling, necessary in the environment of change already set out, and clearly and courageously thought through, will lead to it being increasingly dominated by mailings triggered through 'events' (such as failure to submit an assignment) identified automatically and impersonally by a database, with assistance being offered at anonymous telephone referral points rather than through conversations with known individuals. At its worst, following the pattern of customer care in banking, educational counselling will be replaced by a combination of standardised mailings and desperate telephone calls when something has gone wrong, rather than the developmental continuity of the 'individual and long-standing relationship' seen as so important in earlier systems (Sewart, 1982, p. 28). Peters has voiced the long-term fear that:

> a process of alienation takes place when students are confronted with technical artefacts instead of human beings. Personal relations become indirect, depersonalised and lose much of their reality. (Peters, 1989, pp. 3–4)

Although Sewart has argued that the mediating functions of tutors and counsellors contrasted with the industrialised and mass-produced nature of the learning materials (Sewart, 1982, p. 28), by 1989 Peters was arguing that industrialisation governed far more of the tutor's and counsellor's work than was acknowledged (Peters, 1989, pp. 5–6). Sewart later acknowledges the contradictory forces driving the new developments in counselling in the OU UK, writing that:

> Bureaucracy and formalism are enemies of creativity and innovation but procedures and routines are needed to be able to utilise creative potential in an organisation. (Sewart, 1995)

If the delivery of student services becomes industrialised in the sense of mass-produced, following the model of the production of learning materials rather than contrasting with it, conversation and community will be diminished within open and distance learning as they are in society at large. It is to be feared that, at least to some extent, Peters' pessimistic vision is proving realistic.

New technologies in student support

However, as pressures on established methods of student support lead to more industrialised and bureaucratised systems, new technologies—in particular computer-mediated communication (CMC)—have begun to offer oppor-tunities for the apparently irrepressible human insistence, however low-key it sometimes appears, on interaction. No account of CMC should ignore the warnings in recent publications in this field concerning the crucial issues of how technology is applied for the best interests of learners (Bates, 1993, p. 214), the resistance to technologically-mediated relationships (Von Prümmer, 1995, p. 263), the gendered nature of the new technologies and in particular the gendered nature of access as well as interaction (see Chapter 10), the potential for control as well as liberation of people with disabilities in the use of CMC (Evans and Newell, 1993, p. 90), and the more general concerns about the potential of the new technologies to make education a *'less and less holistic experience in real life, grounded in real communities'* (Menzies, cited in Burge, 1995, p. 160). In addition, it is clear that CMC depends in many ways on industrialisation in its use of technical devices.

However, CMC also embodies many of the qualities which have been associated in the previous paragraph with the terms conversation and community. Indeed these terms are frequently used by writers in this field. We can note, first, Peters' consideration of the role of distance education in a post-industrial society, where he expects the lonely life of distance learners will be considered 'inhuman' as:

> *the additional demands on them divorce them more or less from their families, their neighbours and friends, and reduce their civic, social, and political contacts.* (Peters, 1993, p. 49)

Peters proposes that an increased use of groupwork will be necessary using, in particular, 'telecommunication between the participants' (Peters, 1993, p. 57). Within this broad framework of contemporary development we find in Romiszowski a practical account of *'the effective implementation of group discussion, or "conversational" methodologies on electronic telecommunications networks'* (Romiszowski, 1995, p. 164). Burge suggests that *'we have to create the conditions for "creative volatility of conversation" without producing prattle'* (Burge, 1995, p. 158), neatly embodying some of the qualities, for example, of spontaneity, which it has been proposed make up elements within conversation along with a care for the educational purpose at hand. One of the most authoritative sources in the field notes that:

> *computer conferencing is often more personal, more intimate and more community-making than comparable face-to-face situations ... computer conferencing supports a kind of intimacy which is one feeling of social presence.* (Mason, 1994, p. 34)

So-called 'electronic socialising' (Soby, cited in Mason, 1994, p. 57) evidently has been found to contain many of the elements of conversation and community which it has been suggested are essential elements in education as in social life at large.

Conclusion

In conclusion, it is suggested that in the contradictory ways that social development often plays out, electronic conferencing, in its capacity to engender and support conversation and community, represents a force in counterweight to the increasingly bureaucratised systems of student support. In large distance teaching institutions, dominated of necessity by volume and efficiency gains in recent years and the onward march of technocratic managerialism, student support services may find their ability to complement but contrast with the industrialised production of course materials diminished. In whatever re-engineering of student support systems in this environment is necesssary, the values and characteristics associated with conversation and community should, it is proposed, remain central if open and distance education is to remain a domain which human beings might choose to enjoy and within which they can develop.

REFERENCES

Argyle, M. & Henderson, M. (1990) *The anatomy of relationships* (London, Penguin).

Ball, S. (1990) Management as moral technology: A Luddite analysis. In Ball, S. (Ed.) *Foucault and education, disciplines and knowledge* (London, Routledge).

Barnett, R. (1990) *Improving higher education: Total quality care* (Buckingham, SRHE/Open University Press).

Bates, T. (1993) Theory and practice in the use of technology in distance education. In Keegan, D. (Ed.) *Theoretical principles of distance education* (London, Routledge).

Beevers, R. (1975) The function of the part-time academic staff in the Open University teaching system, *Teaching at a Distance*, 3, pp. 11–15.

Bottery, M. (1992) *The ethics of educational management* (London, Cassell).

Brindley, J. (1995a) Learner services, theory and practice. Paper presented at the University of Umea, Sweden, May 1995.

Brindley, J. (1995b) Learners and learner services: The key to the future in open and distance learning. In Roberts, J.M. & Keough, E.M. (Eds.) *Why the information highway? Lessons from open and distance learning* (Toronto, Trifolium Books).

Brindley, J. & Fage, J. (1992) Counselling in open learning: Two institutions face the future, *Open Learning*, 7 (3), pp. 12–19.

Burge, L. (1995) Electronic highway or weaving loom? Thinking about conferencing technologies for learning. In Lockwood, F. (Ed.) *Open and distance learning today* (London, Routledge).

Earwaker, J. (1992) *Helping and supporting students* (Buckingham, Society for Research into Higher Education and Open University Press).

Etzioni, A. (1995) *The spirit of community, rights, responsibilities and the communitarian agenda* (London, Fontana).

Evans, T. (1994) *Understanding learners in open and distance learning* (London, Kogan Page).

Evans, T. & Newell, C. (1993) Computer-mediated comunication for post-graduate research: Future dialogue? In Nunan, T. (Ed.) *Distance education futures*, Selected papers from the 11th Biennial Forum of the Australian and South Pacific External Studies Association, 21–23 July 1993, University of South Australia.

Ferguson, J. (1975) *The Open University from within* (London, University of London Press Ltd).

Higher Education Quality Council (1995) *A Quality Assurance framework for guidance and learner support in higher education* (London, HEQC).

Holmberg, B. (1983) Guided didactic conversation in distance education. In Sewart, D., Keegan, D. & Holmberg, B. (Eds.) *Distance education: International perspectives* (Beckenham, Croom Helm/St Martin's Press).

Lewis, R. (1994) *Structuring student support to meet changing needs*. Academic board paper AcB/65/18, internal paper (Milton Keynes, Open University).

Lunneborg, P.W. (1994) *OU women: Undoing educational obstacles* (London, Cassell).

Mason, R. (1994) *Using communications media in open and distance learning* (London, Kogan Page).

Moore, M.G. (1983) On a theory of independent study. In Sewart, D., Keegan, D. & Holmberg, B. (Eds.) *Distance education: International perspectives* (Beckenham, Croom Helm/St Martin's Press).

Moore, M.G. (1993) Theory of transactional distance. In Keegan, D. (Ed.) *Theoretical principles of distance education* (London, Routledge).

Paul, R. (1990) *Open learning and open management: Leadership and integrity in distance education* (London, Kogan Page).

Peters, O. (1989) The iceberg has not melted: Further reflections on the concept of industrialisation and distance teaching, *Open Learning*, **4** (3), pp. 3–8.

Peters, O. (1993) Distance education in a post-industrial society. In Keegan, D. (Ed.) *Theoretical principles of distance education* (London, Routledge).

Romiszowski, A.J. (1995) Use of hypermedia and telecommunications for case study discussion in distance education. In Lockwood, F. (Ed.) *Open and distance learning today* (London, Routledge).

Sewart, D. (1982) Individualising student support services. In Daniel, J.S., Stroud, M.A. & Thompson, J.S. (Eds.) *Learning at a distance: A world perspective* (Edmonton, International Council for Distance Education), pp. 27–29.

Sewart, D. (1983) Distance teaching: A contradiction in terms? In Sewart, D., Keegan, D. & Holmberg, B. (Eds.) *Distance education: International perspectives* (Beckenham, Croom Helm/St Martin's Press).

Sewart, D. (1993) Student support systems in distance education, *Open Learning*, **8** (3), pp. 3–12.

Sewart, D. (1995) Regional Advisory Service Working Group, Internal Memorandum from the Director Regional Academic Services to Regional Directors, 29 September 1995. Internal document, Milton Keynes, Open University.

Sweet, R. (Ed.) (1993) *Perspectives on distance education–student support services: Towards more responsive systems*, Report of a Symposium on Student Support Services in Distance Education, Delhi (Vancouver, The Commonwealth of Learning).

Tait, A. (1993) Systems, values and dissent: Quality assurance for open and distance learning, *Distance Education*, **14** (2), pp. 303–314.

Tait, A. (1995a) The end of innocence: Critical issues in open and distance learning, *Open Learning*, **9** (3), pp. 27–37.

Tait, A. (1995b) Student support in open and distance learning. In Lockwood, F. (Ed.) *Open and distance learning today* (London, Routledge).

Von Prümmer, C. (1995) Putting the student first? Reflections on telecommunication and electronic leading strings. In Tait, A. (Ed.) *Putting the student first: Learner-centred approaches in open and distance learning*, Collected Papers of Sixth Cambridge International Conference on Open and Distance Learning (Cambridge, Open University).

Young, M. (1995) The prospects for open learning, *Open Learning*, **10** (1), pp. 3–9.

6

The role of study centres in open and distance education: A glimpse of the future

Roger Mills

This chapter examines the development of study centres in supporting the learner in distance education. It is suggested that there is a need to review the part played by these centres in distance teaching systems, in particular in the context of rapidly developing communications technology.

Heap and Hibbert (1995) quote the Nobel Laureate and inventor of holography, Denis Gabor, as saying *'Futures are difficult to predict but they can be invented'*. Today, with the rapid development and availability of information technology in the home, at least for some students in richer countries, it could be argued that the future for study centres is clear ... **extinction!** The argument would be that each individual student would have his or her own communications technology at home or readily available at work. This would enable them to access the powerful information banks to retrieve data and teaching materials, to contact tutors, course authors and fellow students studying the same course anywhere in the world. In such a situation there may be no need for a study centre where such facilities are provided or where students would meet each other face-to-face. Of course access to communications technology is not total, even in rich countries, and there is some evidence to suggest that even when students report they have access to a personal computer (PC) and modem the quality of access can be quite poor; for example, they may have the use of a PC at work but no access outside office hours or for personal study.

The functions of study centres

It would be interesting to develop a taxonomy of study centres in open and distance education, classifying them according to their different functions and purposes to determine how social, demographic and political factors influence their structure and their role in overall national education provision; but in this chapter a few examples only will be used to illustrate general points. A good deal has already been written (there are over 80 entries on the ICDL database (1995) under the heading 'study centre'), notably by Castro *et al.* (1985) who described the Australian context, and so there is a rich literature about roles, student usage, and costs. This chapter examines some of the issues relating to the use of study centres which distance teaching organisations need to address with a degree of urgency as they plan for the future.

First, there are a number of fundamental questions to be asked about the roles and functions of study centres in distance and open learning. Their main purpose to date has been to provide some or all of the following support and facilities to students and to the general public:

- a place for individual study in appropriate surroundings and at appropriate times

- library facilities

- an opportunity for students to meet with the distance education institution's administrative staff

- an opportunity to meet fellow students on the same or a different course

- a focus for students' association activities

- a source of information, guidance and counselling to the general public in a local area

- access to technology

- access to local guidance and counselling, individual and group tuition, group viewing and listening

- facilities for taking examinations.

Only rarely (and the Indira Gandhi National Open University is an example of this) do study centres fulfil all these purposes. In most other institutions, study centres offer only a selection of these services, although some have 'showcase' centres in areas of high population.

There are major differences between study centres worldwide. These can be grouped under three headings: ownership, financing and collaboration.

Ownership

In some institutions, study centres are owned by the distance teaching organisation and run by its staff. At the other extreme (as in the Open University of the United Kingdom (OU UK)) study centres, for the most part, are suites (if one is lucky) of rooms in another institution's building, usually rented during the evening or on Saturdays. In one or two cases in the OU UK such rented premises are in thriving adult and community centres or public libraries, but all too often they are in dreary, poorly equipped schools or Colleges of Further Education. Some OU regional centres also include study centre facilities, where students may also have access to regional centre facilities, including a library. In a third model, local communities provide and pay for study centre facilities for what they consider to be their local university, as for example in some of the Fernuniversität study centres in Germany, and in the Universidad Nacional Educación a Distancia (UNED) in Spain, where centres may be located in public buildings, e.g. town halls or commercial premises.

Financing

Most study centres are financed by the distance teaching organisation paying rental to the host institution. However, there are some innovative developments. For example, a policy, approved by UNED in 1990, introduced a new form of financing the 53 study centres, whereby 50 per cent of the student enrolment fees are reinvested in the study centre. These study centres are promoted by local and regional, public and private institutions such as town halls and local councils (Tejero and Moreno, 1994). Yet again some study centres may be funded directly by national governments.

Collaboration between distance teaching institutions

The joint use of study centres by distance teaching organisations is surprisingly not as widespread as might have been thought. The South African Institute for Distance Education has been promoting the idea of Community Learning Centres as a way in which distance teaching organisations can share premises for study centres in local community centres which are run by local people involved in the organisation and in policy-making related to such a centre. In this way, the massive distance education systems such as the University of

South Africa and Technikon SA could share the costs of providing an infrastructure for local support and become more involved in the local community.

EuroStudyCentres

In Europe the EuroStudyCentre network has led the way, with the idea that students from all the European distance education institutions can use the same centres across Europe and can access European and worldwide communications.

The aims and objectives of a transnational network of EuroStudyCentres have been set out by Pronk (1994). The shortened and slightly modified version which follows gives an idea of Pronk's proposed functions which are clearly much wider than simply providing learner support:

- quality assurance/improvement, e.g. via
  - adapting and improving the methodology and practice of student support by evaluating ESCs' experience
  - improving of the planning of course production and the composition of study packs *in relation to local and regional need*

- spreading information about open and distance learning facilities *into regions of Europe where it is not already well known*

- catalysing the transnational delivery of courses by members of the European Distance Teaching Universities Association (EADTU), by application of the new technologies

- enhancing access of EADTU's member institutions to different provinces of the European market

- creating multilingual and multicultural service and learning centres.

Lopez (1993), in a visionary address to the European Open University Network conference on 'course delivery, student support and study centres' in Madrid, was able to expand on these aims when he suggested that the EuroStudyCentres should have specialist senior staff who know everything related to study programmes, courses, grants, exchanges etc. available in the European Community, as well as teaching staff trained for tutoring trans-national courses and ready to participate in research projects of an international scope. He went on to emphasise that, although ESCs will develop telematic features to provide students with access to resources, both human and material, the role of the teacher/tutor will still be fundamental in this kind of study centre. The introduction of telematic systems can heighten the importance of the teacher/tutor, who, besides being an expert on content, must also be a dynamic force in the new teaching-learning relationships created by technology.

Centres for individual study

Although many students visit study centres for particular purposes, e.g. to meet other students, to take part in tutorials and self-help groups or for individual guidance and counselling, a significant number use the study centre as a place where they can go to study quietly and undisturbed, if they cannot do this because of home and social conditions. In many countries, too, lack of electric light and space at home is the normal situation for many students, and in some cases even study centres may not have a reliable source of electricity. In contrast, many richer countries, especially in urban areas, can make such a provision through national library services, but the fact remains that some students, working during the week, may need quiet and accessible facilities to study outside their own home at weekends or in the evenings when public facilities are closed. Such a requirement may be especially important for many women who need to get away from the pressures of domestic life.

But does any institution make such provision? It seems the only way such facilities could be provided would be by co-operation between local and distance educational institutions making a real effort to provide pleasant, safe and healthy facilities for all. It is simply wasteful to have institutional facilities with very limited opening hours. In the UK, despite the increasing use of buildings for part-time 'evening' students, there is still a huge waste of education plant and resources because of the inability by institutions to think creatively about the joint use of premises during evenings and weekends, an increasing emphasis on competition, and because of the lack of national and local leadership on educational issues.

The rise and fall of the traditional study centre in the OU UK

Most study centres are not used for 'study' in the sense of an individual working with his or her learning materials. Certainly in the OU UK, the study centre, which, for the most part, comprises rented rooms in another institution, typically a College of Further Education (increasingly on a charge-by-hour basis) began life as a 'Listening and Viewing Centre' with the express purpose of providing access to VHF radio and BBC2 in the days before large numbers of people had such access in their homes. These study centres also provided replay devices to play audio tapes and cassetted film (a precursor of videotape) for those students who had missed programmes which were broadcast nationally by the BBC. Counselling and tutorial sessions were also arranged. At this time, in 1970/71, such was the prestige of the new Open University and its partnership with the BBC that many colleges and Local Education Authorities went out of their way to invite the University to use their premises, charging what was little more than a peppercorn rental for overall usage. In this way, the colleges became linked to the OU and were proud to be study centres. This had enormous positive benefits for the development of collaborative work, for example, in preparatory courses organised by the colleges. Alas, the impact of financial rather than educational success, of competition rather than collaboration, emphasised by the successive Conservative governments since 1979 through their policies to put education on a more business-like footing, has all but destroyed the synergy which was really productive in the early 1970s.

As more and more students gained access to VHF radio, BBC2, and audio and video cassette recorders, the use of the study centre as a listening and viewing centre diminished, and what remained was the access to a computer terminal and to tuition and counselling. But something was lost; there was much to be said for the group viewing of television programmes, especially in the first year of study, and the OU produced a very useful guide to *Learning from Television* (1981), aimed at helping students to use television more effectively. This trend was reinforced some years later when the demand for computer terminals in study centres dropped, as personal computers replaced terminal access to the University's mainframe. A combination of lack of security and increased student ownership or access through their work or friends to PCs led to the University's decision not to locate its own PCs in study centres and to study centre sessions around the computer becoming redundant. The next major step in the use of computing by OU students was the decision by the University, in 1987, to require all its Technology Foundation Course students to rent or purchase a PC (Amstrad 1512 or better) in order to study the course.

Today, most OU UK study centres are simply rented rooms where face-to-face tuition and some individual and group counselling takes place in ordinary classrooms, with little provision for private study outside the rather limited opening hours of the host institution's library, and without any regular access to equipment for computer work, watching television or videos, or listening to audio tapes. Nevertheless, many OU UK students find the group face-to-face tuition and counselling which takes place in study centres an enormously valuable support in their studies, and attendance at these sessions is high in the early years. There is, however, no direct evidence to suggest that attendance at study centre tutorials improves learner performance as measured by assignment and/or examination grades. Indeed such evidence would be extremely difficult to assemble and therefore many institutions rely on the views expressed by students. There are, of course, real problems with renting accommodation in other institutions' premises, not least conflicts of interest when there is competition for students and the lack of a corporate identity for the distance education organisation in the local centre, together with lack of control on issues such as safety, cleanliness, opening hours and staff management. Everyone involved in teaching on other institutions' premises has stories about school keepers and caretakers jangling their keys at the most interesting moment in a tutorial! Service level agreements are being developed between the OU and the institutions which host its study centres in an attempt to be clear about responsibilities and expectations, but it has to be said that many facilities provided by other educational institutions are often of a poor quality; as an indicator they are not usually acceptable to the Open University Business School students who use (and pay for) what they consider to be better facilities elsewhere, for example hotel business suites. Interestingly, although there is no proven direct relationship between attendance at study centre tutorials and learner performance (a multiplicity of factors being involved), both attendance and retention rates for Business School students in the OU UK are higher than on other courses. However, as the OU UK moves towards a more modular structure, students are going to expect parity of treatment and facilities across all Open University provision. This raises the huge question of whether the OU should be looking to move its study centres to conference and business centres, to hotels and company training centres. Apart from trebling the cost of provision (and this would have to be recouped from student fees), such a move may have a significant effect on access (off-putting environments for some students and inaccessibility by public transport) and on the synergy between the OU and its host institutions. Interestingly, it may be that most of the complaints about study centres come from the staff who teach in them rather than the students, and this possibility is borne out to some extent by the relatively positive views about study centres expressed by OU UK students.

Student views

A recent report (Fung *et al.*, 1994) provided data from a sample of over 900 undergraduate students, summarised in Table 6.1.

Table 6.1 Satisfaction with study centres in the OU UK

	Not satisfied (%)	Satisfied (%)	Very/extremely satisfied (%)
Convenient location	21.5	38.0	40.5
Adequate safe parking	14.6	41.2	44.2
Notices and directions clear	18.9	49.5	31.6
Maintenance of rooms	5.7	48.9	45.3
Friendly and helpful staff	9.3	47.7	43.0
Access to a quiet room before tutorials	26.1	59.1	14.8
Availability of refreshments	29.3	52.2	18.5
Location and cleanliness of toilets	7.5	58.3	34.2
Access to room for self-help group	25.2	58.5	16.3

It is always difficult to interpret such figures, but notwithstanding earlier comments, it does seem that most students find their study centre accommodation and location satisfactory, at least in their first year, where local tutorials are provided in most study centres. Students on Open University Committees often, rightly, complain about poor facilities, and regional staff do their best to ensure that, within the budgetary constraints, facilities are appropriate to the needs of adult learners. In the end, however, any extra cost of providing better accommodation would have to be transferred to the student and, given the choice, most students may prefer to see tuition fees kept in line with inflation rather than have better accommodation at a higher fee. Nevertheless, the coming of the University's Student Charter, which sets out the level of support and service the University is committed to providing for students, will certainly mean that more attention will need to be paid to complaints about poor quality study centre facilities. What is needed are more imaginative approaches by the University and its host institutions, and by national and local government to create the excellence of provision which is seen in mainland Europe without excessive cost or inaccessible and inappropriate environments. Unless this happens, the role of the study centre will not develop. As Gough (1980) reported after visiting the OU UK:

in the final analysis, the study centre is merely a convenient base for their [tutor-counsellors'] work. Indeed tutor-counsellors operate effectively in certain areas without such a base; this has always been the case in the north of Scotland and in the Western Isles. If this analysis is correct, then the tutor-counsellor is the vital element in the student support service of the Open University. Study centres are peripheral.

Smith *et al.* (1985), in describing the Victorian Technical and Further Education network in Australia, note how the integration of off-campus students into a college, with full student rights and privileges, was more successful in their view than the Deakin University model, based on the OU UK, where study centres were based in other institutions. They suggested that the reasons such centres had not been successful in terms of student attendance was because:

students do not like to enter and use an 'alien' institution or that the host institutions were not motivated enough to be proactive in assisting Deakin students.

The OU UK has resisted the model of greater integration with other providers, although in 1984 suggestions were made by the polytechnics that the OU should franchise its entire regional service to the polytechnic network. More recently, the University reviewed the possibilities of franchising some of its introductory courses to colleges of further education but decided there would be no advantage in this for its students.

Positive trends

An interesting contrast to the UK and Australia can be found in Slovenia, a small country of some two million people with a geographical area the same as Wales. Here there is already an established network of community centres and, in the past, lecturers from the University of Ljubljana travelled to these centres to give lectures and run tutorials of a similar nature to those on the main campus. With the development of distance education (Mills, 1995), through the Distance Education Co-ordination Point in the Faculty of Economics, part-time staff are now being employed locally to provide support for distance learning materials produced by central faculty. Tutorials will be held in the already existing network of community centres, which also provide a range of other services including general educational advice for a range of individuals and groups in the local community.

One of the most impressive institutional study centre networks is that of the Indira Gandhi National Open University (IGNOU) where over 350 study centres straddle the country, including 86 in Delhi. Although this is not a huge number of centres, given the size of the population and the geographical area covered, the influence and support of the National Government enabled IGNOU to establish its study centres in other colleges, but in its own suite of rooms with its own administrative and support staff. Here students could immediately identify with IGNOU, and the staff of the host institution were able to see clearly what IGNOU was doing. The furniture, the staffing and the books in the library were standard and this, together with the IGNOU logo, gives the centres a really strong corporate image. Students are able to hand in assignments, meet tutors, attend tutorials, pay fees, get advice and counselling about future courses and above all meet each other. Here is a positive move towards establishing a real community of open and distance learners which manages to be both local and national.

So, is it possible to detect a pattern which suggests that study centres on the whole are not successful when they comprise no more than rented rooms in other institutions' premises? Are they more likely to be successful if they are either independently run and administered with permanent staff (albeit using others premises) as in IGNOU, or where there is a true partnership of different organisations involved in education, as in the Slovenian network and in one or two study centres in the OU UK (e.g. Wensum Lodge in Norwich, which is a thriving community adult centre)? The EuroStudyCentre development, where, for example, the OU UK shares some premises with the Fernuniversität in Germany, and the thinking taking place in South Africa with the development of Community Learning Centres, are other exciting developments. It is not surprising perhaps that students like it when OU UK regional centres are used as study centres. Here they clearly feel a greater sense of belonging to an institutional community. Just being tolerated in another institution, in rented rooms which may differ from week to week, and with staff and students not really integrated in the host institution, is very much second best.

A glimpse of the future of study centres in the OU UK

How and in what way will student learning and the role of study centres change? In the OU UK the main driver for change will undoubtedly be the rapid developments in communication technology. This will not only enable links to be made easily between different elements of the teaching system in ways which have not been possible before; it will also mean a new approach to the whole relationship between the student and the University.

Already in the OU UK, the increasing complexity and variety of study programmes—a trend likely to continue rapidly as the University faces increasing competition from others developing distance teaching programmes —and the need for greater flexibility, together with increased possibilities for the accumulation and transfer of credit, has led to proposals to refocus much information provision, advice and guidance away from local part-time staff operating in the study centres towards the regional centres, where staff have computer links with students' records, tools to monitor individual and group progress, and up-to-date information on new courses, fees and credit ratings.

In the 'industrial' model of distance education (Peters, 1983) the economics of the system were characterised by high initial investment (in the production of high quality learning materials by a central 'production unit' or course team, the cost being amortised over the life of the course) and relatively low annual 'running costs' including, as a major element, learner support. In its version of this model, the OU UK stresses the importance of the mediation of study materials to the students by a local or relatively local tutor. The tutor supports students by marking correspondence assignments, by holding tutorials in the study centre, by providing general support and counselling and by being available on the telephone. The fact that a student can contact his or her tutor on a one-to-one basis by telephone at most times during the week is one of the real strengths of the system. Indeed many would argue, as Gough did in 1980, that this individual support is the essential element of the learner support system in distance education; on some courses now this support is being provided, along with group communication, by computer conferencing arrangements, which operate independently from any local base and do not rely on study centre facilities. It is not only the impact of the new communications technologies on learner support that will influence the future of study centres, but also their impact on the curriculum.

The OU UK has the largest number of students in any university in the UK; it also has a relatively restricted curriculum by comparison with other large universities. Students want a greater range of courses, especially at Master's level, and the University is moving to provide these. Clearly the larger the number of courses, the lower the number of students on each course (assuming an equilibrium is reached on the total number of students in the institution). This means that it will no longer be possible, even if we wished to do so, to provide 'local' or even regional tutorials for many of these increasingly specialist courses. It is possible to predict (and there are several examples already) that many courses will have, say, only 50 students or so per year nationally or even internationally, if the University is to broaden its curriculum dramatically. In such circumstances the local tutor will be replaced by the course writer, herself or himself mediating the course from any location by using computer conferencing, audio-graphics or perhaps video conferencing: an approach in principle not unlike that currently used in the University of South Africa where academic staff teach their own courses by correspondence and are available on the telephone to those students who choose and who have the resources to take advantage of this direct support. Indeed, increasingly, students will be able to study distance learning courses from other distance teaching institutions, perhaps with support through the developing EuroStudyCentre network. It does not require much further development of this argument to see that the whole basis of the industrial model, with its course teams working together and its local support, will not be viable in the future except for very large population courses (normally of an introductory nature) which will not require much annual updating.

In such circumstances questions have to be asked about the design of the curriculum and the overall learner support system, including the role of study centres. It is inconceivable that the OU UK can carry on with a single model designed over 25 years ago (think what this would mean if we were talking about motor cars!). The design needs a radical overhaul such that the power of new technology is harnessed to help all its students and not simply those with sufficient resources to benefit from it. What has happened so far has been piecemeal. Several courses have employed different approaches to computer conferencing, some designing the course such that a computer and modem is essential to study, whereas others require the use of computer facilities as part of the course. In the latter case, it is possible for students to rent time on a PC in a local study centre if necessary in order to complete a particular piece of work or an assignment. This piecemeal approach, with individual faculties adopting different policies and practices (and different software), cannot continue. It has led to situations that are confusing and inexplicable to the general public and to students. For example, the new Technology Foundation Course, a large population introductory course, has, as an integral part of its design, the use of a computer and communications modem using SoftArc FirstClass™ software. There is an immediate opportunity for students to be in contact with the academic staff who have written the courses and with all other students and tutors. At first sight this seems to be a real step forward, providing easy links between student and course author; between student and academic expert. It looks certain that this will dramatically affect the balance of study patterns and learning relationships in a distance teaching institution, and change the role of the study centre and also of part-time tutors and counsellors, and the regionally-based academic staff who are responsible for the management of the part-time tutors.

This first-year course, with its week-long summer school and its computer and modem requirements, is likely to cost the student a substantial sum of money, and although there are loan schemes and financial assistance, it is already clear that the cost of the course is a bar to access for many people, especially women.

In contrast, the Faculty of Mathematics and Computing has taken a radical approach to the way in which it introduces students to mathematics, and has completely rethought its strategy for teaching at introductory level, with the consequence that far more women are applying for a new 200-hours course which has neither summer school nor a requirement to purchase a computer, but a simple, cheap, battery-run graphics calculator which is sent to all students and included within the standard course fee.

Clearly there are a number of options facing the University as it reflects on the impact of the new technologies in the design of its curriculum and its learner support patterns for the future.

A possible way forward

In an article written in 1979, Bradford, then Chairman of an OU UK Study Centre Review Group, concluded that *personal relationships are indeed the raison d'être of study centres*. Is this still the case? Undoubtedly, at the time, Bradford understood personal relationships to be face-to-face regular links between students and tutors and of students with each other. To what extent can personal relationships be established through computer-mediated communication without provoking the reaction of Kuno in E.M. Forster's (1913) fantasy 'The Machine Stops', written as a reaction against what he called 'the earlier heavens of H.G. Wells'?

> *I want to see you, not through the machine,'* said Kuno, *'I want to speak to you not through the wearisome machine.'* *'Oh hush!'* said his mother, *vaguely shocked, 'You must not say anything against the machine'.*

The answers to some of these questions will be institution- and country-specific. Even in a world where many people will have at their fingertips all the information and communications possibilities necessary for any educational purpose, there will still be a need for the support and friendship of other people, the humour, the smiles, the concerns, the human contact, in addition to what can be provided through the 'machine' and through the written word. Such opportunities might indeed be provided through the development of Community Learning Centres shared by many institutions and governed by the local communities, as are being planned in some areas of South Africa and which operate already in Slovenia.

The computer communications revolution will dramatically affect teaching and learning; we must make sure it affects our local and academic communities in a completely positive way, by providing an additional learning tool which complements rather than replaces the face-to-face contact which student and tutors consistently find so valuable. We may not be able to predict the future of study centres, but we should at least be trying now to invent it!

EuroStudyCentres are a major development in Europe. The question to be addressed is whether they, like the listening and viewing centres which were the origins of the OU UK study centres, are merely a passing phase until all students have all necessary communication links and data in their own home, or whether local access to such facilities outside the home will become critically important as one of the future key elements in student support and as an opportunity for students to meet face-to-face and support each other.

Distance education is at the forefront of increasing access to education at all levels across the world. The introduction of new technology to support teaching and learning must help to increase access to all and must not be another barrier for some. This is the great challenge.

As for study centres, as students demand a wider curriculum and more opportunities to take courses from other institutions, perhaps in other countries, it will be increasingly difficult to provide local or even regional tutorial support. For example, with imagination and some extra resource, the OU UK could decide that its study centres (perhaps renamed local centres) should be re-engineered to focus more on providing advice and guidance to enquirers and preparatory support for all students, whilst continuing to act as the base for tutors on introductory courses and others where the density of students allows. Such centres would have a critical role in local public relations and in the recruitment of students and would be the genuine local face of the Open University.

The most exciting and imaginative leap forward for the OU UK would be to equip and staff such local centres to provide computer, audio and video communications, perhaps along the developing lines of EuroStudyCentres, or Contact North in Ontario (Sam Shaw, 1995), in an environment conducive to adult study and with access up to 12 hours per day at the weekend and during week-day evenings. Many of the colleges which house existing OU study centres have suites of computers linked to the Internet which are largely unused in the evenings and at weekends. Some colleges are now also linking up by video to enable their own courses to run where there are too few students in any one college; and yet hardly any use is made of these facilities by OU students. If such facilities were made available to the Open University, students studying courses for which local or regional tuition was logistically impossible would be able to link up with each other and their specialist tutor, perhaps in the presence of a general facilitator, without having to purchase their own computing equipment, at least in the first instance. The combination of the availability of telematic and video links with students, tutors and course writers across the country, together with face-to-face meetings with other local students, tutors and counsellors, would again encourage students to use their local study centres more, and in doing so they would meet other students, albeit often studying different courses and in different faculties, thus counterbalancing the potential isolation resulting from studying solely from a home base.

REFERENCES

Bradford, M. (1979) Study centres: The background to the current policy review, *Teaching at a Distance*, 16 (Milton Keynes, The Open University).

Castro, A.S., Livingston, K.T. & Northcott, P.H. (1985) *An Australian casebook of study centres in distance education*, Deakin Open Education Monographs No. 1 (Victoria, Australia, Deakin University).

Forster, E.M. (1913) *The machine stops*. In Barnes, D.R. & Egford, R.F. *Twentieth century short stories* (London, Harrap).

Fung, P., Calder, J. & Monteiro, B. (1994) Monitoring of student satisfaction. A report on completion of pilot research, *Student Research Centre Report 90* (The Institute of Educational Technology, The Open University, Milton Keynes).

Gough, J.E. (1980) *The use of study centres in four distance education systems* (Victoria, Australia, Deakin University).

Heap, B. & Hibbert, A. (1995) Technology foresight: The institute's view, *Biologist*, **42** (4) (London, Institute of Biology).

International Centre for Distance Learning Database (1995) (The Open University, Milton Keynes).

Lopez, A.C. (1993) Prospects of distance teaching in a Europe without frontiers. Internal paper (Madrid, Universidad Nacional a Distancia).

Mills, A.R. (1995) Unpublished report of Slovenian distance education plans.

Open University (1981) *Learning from television* (The Open University and The British Broadcasting Corporation, Milton Keynes).

Peters, O. (1983) Distance education and industrial production: A comparative interpretation in outline. In Sewart, D., Keegan, D. & Holmberg, B. (Eds.) *Distance education: International perspectives* (Beckenham, Croom Helm/St Martin's Press).

Pronk, N. (1994) A transnational network: The development of EuroStudyCentres. In Palank, F. & Pronk, N. (Eds.) *EuroStudyCentres* (Vienna, Zeitschrift für Hochschuldidaktik, Österreichischer Studien Verlag).

Sam Shaw, W.A. (1995) Contact North/Contact Nord: On the leading edge of distance education. In Sewart, D. (Ed.) *One world, many voices: Quality in open and distance learning*, Vol. 1, 17th World Conference for Distance Education (Milton Keynes, International Council for Distance Education and The Open University).

Smith, P., Scorgie, B. & Edge, D. (1985) Past development and an emerging possible future for Victorian distance education. In Castro, A.S., Livingstone, K.T. & Northcott, P.H. *An Australian casebook of study centres in distance education*, Deakin Open Education Monographs No. 1 (Victoria, Australia, Deakin University).

Tejero, L. & Moreno, J.M. (1994) UNED Study Centre Network. In Palank, F. & Pronk, N. (Eds.) *EuroStudyCentres* (Vienna, Zeitschrift für Hochschuldidaktik, Österreichischer Studien Verlag).

7

Computer-mediated learning and its potential

Tony Nixon and Gilly Salmon

Introduction

The rapid developments in information and communications technologies at the end of the twentieth century have provided an array of new tools for open and distance teaching and learning. Overall potentials are huge, but dynamic and difficult to harness for the individual working in and through open learning. Since educational projects involve considerable investment in technological and organisational infrastructures, we need to try to ensure that they can be shaped to meet the overall ethos of supporting open learners. We may need too to consider the fears of those who feel that a computer standing between the learner and the learning supporter may reduce, rather than enhance, opportunities. This article is based on the experience, observations and action research of two UK Open University practitioners.

Computer conferencing systems

In wealthy countries, telephones, television sets, and video cassette recorders are in almost every household, and so it seems likely that this pattern of individual ownership may extend to computers. The uses for which each of these devices was designed are clearly defined. For example, the task of the telephone is to transmit and receive speech. The quality of transmission and reception simply needs to be sufficient for the user to understand and be understood. By contrast, the purpose of computers is less clear and any significant improvement in performance of the device expands the range of use. The theoretical limit of performance for computers is colossal (current theoretical figures give a factor of a billion or so in speed and physical size) and manufacturing technology seems set to advance for some time to come. Increases in speed and capacity change the user-machine interface. Early operating systems were invariably text-driven, now they are usually icon-driven (point and click using a mouse) and in a few years they could be speech-driven. There may be plateaus in computer evolution where popular ownership is feasible, such as in the early 1980s with the Sinclair machines, but in general obsolescence is likely to prove to be a major obstacle in the future.

In this chapter, we are using the notion of a 'computer conferencing system' to mean a server (a single device which acts as a central hub to the conferencing network) and a series of nodes (usually referred to as clients) from which the system may be accessed. This type of conferencing system allows for conference moderation, which is necessary in an educational context. The alternative would be a peer-to-peer system which is largely unstructured and would not provide the degree of control required to orchestrate Computer Mediated Learning (CML). Such systems usually allow word-processed documents or spreadsheets to be attached and posted. This makes it possible for students to produce joint documents by working successively on a single text which is passed back to the conference at each stage of its production.

Electronic conferencing is a way of supporting open learning through exploiting the advantages of wide-ranging access to computers connected by telephone, cables or network, in students' homes or local study centres. Conferencing works like a series of notice boards, each with a title and purpose. For example, a tutor may set up a conference and post a directional message on it to begin with. This message could be: 'This area is for our discussion on your next assignment'. Each student then logs on through his or her individual computer, reads the message and can post one of his or her own. Students can access this electronic conference at any time of day or night, including when the tutor is sleeping or working elsewhere. So, when the tutor returns to the conference a few days later, 20 students may have made their contribution to the discussion, often answering each other's questions. The tutor may then summarise the discussion and post more questions. Students continue to log-on, read the contributions of others and the discussion begins! This type of access to electronic learning opportunities is known as *asynchronous*, compared with the synchronous nature of telephone or video conferencing.

The potential of computer-mediated learning

The challenge of educating through 'uniting action and reflection' is thrown much into focus by this way of teaching and learning (Freire, 1985). McConnell (1992) describes how useful knowledge can be gained through dialogue with others. This knowledge takes various forms and allows the surfacing of tacit, personal and experiential understandings (Kolb, 1984).

Electronic conferencing is in some ways a unique medium (Mason, 1993). The social and contextual cues that regulate and influence group behaviour are largely missing, or can be invented, during the life of the conference. A major shift can be observed from tutors to students, as the locus of authority and control accelerates rapidly when learners become more competent and confident (Kiesler, 1992). Face-to-face identities become less important and the usual discriminators such as race, age and gender are almost hidden. Existing hierarchies and relationships fade (Mason, 1992).

Learners' ultimate use and appreciation of computer-mediated learning does not appear to depend on previous computer literacy and it often appeals to inexperienced users. The spirit of access and openness that we strive for with open learning is therefore well served (Mason, 1994). This does, however, have considerable support implications, both in terms of technical access and learning support (Jennings, 1995).

Learning through computer conference mediation involves a hybrid of previously familiar communication. It has some of the elements of writing, with its associated thinking and publishing, but it resembles less formal and more transient verbal discussion (Mason, 1992). Most tutors using computer conferencing systems employ metaphors from real life for the on-line situation, e.g. 'common room' for chat and informal aspects, and 'seminars' for course-related discussions, which has led to the use of the term 'virtual teaching' (Nixon and Salmon, 1995).

Model of student use and learning support

Understanding the way in which students at undergraduate and professional levels of study use computer conferencing was developed by the authors through participant observation and focus groups of users from 1990 to 1995. The computer conferences from which this model was derived were provided as additional, optional and complementary to more traditional distance learning devices such as text and video, and therefore describe unstructured or 'natural' use (Nixon and Salmon, 1995).

The gradual process of moving from new student to independent learner on-line is continuous but can be approximated as a series of discrete steps. We have identified five stages in this process. Viewing computer-mediated learning in this way allows us to understand the support and learning needs of the student within the virtual learning environment and enables us to interpret and adjust the interaction between student and tutor.

Learning through computer mediation is an experiential, self-determined and largely self-motivated process. It cannot be legislated for in advance nor totally controlled at the time. This model suggests the way in which an individual student may use a computer-mediated networking or conferencing opportunity, and demonstrates how each stage depends on the preceding one. Some student support needs to be available at all stages, as each individual will move through at a different pace. At each stage of the learning process, some students become demotivated and 'drop out'. Therefore it is suggested that learner support be concentrated at the early stages. However, the rewards are greatest for those who persist and start to use the conferencing opportunities for information seeking and interaction: a stage when much less support and teaching is needed.

The computer-mediated learning context provides an opportunity for learners to self-manage in a somewhat unique way. The role of the tutor and other kinds of supporters is rather more diffuse and integrated than we have been used to in distance learning. The tutor takes on specific stimulating and boundary-setting roles. A 'virtual environment' can be created that is context-sensitive and yet transferable across cultures (Mason, 1994).

Stage 1: Access

At the first stage of CML use, the student needs information and technical support to get 'on-line' and motivation to commit to the time and effort involved. Hardware, software and the network or remote access (telephone line and modem) need to be available at a time when students have freedom to use them. High motivation is a prime factor at this stage to encourage tackling of technical aspects. As the student masters the enabling technology, he or she needs also to be assured that it is the *use of the technology* by *people* that makes it fun, fascinating and ultimately a learning experience. It is at this time that sitting in a classroom and having the words of the teacher 'wash' over them seems very attractive. Therefore, in addition to technical support, 'selling' of this potentially new and strange medium is most important. It can be demystified for students and tutors by providing continuing encouragement and motivation. This stage can be considered to be over at the point at which the student posts his or her first message.

Support is needed at this stage in providing hard, soft or net links and, in particular, solving technical problems. Access to support needs to be available at the times at which students are likely to be struggling to get on-line on their *own*. Attempts at forced responses are unlikely to be productive at this stage and cause much frustration and anguish, e.g. linking the use of electronic conferences with assessment.

Stage 2: Induction and socialisation

Every grouping of people develops its own culture, i.e. formal and informal rules, norms of behaviour, ways of operating and of sanctioning those who fail to understand or conform. On-line communities and learning groupings are no exception. The new on-line student can easily make behavioural mistakes and supporters need to provide information, usually called 'netiquette'. Each individual conference will also develop its own norms; therefore, what is acceptable on one will not be on another. Furthermore, basic skills instructions, such as keeping to one topic per message (much easier reading and responses) and keeping the message itself short (people are often paying telephone call time to download), can help a great deal. Advice and encouragement can be given to read and enjoy conferences for a short while before posting messages. This is known as 'lurking'. Some tutors become annoyed with lurkers, but it appears to be a natural and normal part of the socialisation and should therefore be encouraged for a while. The student will usually contribute as soon as he or she is ready.

At this stage, the student needs congratulations and welcoming to the virtual environment, together with information on how to behave in conferences and how to become comfortable enough with the medium to make effective use of it. Now it is important to be tolerant of 'chat' conferences and informality (McCreary, 1989). Most netiquette mistakes can be gently corrected on-line. Students can be encouraged to post information about themselves in special 'contact' conferences to identify others with similar interests or locations, and to describe themselves by posting their 'CV'. It helps to have conferences specifically for newcomers to answer frequently-asked questions and deal with technical aspects.

Early student messages may be formal and appear in the style of written letters to be posted in the conventional way. As confidence grows, users become more tolerant of poor layout, short form or abbreviations of words and phrases, spelling and typing mistakes. 'Say-writing' has begun! Conveying emotion and responses such as humour or anger is difficult to achieve in computer conferencing and students and tutors need advice and support on-line to avoid offending others. At the point of feeling 'at home' with the culture, and reasonably comfortable with the technology, the student is free to move on.

Issues of intellectual ownership, copyright, privacy and freedom of speech should be considered and explained to students and tutors. Electronic conference extracts are open to wide use and copying, and rights in new electronic frontiers have yet to be established. There are fears that the constraints associated with legislation may dampen the potential of wide-spread dissemination and debate of information and ideas (Branscombe, 1991). It is important that conference participants are directed to on-line Codes of Practice, and students are encouraged, as always, to acknowledge all sources and avoid copying extracts without the author's permission.

Stage 3: Seeking information, finding new pathways

At this stage, the student realises that he or she has access to wider, more diverse groups of people and information than ever before. This may create excitement but also some frustration, and responses may still be quite passive. The proliferation of messages and conferences leads students to expect to be able to shift and sift around to find what they *really* want. The cry soon arises, 'Help! I need a Guide through all of this stuff!' The student will look to the tutor to provide direction through a mass of data and encouragement to start using the most relevant material. The support skills related to the task focus of the group become important for the tutor. Tutors can direct students to useful conferences, summarise others and open new conferences where discussion topics and interests change, as well as taking part in the processes of discovery. This is known as 'netweaving'.

The student typically starts to understand the potential of forming interest groups through writing and posting on-line. He or she may discover the joy of writing a message—and getting responses. Altruism grows quickly. Most notable is the extent to which conference participants respond to requests for information and advice, even from apparent strangers. Students soon start to ask 'Can anyone tell me?' questions. Such use of the conference frequently reaps a proliferation of answers and subsequent debates and benefits, not only for the questioner, but for many other readers. Sproull and Kiesler (1991) suggest that the cost of responding is low in terms of time and effort, and consequently computer conferencing promotes the free flow of information.

At this stage, the tutor needs to do rather less, but somewhat more carefully, which can pose difficulties. Essentially the tutor sets the climate of what the students can expect and sensitively allows the maximum possible interaction and discussion to occur within that framework. A 'hands-off' approach to support and teaching is required. Remaining 'silent' for a while is often appropriate to enable students to support each other. The tutor may then find that he/she disagrees with the information given. One technique is to build on what has been said in summary form at appropriate time intervals, perhaps including statements such as, 'I agreed with Anne in message 200, but less so with John in message 206. My view is . . .'. Empathy templates, such as those discussed in Alexander and Mason (1994), have a role to play in this context.

Without the usual non-verbal and face-to-face cues of speech, problems may arise over keeping the discussion going and, particularly, keeping it on track. Although it is accepted that face-to-face conversations may twist and turn, this is less acceptable on-line, when participants log on expecting to find a particular topic discussed. The tutor may become frustrated at the near impossibility of students keeping to the designated subject. Rather than impose sanctions on those who do not conform with the conference intentions, the solution can be to open new sub-conferences and encourage participants to 'move' there. Ultimately, the students will find their own way around and develop personal shifting and choosing mechanisms. At the point at which they resist direction, they are almost certainly entering the next stage.

Stage 4: Interaction

At this stage the students start to interact with each other, often in a highly exposed and participative way. The act of formulating and writing down an idea, or understanding then reading and responding to peers, is a most important cognitive skill (Harasim, 1989). Once this begins, it has its own momentum and power. The best processes of computer conferencing demonstrate the power of open discussion with the value of written recording of the flow of thought and interchange.

In this phase, the tutoring aim can be to achieve interaction for as many participants as possible. Collaborative learning can be seen to happen in very visible and often exciting ways (Kiesler, 1992). Ong (1982) describes how interactive writing introduces both division and a higher form of unity. Both can be observed in computer-mediated conferencing. At this stage, very active learning, especially the widening and appreciation of differing perspectives, and the understanding of application of concepts and theories, happens very obviously as conferences unfold and develop.

The student needs enabling tutors to stimulate conferences, summarise wide-ranging views, provide new topic areas where discussions and interactions go off track, and stimulate new strands, themes and approaches. Tutoring skills related to group building and maintenance become important. The tutor typically undertakes 'weaving' the student contributions together, e.g. collecting up statements and relating them to concepts and theories taught in the course, and to forthcoming assignments.

Enabling students to get through to this stage often brings great rewards. Ideas often emerge and provoke responses of interest and vitality and these are shaped in a dynamic way. Regardless of the designated subject, it is common for participants to reflect on and discuss how they are networking and how they are learning. At this stage, the students are taking control of their own learning processes (Marantz and England, 1992).

Stage 5: Boundary shifting

At this stage, the student becomes responsible for his or her own learning through computer-mediated opportunities, and little learning support, beyond what is already available, is necessary. Indeed, he or she may resent interference and ask the tutor to withdraw. The students may ask to start conferences of their own. The role of the tutor, when students achieve this kind of use, is sometimes a difficult one to negotiate. Tutors need to continue to be as open and receptive as possible. The students will often be confident enough in the medium to confront a tutor when interventions seem unhelpful or out of place. Interpreting a silence on-line at any stage may be difficult (McConnell, 1992). It may be necessary to contact and discuss with previously enthusiastic participants which aspects of the system are getting in the way of learning.

At this stage students may find ways of producing and dealing with humour and more emotional aspects of writing and learning. The reflection involved in this is considerable and it may impact other more usual day-to-day communications.

The students may start to challenge the basis of the conferences or system. They typically start to demand better access, faster responses, more software. Tutors may be accused of 'gatecrashing' on the learning processes and failing to understand the power of the learning going on. This may be very difficult for the hard-working tutor or those teachers more used to higher status, but essentially it is time to 'let go'. It is relatively common for conflict to arise on-line, particularly in terms of control of conferences. Conflicts played out in this medium have the potential to escalate, since many users may read the messages and they themselves respond and fuel the rising debate. This is known as 'flaming'. It may be necessary to set up conferences to facilitate discussion on the system and be prepared to hand over some moderating rights to students and alumni.

At this point, the blurring between learning and teaching results not only in frequent changes of roles, but also in lack of need to define roles. It can be difficult for tutors to find that they have enabled the independent learners they desired to create, but, in doing so, have lost control of the teaching processes! However, students who have been through the five stages may be invaluable as supporters to those still at the earlier stages. They are often most tolerant and understanding of the difficulties faced and encouragement required by newcomers.

By this stage, course designers, teachers and learners will have invented something new, and the technological opportunities will be offering yet more enticing possibilities. Computer-mediated learning evolves, develops and continues to offer surprises.

Staff development can be provided by using the model of student use. It is essential to ensure tutors have good access, motivation to undertake their own learning, and a good feel for the appropriate opportunities and difficulties of teaching on-line. Tutors then respond well to understanding computer-mediated conferencing as a 'virtual' environment and to appreciating aspects of tutoring and student support that transfer happily to the new medium, as well as those that do not. It is important to undertake training programmes 'on-line' to enable maximum possible experiential learning for tutors.

Examples of successful computer-mediated conferencing on a large-scale distance education course

Where active reflection occurs, the individual learner will reconstruct his or her understanding of the world as part of the learning process (Dewey, 1910). This reconstruction has an impact on future actions (Kelly, 1955). Networking can be defined as reflecting, interacting and learning through other interested individuals. It is especially suitable for students looking to increase their knowledge and their ability to affect their work organisations through action. The Open University Master of Business Administration (MBA) offers a structured learning package including written texts, audio and visual materials, residential schools, correspondence tuition, face-to-face local tutorials and day schools. It was realised that supporting and encouraging networking through computer mediation could widen and supplement this package and ultimately enhance the learning processes. This became more urgent with the advent, in 1992, of the MBA being made available outside the UK throughout European Union countries and the need to widen geographical access and offer asynchronous networking.

The student registration pattern concentrated on the major international cities, but with a few further flung students, such as those on Spanish islands. Much of the learning 'package' was successfully transferred from the UK to the continent of Western Europe, but some students had difficulty in getting regularly to face-to-face tutorials or demonstrated the need for wider links with co-students and tutors outside their home country. Also, those who had experienced more traditional education were looking to interact with others and for opportunities to acquire new knowledge and learn from a diversity of interactions.

From 1992, computer-mediated conference access was offered to all MBA students, using CoSy™ and Wigwam™. Software and local dial-in points were provided free of charge. The student needed to supply a personal computer and modem from home or work and pay telephone costs. Wigwam™ provides an off-line reader, enabling all unread messages within a conference to be downloaded in seconds or minutes to a hard disk. The software then provides a familiar Windows™ environment, including the opportunity to structure the messages within threads or themes. Replies can be prepared off-line and then later uploaded rapidly on-line. This facility dramatically reduces telephone costs for remote users and provides a rich environment for tutors to 'weave' and summarise.

By 1995, three MBA courses were using the CoSy™ conferences in an explicit and supported way as a thrust of their teaching strategy. Eight other courses saw conferencing as an optional and supplementary part of learning. A small number of tutors were able to 'teach' potentially large numbers of students in this way but rapidly became adept at promoting student reflection and interaction, as well as gradually moving students on-line to more independent learning.

In 1992, B885, the 'Challenge of the External Environment' course, used the electronic networking environment in a number of explicit ways. Student independence and self-help was encouraged in order to 'find' and network with others on-line. Two of the four assignments on the course offered assessment for collaborative team working. Although students did not have to use electronic means to achieve team work, it proved one popular and effective way of working together: a demonstration of 'interaction' from the model of use. This course quickly discovered that the skills needed to tutor on-line were not common among its large band of part-time distance teachers, and 'special' on-line tutors were selected with good motivation as well as group-tutoring skills.

In 1995, one committed and competent tutor, living in Eastern England, and logging on in the evenings from home, achieved 1844 messages over seven months with an international group of students all studying B881 (1990), 'Strategic Management', on the MBA programme. Approximately half the messages were associated with gaining access, or the 'socialisation' phase of use, particularly in norms of behaviour and gaining skills within the system. The students were approving and appreciative of the tutor's focus on course issues and had great need of his input for information seeking, especially in looking for direction for the assessed elements of the course. However, they also demonstrated considerable interactive ability and frequently stimulated debates and answered questions for themselves without his involvement. A group of students set up their own conference around half way through the year in order to share materials. This demonstrated some evidence of the 'autonomy' phase, although in practice over half of the 300 messages were about developing technical and data-handling skills rather than strategic management.

An example of an innovative international experimental CML course

In 1992 conferencing software called FirstClass™ (manufactured by SoftArc) was used on a small-scale experimental course on renewable energy (Alexander and Mason, 1994). The course had 24 students from the UK, Finland and Australia. Students used their own computers (Apple Macintosh®) but were loaned modems and CD-ROM drives by the University. This course was to provide an interactive learning support environment using the metaphor of three 'rooms', each with its own purpose.

There was a *Study* for individual work, containing tools such as word-processors and spreadsheets. A *Library* held learning resources on CD-ROM, including an audio-visual introductory lecture and copies of the course study guides, a 'media library' holding photographs, diagrams, sampled sounds and animations, which the students could use to create hypertext documents, and a series of documents prepared specially for the course.

In addition, there was a *Meeting Room* for collaborative work which used the FirstClass™ computer conferencing system. FirstClass™ was chosen primarily for its ease of operation, particularly with respect to attaching documents, since one objective given to students was to produce a joint document. The software proved to be very popular with the students, who found it easy to use.

It was possible to include a number of innovative facilities which the course team felt would be of value to the students. These included *electronic faces*, *virtual circles* and *empathy templates*. The 'electronic faces' provided a means for students to generate a picture to represent themselves, which they could attach to documents. In fact this was in the form of a caricature assembled from a set of editable face parts in a 'Face Maker' program. This mechanism was used to break down some of the potential barriers created by the lack of face-to-face contact. A 'virtual circle' (Johnson-Lenz and Johnson-Lenz, 1991) called for every member of a group to make one statement and to input this message to a conference within a given time period. This provided a method of checking the general status and progress of students. The 'empathy templates' were a set of protocols intended to enhance creative co-operation. These took the form of a set of phrases, designed to avoid the bad feelings caused by clumsy or dismissive replies, e.g. 'What I think you mean is . . .', 'My own view differs . . .' (to differ without dismissing).

The collaborative learning approach was successful in terms of creating motivation and enjoyment and the students produced a joint document. Additionally, the student group combined their breadth of experience to act as a resource in its own right. The project demonstrated how topics, such as 'Renewable energy', which suffer from a shortage of expert tutors, could benefit from this type of approach. Furthermore, subjects which would attract only small numbers of students could be made practicable when run as global courses.

(A further description of the use of FirstClass™ is given in Chapter 8 of this book.)

Conclusions

With supported and planned computer-mediated conferencing, there is less teaching and more learning, more self-help, a greater focus on the message, rather than the messenger, and the opportunity to engage in learning interactions more easily and at any time of day or night.

To achieve such worthy aims, sympathetic and effective technical 'getting in and problem solving' support is needed at the earliest stages. Tutoring and support should be aimed at providing a worthwhile purpose for being on-line and broadly steering work objectives and goals, stimulating and helping students to move through the steps, and being prepared to encourage and support autonomy in learning for those who continue to climb. 'Virtuality' can be exploited to enable students and tutors to identify with the learning environment and understand the purpose of activities and conferences.

Geographically-isolated students can interact and experience tutoring and support if appropriate help is given to enable them to climb the electronic steps. Students disadvantaged in other ways can benefit enormously from prejudice-free and mobility-independent learning of a unique and productive kind, if they are helped and supported through the first steps of the process. Creativity and innovation in learning can flourish at midnight, without teaching, without paper and on a huge scale, if the basics are made available and support is provided at the early stages. Computer-mediated learning can supplement tried and tested ways of open and distance teaching; or, if we face the challenge, replace many aspects of it that might be due for review. Overall, it can operate successfully and comfortably within the spirit of openness, and offers opportunities for student-centred, multinational and interactive learning on a massive scale.

REFERENCES

Alexander, G. & Mason, R. (1994) Innovating at the OU: Resource-based collaborative learning on-line, *CITE Report No. 195*.

B881, *Strategic Management*, 1990, Open University.

B885, *The Challenge of the External Environment*, 1992, Open University.

Branscombe, A. (1991) Common law for the electronic frontier, *Scientific American*, **265** (3), pp. 112–116.

Dewey, J. (1910) *How Do We Think?* (London, Heath).

Freire, P. (1985) *The politics of education: Culture, power and liberation* (Basingstoke, Macmillan).

Harasim, L. (1989) On-line education: A new domain. In Mason, R. & Kaye, A. (Eds.) *Mindweave: Communication, computers and distance education* (Pergamon).

Jennings, C. (1995) Organisations and management issues in telematics-based distance education, *Open Learning*, **10** (2).

Johnson-Lenz, P. & Johnson-Lenz, T. (1991) Post-mechanistic groupware primitives: Rhythms, boundaries and countainers, *International Journal of Man-Machine Studies*, **34**, pp. 395–417.

Kelly, G.A. (1955) *The psychology of personal constructs* (New York, Norton, reprinted by Routledge, 1990).

Kiesler, S. (1992) Talking, teaching and learning in network groups: Lessons from research. In Key, A. (Ed.) *Collaborative learning through computer conferencing*, NATO ASI series (Berlin, Springer-Verlag).

Kolb, D.A. (1984) *Experiential learning: Experience as the source of learning and development* (NJ, Prentice Hall).

McConnell, D. (1992) Computer mediated communication for management learning. In Kaye, A. (Ed.) *Collaborative learning through computer conferencing*, The Najaden Papers, NATO ASI series (Berlin, Springer-Verlag).

McCreary, E.K. (1989) CMC and organisational culture. In Mason, R. & Kaye, A. (Eds.) *Mindweave: Communication, computers and distance education* (Pergamon).

Marantz, B. & England R. (1992) Closing the distance, A CMC learning contract tutorial, *DEOSNEWS*, **2** (4).

Mason, R. (1992) Written interactions. In Mason, R. (Ed.) *Computer conferencing: The last word.* (Victoria, BC, Beach Holme).

Mason, R. (1993) Computer conferencing: A European perspective. In Harasim, L. (Ed.) *Global networks, computers and international communications* (Cambridge, MA, MIT Press).

Mason, R. (1994) *Using communications media in open and flexible learning* (Kogan Page).

Nixon, T. & Salmon, G. (1995) *Spinning your web*. Paper presented to Society for Research into Higher Education conference, Edinburgh, Scotland, December 1995.

Ong, W. (1982) *Orality and literacy: The technologizing of the word* (London, Methuen).

Sproull, L. & Kiesler, S. (1991) Computers, networks and work, *Scientific American*, **265** (3), pp. 84–91.

8

Learning in practice: Support for professional development

Jenny Leach

We need to concentrate not on the product of development but on the very process by which higher forms are established ... To encompass in research the process of a given thing's development in all its phases and changes—from birth to death—fundamentally means to discover its nature, its essence, for 'it is only in movement that a body shows what it is'. (Vygostsky, 1978, pp. 64–65)

Professional development in education is a career-long process. It is on this view of teacher education that this chapter will rest. It is not a single event, or a course of study, though both may form a part of the overall process. Rather it is a continuum: a complex, often uncertain but potentially creative journey from the earliest stages of initial teacher education, through to the latest stages of being an educational professional. For if professional development is about real change, it can only realistically take place over time and in the context of continuity of personal goals and aspirations as well as institutional purposes. It will almost always include periods of supported training, study or research; sometimes involving risks, almost always doubt, but hopefully also exhilaration and insight.

For real professional growth, however, there must be a direct relationship between such education and practice itself. Professional development, as this chapter will argue, is also essentially a social as well as a personal practice. If its fundamental purpose is ultimately not only to question, challenge and develop the individual teacher but also to consider the kind of teaching and learning that young people experience, it cannot be done in isolation. Teacher education, in whatever context it takes place, needs to be rooted in a theory of learning as social practice. The pattern of relationships evolved to support 'distance' professional development programmes will therefore be critical, and can in turn provide a dynamic model in general for teacher education and change. Drawing on this broad view of professional development, this chapter begins by briefly outlining current debates about teacher education, moving on to examine the concept of student support and its role in the context of distance programmes.[1] Two case studies of innovative, distance teacher education programmes follow which focus on frameworks for student support: an initial teacher education programme in the UK and an in-service education programme in Eastern Europe. The chapter concludes by outlining some key issues for student support in open and distance teacher education.

Professional development and distance education: global issues

Over the past decade, debates about both the nature and quality of teacher education and development have been accompanied by widespread educational, political and social change. Education systems across the world are undergoing transformation and traditional forms of teacher education are being questioned. In many areas, such as Eastern Europe and South Africa, the scale of need for both initial and in-service education is colossal. It is also high on political agendas (Glennie, 1995; Breger, 1995). Such change has been accompanied, and in some places facilitated by, the revolution taking place in technological communication, which gives new meaning not only to the way in which knowledge and new ideas can be accessed but also to the way individuals and institutions, although distant in place, can be instantly linked in time via cable, satellite or computer networks. In this context there is growing acknowledgement worldwide that all teachers are entitled to high quality, up-to-date programmes of professional development.

Another parallel change in thinking is taking place in many parts of the world: namely, a debate about the increased significance that schools should play in professional development at all stages. This dialogue, both in Europe and across the USA, has been well documented (Booth *et al.*, 1990; Hargreaves and Fullan, 1992). Hargreaves (1995) has drawn attention to the new 'social geography' of teacher education as it rapidly becomes de-institutionalised and dispersed across a variety of schools and clusters: 're-embedded in other sites and spaces'. The rationale for this shift of focus has varied from system to

---

[1] The term *'student support'* is used interchangeably in this chapter with *'learner'* support and *'teacher'* support. The term 'student' has traditionally been used in the Open University to refer to *any* course user. Although in some ways it seems an inappropriate term for experienced teachers engaged in continuing professional development, the interweaving here of the terms student/learner/teacher highlights the fluidity of these roles in the teaching and learning process.

system and, as Moon points out, within both national and regional systems diverse models exist, as our two case studies illustrate. In this new context he argues:

> the school as a site for training is unambiguously central to the task of establishing new and more challenging expectations (Moon, 1996, p. 12).

Open and distance teaching and learning (ODTL) has, over the last twenty-five years, offered an important routeway to professional development for many teachers across the world. This changing global educational context, however, provides a new and even more significant role for open learning. Its underlying methodology is ideally placed to facilitate a responsive and flexible model of teacher development, shifting the focus as it does from what institutions provide to how learners can be actively engaged in the process of their own learning through a wide variety of teaching and learning strategies. Indeed, if we define open and distance education as an underlying methodology, rather than seeing it as uniquely something that happens 'at a distance', then it has as much applicability for teaching and learning in the face-to-face setting of conventional institutions, as it has for students who are home-based or studying independently with little face-to-face contact. In addition, debates about the provision and nature of support for teachers engaged in professional development are becoming increasingly pertinent across all institutions, not just those engaged in 'distance' teaching and learning.

Conceptualising student support in distance education

Tait (1995) asserts that the rationale for student support in ODTL 'has been weakly conceived over the last twenty years'. Despite the widespread growth of commitment by many open learning institutions to its provision, the many examples of excellent practice in different countries are 'born out of educational instinct rather than theoretical understanding'. He argues that those activities which are commonly referred to within distance education as 'student support' (e.g. tuition, whether face-to-face, by correspondence, telephone or computer; counselling; the organisation of study centres and interaction though video) should have as a 'key conceptual component' the notion of supporting individual learning. Such provision stands in contrast to resources such as printed course units, audio and video materials, course readers and set books that have so often been seen as characterising distance education. Student support, whether provided in an individual or group setting, or both, is essential and complementary to the mass-produced materials which are provided for students regardless of prior experience, personal needs and preferred learning styles.

Placing learning at the heart of any discussion about student support is clearly vital. It is all the more pertinent in the context of teacher education programmes where the learning process itself is a main object of study. It would seem important, therefore, to explore Tait's argument further. Is there broad consensus about what 'supporting individual learning' might mean in distance education? Thorpe suggests there is:

> ... the concept of *facilitating learning* ... has attained such popularity that teaching and its role threatens to be displaced by the idea of the management of learning.

She goes on to argue:

> In place of a transmission model of teaching we now have the facilitation of learning, which may in practice take on a variety of less than satisfactory forms. It is all too possible, for example, to hand back to the learner all the responsibility for what and how to learn, while retaining all the power to judge whether or not that learning has been successful.
>
> The other source of danger, in shifting attention wholly away from teaching and on to learning, is that we know as yet too little about the process of how confident independence is achieved, and about the proper role of teaching in that process. (Thorpe, 1995, p. 176)

Such debate is vital, raising as it does crucial issues in relation to student support and the nature of the learning process. For those involved in teacher development it must be the heart of the venture.

Teacher education programmes have drawn extensively on social theory over the last decade in their account of the learning process. Social constructivism has moved thinking away from purely individual perspectives, focusing as it does on how knowledge is developed in contexts of shared learning. As a theory of intellectual development, it is well known. It suggests that human learning presupposes a specific social nature: the ways in which children's and adults' reason has been shown to be closely bound up both with the nature of social transaction and the discourse with which this reasoning is done. In dialogue, knowledge is continually not only constructed but transformed: thus when two or more people communicate, there is a real possibility that, by pooling their knowledge and experience, they achieve a new level of understanding beyond that which either had before (Edwards and Mercer, 1987). In addition, by taking into account the differing goals, contexts, experience, knowledge and cultures of every learner, constructivism places firmly on the agenda issues of social diversity, inequality, co-operation and conflict, differences of power and knowledge, and the way in which these are socially produced, reproduced and transformed in educational institutions as well as everyday settings.

Constructivism also provides a rigorous theoretical basis for pedagogy that moves beyond generalised concepts such as the 'facilitation of learning'. The concept of the 'zone of proximal development' (Vygotsky, 1978), for example, familiar to many through Bruner's (1986) account of 'scaffolding', provides a clear role for the teacher, whilst showing the familiar dichotomy between a transmission view of education and a learner-centred view to be false. Although this theory is most developed in accounts of childhood learning, it remains an important concept for adult development too, an interactive system:

> *within which people work on a problem which at least one of them could not, alone, work on effectively. Cognitive change takes place within this zone, where the zone is considered both in terms of an individual's developmental history and in terms of the support structure created by other people and cultural tools in the setting.* (Newman et al., 1989, p. 61)

The process of teaching and learning from this perspective becomes a dialogue, a constant meeting of minds, which Bruner has called a 'forum' in which teachers and learners engage in a negotiation of shared meaning:

> *The language of education, if it is to be an invitation to reflection and culture creating, cannot be the so-called uncontaminated language of fact and objectivity. It must express stance and counter-stance and, in the process, leave place for reflection, for metacognition. It is this that permits one to reach higher ground: this process of objectifying in language and image what one has thought and then turning around on it and reconsidering it.* (Bruner, 1986, p. 129)

This theory critically extends the role of 'teacher' or more experienced peer in the learning process well beyond that of mere 'facilitator'. Although the courses within our case studies draw widely on theories of learning, it is this perspective that centrally informs their structure and which provides a model for learner support, both as an overarching concept and as a teaching methodology within specific settings such as face-to-face tutorials, correspondence tuition and electronic communication.

Perhaps the greatest challenge, however, for distance programmes of teacher education is to develop frameworks of support not only for the study of course materials but also for school-based learning. This challenge moves us straight to the heart of important questions about the nature of teacher education and the interrelation between theory and practice: an ongoing and international debate, as our case studies illustrate. The questions are many and diverse but they include:

- **For course development:** To what extent should students be presented with theoretical knowledge, such as theories of learning or child development, in advance of practical experience? What is most appropriately taught in the context of school practice, what by university or colleges? How, if at all, should this interrelate?

- **For support and training:** What knowledge and skills are needed for those involved in the training of teachers? How, if at all, does the knowledge differ for those engaged in supporting school experience and theoretical studies? Does the nature of support differ also?

The questions of course intermix.

The practical dimension of teacher education has led to the development of the concept of *partnership* between institutions responsible for teacher education courses and schools which provide experience of practice. It has also led to the concept of *mentoring*:

> The **mentor** within the **practicum** provides the crucial link that mediates the beginning knowledge and skills of the teacher with practical experience in schools. In school-focused professional development programmes the role of more experienced teachers in assisting the professional growth of their less-experienced colleagues is becoming increasingly acknowledged. Most significantly the mentor role is crucial to the forging of pedagogic knowledge and academic or subject domain knowledge. (Moon, 1996, p. 18)

Those involved with the development of mentoring as both a concept and a practice have drawn substantially on *experiential learning theory* which focuses primarily on the professional aspect of teaching. Schon's (1987) concept of the 'reflective practitioner' has been influential here, particularly for those directly engaged in supporting students in school-based experience. Schon's work has established an epistemology of practice based on a process of interaction and reflection on the part of the learner and structured feedback from a teacher or 'mentor'. Indeed the concept of 'reflective practice' has become commonplace in models of mentor support. It accords much needed status both to 'knowledge in practice' and to the mentoring role.

As an account of learning, however, this concept of reflective practice demands close attention. The notion of 'reflection in action', for example, relies on a learner's ability to make solitary reflections on his/her own and others' practice. But as McIntyre points out:

> the limitations of student teachers' perceptions, information-processing, understanding and awareness of alternatives are likely to restrict their learning about teaching as much as they restrict their teaching. (McIntyre, 1990, pp. 124–125)

Similarly, applications of the concept of 'reflection on action' can divert attention away from the major issues for mentoring practice which Moon locates. Research by Burgess and Harris (1995), for example, has highlighted the high degree of personal responsibility some mentors feel for novice teachers, particularly those involved in a school-based programme. The mentoring role becomes identified in these cases with 'counselling' and 'empathising', whilst continuing to be informed by generalised notions of 'reflective practice'. Personal relations thus predominate at the expense of the systematic challenge and evaluation of novice teachers' progress and development. In searching for models of learning that will inform student support, not only in relation to the theoretical aspects of teaching, but also in school practice and professionalism, we need to embrace those models which enable rigorous attention to be paid to the process of teaching and learning. How, for example, can experienced teachers make pedagogic strategies and their practice in action explicit to 'novice' teachers (Banks *et al.*, 1995)? What role can collaborative teaching and classroom observation play in teacher development? Here, too, constructivist approaches would seem to have as much to offer as theories of reflective practice.

Recent critiques of cognitive theory help to connect what might seem to be otherwise important but distinct perspectives for support of teacher development: parallel furrows which tend towards seeing learning theory and professional practice as separate and distinct (Lave, 1988; Chaiklin and Lave, 1993). Extensive research into adult learning in 'everyday life' has led Lave to propose that:

> *cognition is distributed—stretched over, not divided among—mind, body, activity and culturally organised settings (which include other actors), across persons, activity and setting.*

She argues against persistent formulations of theory that create gulfs between minds and their 'environments', between public and domestic domains, theory and practice:

> *the everyday world is just that: what people do in daily, weekly, monthly, ordinary cycles of activity. A schoolteacher and pupils in a classroom are engaged in 'everyday activity' in the same sense as a person shopping for groceries in the supermarket after work and a scientist in the laboratory.* (Lave, 1988, p. 15)

In this theory of cognition, situated knowledge becomes the crucial component which drives reflection and in turn the process of learning. This perspective challenges traditional dichotomies: between theory and practice, institutional (or school) learning and 'everyday learning', between thinking and doing, mind and body. As an account of learning it presents a view of cognition as ongoing, unfolding and experiential, which has important insights not only for curriculum development but also for learner support in teacher education.

We would wish to argue that although support for professional development should draw on a range of theories of learning, *it must be centrally grounded in social practice*, recognising that knowledge is constantly created and transformed at the intersection of dialogue between people, their collective knowledge and experience, in particular settings and context. It follows that support should be set in a framework which provides for a range of opportunities: of relationships and activities in a variety of settings, which include schools and classrooms. We would also argue that support in the professional development context must ensure that opportunities for learning continually challenge traditional dichotomies of theory and practice, teacher and learner, institutional learning and 'everyday' experience. The variety of opportunities provided by such support are not a series of unconnected events but should provide, in an ongoing, unfolding way, the basis for 'learning in practice' that stretches across time and space. The nature and quality of these opportunities are key, whether they be large day schools, co-teaching in classrooms, one-to-one discussion on the telephone about written assignments, or electronic conferencing across national borders. This is a shared endeavour and has important implications for course construction and for ongoing developments in mentor and tutor training. In establishing such a framework of support we are, of course, also describing a model framework for learning: for we would argue that support for professional development should fully mirror what is expected of the best practice in students' own schools/teaching contexts (see Fig. 8.1).

In the case studies of innovative distance programmes of teacher education that follow, we will focus in particular on learner support.

Initial teacher education at a distance: a study in innovation

The UK context

Broad educational debates about teacher development in the UK have taken place against the background of radical changes in government policy in relation to both initial and in-service training. Since the early 1970s, initial teacher training has been compulsory for all except maths and science graduates in England and Wales and, until recently, was seen primarily to be the responsibility of colleges or university departments of education, who in

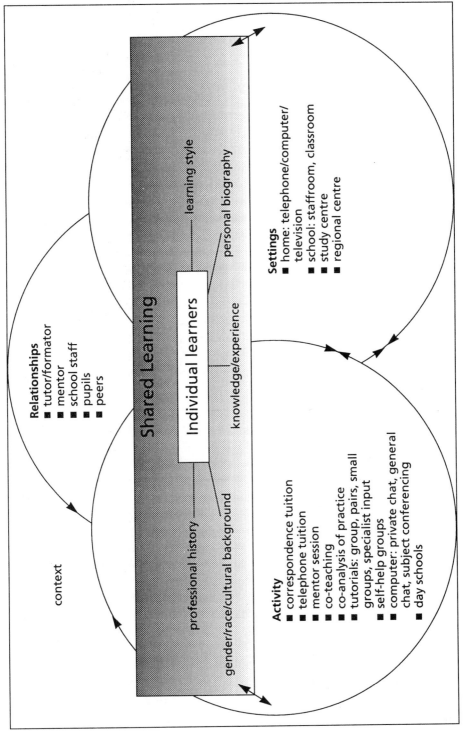

Relationships
- tutor/formator
- mentor
- school staff
- pupils
- peers

Shared Learning

learning style

Individual learners

personal biography

knowledge/experience

professional history

gender/race/cultural background

context

Settings
- home: telephone/computer/television
- school: staffroom, classroom
- study centre
- regional centre

Activity
- correspondence tuition
- telephone tuition
- mentor session
- co-teaching
- co-analysis of practice
- tutorials: group, pairs, small groups, specialist input
- self-help groups
- computer: private chat, general chat, subject conferencing
- day schools

Figure 8.1 New knowledge in practice

turn made individual decisions about the way in which students would gain practical experience of school. The establishment of the Council for the Accreditation of Teacher Education (CATE) in 1984, however, made partnership between Higher Education Institutes (HEIs) and schools more systematic and wide-ranging, requiring that teachers be involved in course planning and writing and interviewing of students, as well as playing an increasingly influential role in the assessment of school experience (DES, 1984). Wilkin (1990) has argued, however, that the underlying impetus towards a more significant role for schools in initial teacher education over the last decade in the UK grew primarily out of the theory/practice debate, being both a testing in practice of that relationship and a response to critical argument. The wider political context has cut across this key educational debate, polarising and at times side-tracking important dialogue concerning the nature of the relationship between schools and teacher education. In 1992 the government implemented new procedures for the accreditation of initial teacher education, which in a single move more than doubled the statutory period of time that teachers in training were required to spend in schools; simultaneously, a competence model was introduced on which accreditation was to be based (DFE, 1992). Thus, whilst many educational professionals had been concerned with developing a broad view of teacher education, that took into account the personal, intellectual and cognitive dimensions of learning and the importance of developing teachers who could critically engage in the 'reflective practice' previously described. Conservative policies implemented far-reaching legislation, rooted in a predominantly skills-based, functional view of teacher education. Ironically, many of those who had both argued for and implemented more school-based programmes of teacher education found themselves opposing this very policy. Such opposition arose in part from disquiet about the narrow concept of teacher education and learning on which such policy was grounded, as well as concern about the way in which an explicitly political agenda was driving a fundamentally complex and critical educational debate about the interrelationship between theory and practice.

Recent government policy in the UK has also foregrounded the responsibility of the school for continuing professional development, whilst simultaneously weakening the leading role that Local Education Authorities (LEAs) have traditionally played in this aspect of teacher education. Parallel debates to those taking place in initial teacher education in the 1980s had led many HEIs and LEAs to acknowledge teachers' responsibility for their own professional development and the importance of schools as the site of professional training. Here, too, broader, holistic models of professional development, conceived and implemented in partnership with teachers and schools, were strongly influenced by the increasing interest in experiential learning and Schon's concept of the 'reflective practitioner'. Swingeing government cuts in the early 1990s, however, and the devolving of funding for professional development to schools put an end to numerous authority-wide initiatives, effectively removing local authority structures that in many places had facilitated the articulation of wide-ranging discussions about effective professional development and had also provided vital support for exploratory developments of practice in schools. Political intervention has thus enforced a school-based agenda in both initial and in-service education, whilst simultaneously removing many of the mechanisms of support that schools relied on in developing their new and critical role in teacher education.[2] One of the challenges for both schools and partner institutions in this new climate is to continue dialogue and research into the ways in which teacher development can be continually improved and renewed.

The OU PGCE

The development of the Open University UK's new Postgraduate Certificate in Education (OU PGCE) was coincidental to the move to school-based teacher education. The OU PGCE was launched in February 1994 and is currently one of Europe's largest programmes for the initial education and training of teachers. The impetus for the programme lay principally in the findings of two research exercises carried out in the late 1980s which indicated that there were a significant number of graduates with a real interest in a part-time distance education route to teaching, a large proportion of whom were specialists in science and technology (Moon, 1992). It is an eighteen-month, part-time postgraduate course which includes eighteen weeks of full-time school experience. A key priority for the course team from the outset was the development of a clear conceptual framework for student support which would be integral to the programme.

The majority of OU PGCE students are mature people who come to the course from a wide variety of employment and life experiences? Just 20 per cent of them are under 30 years old, compared to the national PGCE profile which indicates that 52 per cent of students are under 26. OU students have also, for reasons of work, personal circumstances or learning preference, deliberately chosen a part-time distance education course. Seventy-five per cent of them are women, many of whom are intending to return to paid employment after time at home employed in full-time parenting (see Fig. 8.2).

We emphasised at the outset the importance of teacher development as a

---

[2]A Teacher Training Agency has now been established by the Secretary of State for Education, committed to school-based training and charged with administering the central funds for initial teacher education in England. The Agency has also taken responsibility for establishing national standards for continuing professional development (DFE, 1995; TTA, 1995).

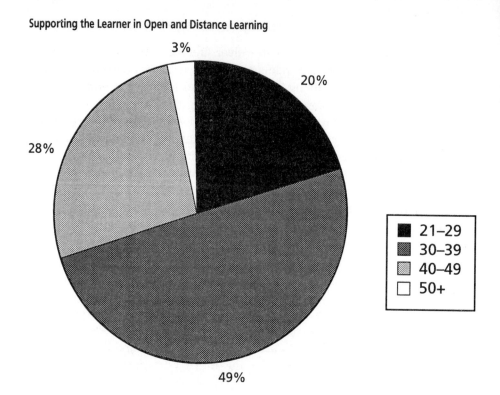

3%

20%

28%

49%

	21–29
	30–39
	40–49
	50+

Figure 8.2 1995 Open University PGCE students—by age

lifelong process. Recent work on teacher development has begun to look at the implications of life span or life cycle research in relation to teachers' careers: Huberman (1992) has suggested that life cycle concerns are deeply implicated in teachers' approaches to instruction. However, the OU PGCE student challenges the notion of a traditional teaching 'career cycle' which defines those involved in initial teacher education, for example, as:

> *usually young adults, still in the process of establishing their personal identities and independence, frequently insecure and vulnerable.* (Alexander, 1990, p. 66)

In fact, evidence testifies to the *'definite expectations, strong motivation to succeed and high level of personal independence and organisation'* displayed by students on this course (Bourne and Leach, 1995).

A common course framework runs across the whole PGCE programme; although the different course lines (primary/secondary) and subjects (English, mathematics, music, science, technology, history and French) have distinctive activities and materials, the order and sequence in which they are addressed is common. A feature of the course is the emphasis placed on understanding pupil learning. Students are therefore introduced to the main theories of learning and, progressively, as the course develops, they observe these ideas and practise integrating them into different teaching strategies. A 'School Experience Guide' is a key element in the course, structuring the school placements through a range of directed activities which cross-reference to the study programme as a whole. This provides a basic 'entitlement' which each student can expect from their school experience.

Students are provided with a wide range of open learning materials and resources to support their study. Some of these are commonplace in distance education programmes: a course study guide; video, audio materials and audio-visual guides; course readers and set books. Other aspects of provision are unique to the OU PGCE. First, students are given substantial resource packs for each phase and secondary subject line, which contain a wide range of documents, facsimile material and other texts. Second, an Apple Macintosh® computer, printer, keyboard, modem and associated software are lent to the student for the duration of the course.

Student support

Although these extensive resources constitute a fundamental element of the PGCE course, the other 'complementary but essential' provision is its wide-ranging student support. This aspect of the programme involved the Open University in the development of new structures, as well as the modification of existing forms of support.

The PGCE is administered on a day-to-day basis by academic staff located in twelve regional offices across England, Wales and Northern Ireland. These regional *staff tutors*, like their counterparts in other faculties, are responsible for appointing and training local part-time OU tutors for the course. A unique aspect of their role in terms of the OU structure, however, is the direct, face-to-face contact with schools and students: sample monitoring the interviews of students by schools; briefing mentors; supporting partner schools and moderating the assessment of school experience. Staff tutors thus provide a vital link between regions and the central academic team.

A crucial new element of student support for the OU is based on its partnership with schools. The PGCE's 'partner schools' are essentially those schools which, in collaboration with the OU, implement the PGCE course for over 1000 students each year, providing student support during full-time school placements. As the eighteen-month course cycles overlap, the OU can, in theory, have up to 3000 schools involved in the partnership scheme for six months of the year. Such a large enterprise requires a clear framework of responsibilities and student entitlements, but one within which local strengths must be accommodated. A simple but rigorous framework sets out the roles and responsibilities of the institutions and the people involved (Open University, 1995).

Within this partnership the *mentor* plays a key role, with responsibility for support and training as well as assessment of the students' three school experiences. As we have emphasised, it is the School Experience Guide which provides for consistency of experience and acts as a tool for negotiating a variety of teaching opportunities within and between schools in the programme. These include involving the students in extensive classroom observation and evaluation, as well as giving them the opportunity to teach collaboratively with their mentor and engage in 'co-analysis of practice'. This Guide is one element of a substantial pack of mentor training materials which is given to every partner school and which guides the mentor in his/her various roles. To support both mentor and student, the partner school nominates a senior member of staff or *school co-ordinator*, who also acts as a management link to the University, ensuring the student can experience school-wide activities as well as validating school-based assessments of the student's progress.

The PGCE *tutors* are also experienced teachers and provide readily accessible personal support for individual students throughout the course, as well as through regular group tutorials and day schools. Although the mentor provides in-depth knowledge of classroom teaching and the opportunity for students to observe and discuss practice with an experienced teacher, the role of the tutor complements that of the mentor by drawing links, in tutorials and in correspondence tuition on written assignments, between the student's experience in schools and the course materials. This support provides breadth as well as depth of experience, and gives students the opportunity to analyse a range of practice outside the pressures of the school context. In regional day schools and tutorials, students share experiences and draw support from their peers.

The variety of opportunities for student support that the PGCE programme provides is integral to the course. Statistics show that in the first two years of the programme, attendance at both optional tutorials and day schools has been far higher than in conventional OU courses: 80 per cent nationally. All those involved in student support are not only given written briefing materials but are provided with face-to-face training in their respective roles. Tutors and mentors are briefed together before each school experience, and so although their roles are separate and distinct, they are able to share a common approach to both the course's methodology and the interpretation of the assessment framework. The nationally prescribed framework for briefing and training, along with the monitoring of tutorials and school experience, is an important aspect of the programme's extensive quality assurance procedures.

There is a similarly high participation rate in the other innovative element of student support within the OU framework: the provision of *electronic communication* via a personal computer and modem, controlled by the FirstClass™ program. The system is facilitated by a team from the Open University's Academic Computing Service whose aim was to make the Internet available to all OU students by the beginning of 1996. The PGCE environment within the FirstClass™ system is managed by members of the central academic team, including the director of the programme, the IT co-ordinator, the course writing team, course managers and administrators, as well as the regional academic staff tutors. FirstClass™ enables access to electronic mail, computer conferencing, 'real-time chats', and the facility to attach and send documents. Students can operate in numerous environments depending on need: access to 'read only' bulletin boards providing course-related details; general conferencing; an e-mail facility; discussions about their subject specialism; and private synchronous on-line 'chat' (see Fig. 8.3).

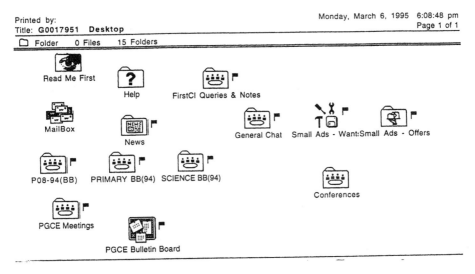

Figure 8.3 Facilities offered by FirstClass™ conferencing system

The system's pervasiveness over time and space, as well as its capacity to provide for both synchronous and asynchronous communication, makes it a fascinating and highly flexible mode of student support, unexplored in most traditional teacher education courses. Log-in times reveal patterns of use which illustrate well the medium's accessibility for students with differing time constraints for study. This is reflected in a secondary (Modern Foreign Languages) student's contribution in the 'General Chat':

I've noticed that people tend to log in at particular times. I'm usually a night person, and there are several 'people' I 'meet' regularly. I logged in this morning, and I didn't recognise a single name.

The 'permanent' nature of student contributions on screen means that the variety of purposes which this mode of support fulfils is transparent. Contributions also provide an insight into the way different aspects of the course interrelate; for this reason, FirstClass™ is described here in more detail.

Over a two-month period, the monitoring of contributions made by PGCE students within the English subject conference alone showed more than a hundred students logging in regularly and 39 active contributors. One advantage of asynchronous communication is that students can plan and edit a contribution to an on-line conference without the pressure that the immediacy of live discussion can entail: clearly helpful for less confident students. Discussion included references to 140 individual texts or authors, ranging from Spencer's sixteenth-century poem *The Faerie Queene* to contemporary media texts and teenage 'point horror'. Monitoring also revealed exchange of information about events nationally from Edinburgh and Dublin, to Armagh in Northern Ireland and West Stow in Sussex. Students were shown to be engaged in a wide range of activities including queries about course materials, arrangements for the exchange of correspondence between pupils in Cumbria and Essex, debates on issues such as gender in the teaching of reading, as well as discussion of individual pupils' problems, such as spelling. Patterns of use illustrate the way in which the personal and public, the intellectual and affective, the trivial and humorous, as well as the highly serious, interweave in a form of support that is accessible twenty-four hours a day.

This variety of purpose is illustrated by evaluations made by a group of students electronically during the course of subject conferencing:

I use FirstClass™ because it's something related to the course which I can accomplish in 3 to 20 minutes (not normally a useful size block of study time).

Course content related

I have drawn some relief from finding that others are in the same boat with regard to overload.

Study support

I have traded ideas for teaching which has been stimulating of further ideas for me.

School experience related

I like private chat for meeting peers: sometimes it is hard to have a strong sense of achievement, or humour.

Personal relationships

I find direct contact with people (like the course team) is very helpful (they have been very supportive).

Personal and course related

I am just beginning to talk about exchanging lesson plans and materials with a couple of MFL students.

School experience related

. . . and it does give one the feeling of belonging to a community: providing support, chat and a feeling that one is not alone.

Personal relationships

Such evaluations illustrate the interplay between private and professional, course-related and personal, affective and cognitive engagement with the whole person, the learner. This theme is reflected in a conference contribution which simultaneously links the student's engagement with her subject study (English poetry conference), relationships with fellow students, her role as a single parent, and the setting (11 p.m. at home across the hall from her sleeping 5-year-old daughter):

I think nearly all we regular users are mothers, using this in lieu of meeting flesh and blood people. I attach Fleur Adcock—though I don't think this poem would work in school:

FOR A FIVE-YEAR-OLD

A snail is climbing up the window-sill
Into your room, after a night of rain.
You call me in to see, and I explain
That it would be unkind to leave it there:
It might crawl to the floor; we must take care
That no one squashes it. You understand,
And carry it outside, with careful hand,
To eat a daffodil.

I see, then, that a kind of faith prevails:
Your gentleness is moulded still by words
From me, who have trapped mice and shot wild birds,
From me, who drowned your kittens, who betrayed
Your closest relatives, and who purveyed
The harshest kind of truth to many another
But that is how things are: I am your mother,
And we are kind to snails.

Fleur Adcock (1994)

117

The OU PGCE illustrates one framework of support for professional development in a distance context. We have emphasised the range of learning opportunities the programme seeks to provide, which operate both across and throughout the course in an unfolding, interrelated way. FirstClass™ has been used to illustrate the constant dialogue that student support can and must engender between course 'theory' and 'practical' school experience, the public and the personal, between learners, and between teachers and learners and their collective knowledge and experience. Key areas for the development of the PGCE programme clearly lie in the refining and constant evaluation of each and every aspect of student support within the programme. By turning now to an in-service teacher education programme in Eastern Europe for our second case study and its framework for teacher support, we emphasise the centrality of *continuing* professional development in our view of teacher education. In contrast to the OU PGCE, those involved in this programme have access neither to advanced technology nor to sophisticated mechanisms for course production and publication.

In-service teacher education at a distance: An Eastern European experience

The Albanian context

Recent changes in teacher education in the UK throw into sharp relief the educational context in Albania, Eastern Europe, the focus of the second case study of this chapter. There, teacher training is not routine and no national assessment policy exists. There too, however, broad debates about teacher education are taking place against the background of fundamental political and social change. After years of enforced economic, political and cultural isolation, such change has propelled Albania into contact with the rest of Europe and the international community, yet it remains Europe's poorest country. The grave economic situation faced by Albania not only impedes desperately-needed teacher education programmes but educational reform in general. Indeed, priorities are difficult to establish when the needs are so varied and pressing. In 1994, for example, reports showed that 60 per cent of basic and secondary school classrooms needed repair or complete replacement, having seriously deteriorated during the interregnum which followed the demise of the communist system. There is a severe shortage of basic textbooks and paper. There is no educational technology. Vital infrastructures such as roads and telecommunications remain fragile and unreliable.

In a country where almost one in three of the population is of school age, recent declines in school enrolment testify to a potentially serious breakdown in the education system. This situation is most acute in remote areas. Multiple factors contribute to enrolment decline nationally: one issue is that of re-engaging popular commitment to education which has traditionally been associated with a controlling and punitive regime. In the north and east of Albania the Ministry of Education faces difficulty in recruiting teachers; 64 per cent of the population live in rural and mountainous districts and the quality of education provided is often poorer in these areas. Only 19 per cent of teachers in rural areas, for example, have a high school qualification at senior primary level (10–14 years); the figure nationally is 30.6 per cent. Poor public transport makes aggregating students or moving teachers among schools on a daily basis difficult. This is another factor which is crippling small village schools' ability to provide quality instruction (World Bank, 1994).

Prior to 1991, educational policy was prescribed by a national education plan co-ordinated with the national economic plan; its administration was highly centralised. So too was the curriculum, with its 'red threads' of political doctrine particularly evident in philosophy, civics, history and geography. Albania's political and geographical isolation meant that educationalists have been unable to keep abreast of modern developments in curriculum and pedagogy. Teacher educators thus face a long-term need to create curricular frameworks that reflect current subject knowledge and the best pedagogical practice within the Albanian context.

All aspects of education, including the curriculum, are under review: a major priority for the Ministry of Education is teacher education and retraining. Discussion, however, about how such professional development might best be achieved is painful and parallels the UK debate. Although an ambitious national policy has been formulated, with the country's Pedagogical Institute responsible overall for the development of this aspect of educational policy, there are certain key decisions to be made against the urgently felt need in some quarters to shift the focus of debate towards schools, and towards the development of new knowledge in the context of classroom practice. How, for example, will intending teachers gain experience of new ideas and real classrooms? What strategies are best used for in-service education? Should there be demonstration schools where innovative ideas can be piloted before introducing them 'system-wide'?; if so, how can good practice spread beyond such schools, and what incentive is there for teachers to seek out and use better practice? Where does the cascade model of in-service education fit in as it is currently delivered? What of the 'formators' who have responsibility for such programmes, many of whom are associated with outdated approaches and thinking? A World Bank strategy report on educational development in Albania summarises the 'retraining challenge' facing the country thus:

> cascade training can behave like gossip, the message becoming increasingly distorted as it travels from person to person. More fundamentally, unless training combines new knowledge with its guided and corrected application (for example in simulated classrooms), it will change teachers' verbal repertoire but not their practice. Thus the retraining challenge will be to design curricula that help trainees transfer what they know into what they do, and to design school or district-level mechanisms that reinforce the new learning. (World Bank, 1994, p. 64)

This dialogic relationship between theory and practice, as we have already seen, remains the challenge for teacher education and development worldwide.

Kualida Education Development Project

Kualida Education Development Project is a pilot project for the in-service training of elementary teachers (Grades 5–8) in three districts of Albania. The impetus for the development of this three-month programme arose from the urgent need for teacher retraining in Albania, as previously described. The specific courses which are being piloted arose out of a feasibility study into the potential for using open learning in the Albanian context. The study was commissioned by the Albanian Education Development Project as part of the Ministry of Education's development strategy. Although there is no experience of open and distance learning in Albania, the study found a wide interest in such a methodology amongst members of the universities and pedagogic institutes, teachers themselves and members of the teaching unions (Moon and Leach, 1995).

The course is designed for 815 teachers of English, history, geography and French: subjects that members of the pedagogic institute and teachers had identified as most in need of in-service programmes. The course materials include four study texts: *Aspecte Te Mesimdhenies Gjuhe Frenge/Angleze/Histori/Gjeografi* (Aspects of Teaching in French/English/History/Geography) (Musai, 1995). There is one text for each subject area, and each is designed round a common framework. There is a two-part introduction: 'Why change?' and 'Distance education as a methodology'. The first main section focuses on *Metodolgji* (methodologies) which are new to Albanian teachers generally, such as strategies for teaching and learning (e.g. problem solving, brainstorming, role play), the use of questioning, and pupil assessment. The second section, *Veprimtari* (activities), provides teachers with exemplar material to be adapted to their own teaching contexts. Each study text is bound in a plastic folder containing A4 notebook and pen to be used by the teachers for written assignments; the texts' layout, graphics, print and binding are far superior in quality to those of the subject-focused text that teachers have routinely been issued with. Three 45-minute television programmes to complement these study texts have been filmed in Albanian classrooms, illustrating the new teaching approaches and accompanied by interviews with teachers and pupils about this classroom innovation. The programmes have been aired on national Albanian television at peak viewing times (Fridays at 5.15 p.m.) and also on satellite television, in order to generate wide public discussion about educational change. They include video sequences that have been recorded for replay in the newly-equipped study centres in each of the three pilot regions.

The materials are innovative in two respects in the Albanian context. The first is that they have been written by academics drawn from the pedagogic institutes in collaboration with practising teachers in each of the four subject areas. Hitherto, teachers were used to an imposed curriculum. These writing teams were trained in open learning approaches and wrote to a very tight three-month deadline, which reflected the urgency of the task. The second respect is the way in which methodology and practice are interlinked in the programme. Teachers are invited to try out new approaches to teaching and learning in their own classrooms and then to evaluate these in discussion with colleagues and pupils themselves.

Teacher support

Not only is open learning a completely new concept in Albania, the whole constructivist agenda on which the course rests is unfamiliar to most teachers. It has not been customary for Albanian teachers to make choices about teaching and learning strategies, even less common to involve pupils in activities that demand active approaches in the classroom. The Kualida writing team was well aware that the teaching methodologies being introduced would present a challenge to many teachers. Indeed they acknowledge this directly in the introduction to the course materials:

> *I dashior mesues . . . Dear teacher*
>
> *Recent years have seen many changes. We have both a need and a desire to change things in our profession. But it has been hard to respond to the many questions such as What is change? Why change? How do we change? . . . Our society is changing in many different directions. There are new requirements ahead of us. We cannot meet these demands with old concepts and practices.* (Musai, 1995; Translation from the Albanian by Zana Lita, Kualida project officer)

For all these reasons the provision of teacher support for Kualida was carefully considered by the project team. This was seen as crucial to the success of the pilot programme. Any chosen infrastructure of support for teachers involved in the project needed to be consonant with the existing culture, providing stability at a time of change and a secure framework for reflection and evaluation. The project team judiciously decided to work within the existing regional networks of formators. There were some obvious drawbacks to this plan: we have already mentioned, for example, that some formators are identified with the controversial cascade model of training.

Teachers involved in the pilot project are therefore assigned to a subject-specific formator in groups of twenty-five. Three tutorials are provided—at the beginning, in the middle and towards the end of the programme—led by the formator, who is also responsible for assessing the teachers' written notebooks according to agreed criteria. As with the PGCE programme, links are made in tutorials between school Activities and the course materials, and teachers are given the opportunity to analyse new practice outside the pressures of the school context. Early monitoring shows that attendance at the tutorials has been high and most formators have taken their new role seriously.

All formators in the pilot regions have been given extensive face-to-face training: in open learning methodology, in the course materials and in 'tutorial' provision. This training has taken place centrally in Tirana, followed by regional briefings in the three pilot districts: Elbasan, Skodra, to the north, and Girokastra in the south of the country, encompassing both rural and town communities. Some members of the writing team are also formators, therefore regional teams are able to benefit from their detailed knowledge of the course materials. Formators have also been provided with clear written guidance, including notes on their role and how tutorials can be planned and run. Members of the programme team visit a proportion of tutorials to evaluate and review the programme. The combination of country-wide training, written guidance and tutorial monitoring forms an important component of quality assurance within the Kualida project.

As noted earlier, a course that interlinks methodology directly with classroom activities is innovative in Albania. School-based support was clearly vital within the Kualida programme, but what form should it take at this pilot stage? No formal mentoring system currently exists in Albanian schools and although expertise in classroom methods is being developed, support operates on an informal basis. It was decided to combine this informal approach with the work of formators. The programme therefore explicitly urges teachers to invite formators to visit their classrooms to discuss the school-based work, whilst also encouraging them to build on traditional practice by meeting with colleagues from neighbouring schools and visiting each other's classrooms.

As with the PGCE School Experience Guide, the Activities in the Kualida course materials provide a common frame of reference both for teachers working together and for visiting formators. Traditionally, formators have attended schools without warning, but the programme emphasises that visits to discuss course activities are by invitation of the teacher concerned and in a context of professionals working together. It is hoped that this new approach will inform and modify relationships between formators and teachers in positive ways; it remains to be seen how those involved adapt to change. Inevitably some teachers and formators are resistant to the new ideas and methodologies, but early indications show a groundswell of interest in and commitment to the programme, both from the grassroots and amongst formators themselves. Vigorous debate about the new approaches to teaching and learning is taking place in the pilot districts. This debate has been fuelled by the screening of the Kualida television programmes on the mainstream television network, as well as by a national television programme focusing on distance learning and innovation in teacher education. The establishment of new study centres in each of the regions creates a further context in which teachers can work together.

The creation of new knowledge 'in practice' is nowhere more acutely realised than in the Kualida project, where the transformation of both pedagogical understanding and teachers' classroom activities are profoundly open-ended processes. Most of the Albanian teachers in this programme are, for the first time in their professional lives, being encouraged to actively engage with new approaches to teaching and learning. How such approaches, in individual schools and classrooms, will develop in the longer term is as yet unclear. But for those that engage in this unfolding dialogue stretched across 'everyday activities'—including tutorials, watching and discussing project television programmes at home, school-based meetings and classroom teaching—new learning in practice is inevitable. Engeström has suggested that when people learn to do things that they have not done before:

> zones of proximal development are collective, rather than individual, phenomena ... 'the new' is a collective invention in the face of felt dilemmas and contradictions that impede ongoing activity and impel movement and change. (Chaiklin and Lave, 1993, p. 13)

This is an appropriate metaphor for the potentially radical change we have described.

Student support: Some conclusions

Student support would seem to be a process through which understanding is both created and transformed, rather than a 'provision' to be 'managed'.

Within teacher development it is an essential and integral part of the overall learning process and the quality of its constituent elements are key. Essentially a social practice, it occurs at the intersection of:

- **setting** (be it home, school, classroom or study centre)
- **relationships** between learner(s) and teacher(s)
- the **activities** taking place
- the **knowledge and experience** brought to bear by participants (we can include as 'participants' the invisible authors of course materials, school experience guides or video tapes)
- **context**.

In conclusion, six key issues for professional development arise from this study. Although the context is teacher education, the issues raised are common to other vocational and professional areas.

1 Support should provide model learning environments: Teaching and learning should fully mirror that which is expected of the best practice in students' own school/teaching contexts, be it in face-to-face provision, written communication on course assignments, one-to-one support or electronic conferencing. This has critical implications for the provision and development of tutor and mentor training.

2 Support should build on existing frameworks as far as possible and be consonant with the culture in which it is developed: We have shown the way, for example, in which the role of formator has been used and developed in new programmes in Albania.

3 Support should be developmental and exploratory, providing experience of a wide variety of teaching and learning opportunities: It should seek to challenge over time traditional dichotomies such as the distinction between the transmission of knowledge and learner-centred approaches, theory and practice, teacher and learner. We have noted, for example, the need for more research into how mentors can successfully make pedagogic strategies and their practice in action explicit to novice teachers.

4 Support should recognise and build on the variety of professional experiences of its participants: Distance learning courses traditionally attract adults from a wide variety of life experiences and with a range of expertise. Such experiences powerfully affect frames of reference, some of which will conflict with new knowledge and experience, as we have seen in the implementation of the Kualida programme.

5 Support should acknowledge both the private and professional aspects of learners' experiences and their interconnectedness in the development of learning: The Open University students' use of the FirstClass™ system illustrates the ongoing, unfolding nature of learning and the importance of the interrelatedness of the personal and professional in the development process.

6 Support should have a firm base in schools and classrooms: It should be seen as an ongoing process across initial, induction and ongoing phases of teacher development.

REFERENCES

Adcock, F. (1994) For a five-year-old. In Hall, L. (Ed.) *An anthology of poetry by women: Tracing the tradition* (London, Cassell).

Alexander, R. (1990) Partnership in initial teacher training: Confronting the issues. In Booth, M., Furlong, J. & Wilkin, M. (Eds.) *Partnership in initial teacher training* (London, Cassell).

Banks, F., Bourdillon, H., Leach, J., Manning, P., Moon, B. & Swarbrick, A. (1995) Knowledge, school knowledge and pedagogy: Defining an agenda for teacher education. Paper presented at a symposium for the 1995 European Conference of Educational Research, Bath, UK, Centre for Research in Teacher Education (Milton Keynes, Open University).

Booth, M., Furlong, J. & Wilkin, M. (1990) *Partnership in initial teacher training* (London, Cassell).

Bourne, J. & Leach, J. (1995) Open learning and the PGCE: A primary experience. In Griffiths, V. & Owen, P. (Eds.) *Schools in partnership: Current initiatives in school-based teacher training* (London, Paul Chapman).

Breger, B. (1995) *Report on the NIS transformation of the Humanities Conference*, Minsk, 6 June 1995.

Bruner, J.S. (1986) *Actual minds, possible worlds* (London, Harvard University Press).

Burgess, H. & Harris, A. (1995) Concepts of the mentor role in open and distance learning teacher education. Paper presented at a symposium for the 1995 European Conference of Educational Research, Bath, UK, Centre For Research in Teacher Education (Milton Keynes, Open University).

Chaiklin, S. & Lave, J. (1993) *Understanding practice: Perspectives on activity and context* (Cambridge, Cambridge University Press).

Department of Education and Science (1984) *Initial teacher training: Approval of courses* (Circular 3/84) (London, DES).

Department for Education (1992) *Initial teacher training (Secondary Phase) (Circular 9/92)* (London, DFE).

Department for Education (1995) Inspirational teachers key to future: Shepard, *DFE News*, 27 March 1995, London.

Edwards, D. & Mercer, N. (1987) *Common knowledge: The development of understanding in the classroom* (London, Routledge).

Glennie, J. (1995) Towards learner-centred distance education in the changing South African context. Keynote address to the Cambridge International Conference on Open and Distance Learning, 3 July 1995, Cambridge.

Hargreaves, A. (1995) Towards a social geography of teacher education. In Shimahara, N.Z. & Holowinsky, I.Z., *Teacher education in industrialised nations* (New York, Garland).

Hargreaves, A. & Fullan, M.G. (1992) *Understanding teacher development* (London, Cassell).

Huberman, M. (1992) Teacher development and instructional mastery. In Hargreaves, A. & Fullan, M.G., *op. cit.*

Lave, J. (1988) *Cognition in practice* (Cambridge, Cambridge University Press).

McIntyre, D. (1990) *The Oxford Internship Scheme and the Cambridge Analytical Framework: Models of partnership in initial teacher education.* In Booth, M. *et al., op. cit.*

Moon, R.E. (1992) A new routeway into teaching: The Open University and school partnership, *Education Review,* **6** (2).

Moon, R.E. (1996) Practical experience in teacher education: Charting a European agenda, *European Journal of Teacher Education,* **19** (2).

Moon, R.E. & Leach, J. (1995) Open and distance learning and teaching in the education and training of Albanian teachers: A feasibility study, Mimeo, Open University, Centre for Research in Teacher Education.

Musai, B. (1995) *Aspecte Te Mesimdhenies Angleze* (Tirana, Albania, Education Development Project).

Newman, D., Griffin, P. & Cole, M. (1989) *The construction zone: Working for cognitive change in school* (Cambridge, Cambridge University Press).

Open University (1995) *PGCE course handbook for schools* (Milton Keynes, Open University).

Schon, D.A. (1987) *Educating the reflective practitioner* (San Francisco, Jossey Bass).

Tait, A. (1995) Understanding student support in open and distance learning. In Lockwood, F., *Open and distance learning today* (London, Routledge).

Teacher Training Agency (1995) *Initial advice to the Secretary of State on the continuing professional development of teachers,* July 1995, London.

Thorpe, M. (1995) The challenge facing course design. In Lockwood, F., *Open and distance learning today* (London, Routledge).

Vygotsky, L. (1978) *Mind in society: The development of higher psychological processes* (Ed. Cole, M., John-Steiner, V., Scribner, S. & Souberman, E.) (Cambridge, MA, Harvard University Press).

Wilkin, M. (1990) The development of partnerships in the UK. In Booth, M. *et al., op. cit.*

World Bank (1994) *Strategy note: Albania education system.*

Part 3

Recognising and supporting difference

9

Equal opportunities in open and distance learning

Diane Bailey, Gill Kirkup and Lee Taylor

Introduction

The rationale for developments in open and distance learning (ODL) has often centred on their potential for overcoming educational disadvantage and for providing opportunities for groups hitherto excluded. This rationale has two main strands. First, distance education, progressing from a long history of correspondence teaching to its current state of multi-media pluralism, has been seen as creating new opportunities for those previously excluded by geographical isolation, disability, and work or caring responsibilities, or the cost of full-time study. Second, versions of open learning which require no previous entry qualifications or which accredit prior learning gained outside formal education have evolved to overcome the rather different barriers of 'credentialism'. Such schemes, by allowing people to leap-frog the qualifications hurdle, create opportunities especially suited to those who by gender, class, poverty and age have missed out in selective educational and training systems. Allied to these arguments has run the theme that ODL is cost-effective to the student and to the state and, therefore, is suited to economies demanding a rapid expansion in the training of the workforce. By adapting industrial models of mass production in which a high investment in materials production is offset by modest delivery costs, ODL, it is argued, can reach more students than is affordable by traditional forms of learning.

In essence, then, the broad rationale for ODL has focused on its democratising potential. This has remained largely true as ODL has diversified and colonised areas of education in the developed world previously dominated by face-to-face teaching, such as schools, professional updating and work-based learning. It is also true as ODL has extended access in the developing world to cohorts who are without alternatives. Current incarnations of ODL, including resource-based learning (Laurillard, 1993) and the use of global information systems and 'virtual classrooms' (Tiffin and Rajasingham, 1995) likewise stress the potential of these initiatives for widening access, though for widely differing target groups. This liberal, emancipatory dimension of ODL is saluted in a recent survey of second and third generation systems which offer *'new ways of accessing knowledge and skills that can liberate millions of human beings'* (Daniel, 1995).

But consideration of equality of opportunity and even more of equality of outcome make us question this assumption that ODL is invariably liberating. Theoretical critiques of openness, as well as evaluations of specific systems in terms of their inclusivity and their effectiveness in serving disadvantaged target groups, are, of course, well advanced. For example, Lewis (Lewis and Spencer, 1986) has modelled dimensions along which all ODL systems are relatively open or closed. Harris (1987) has analysed the far-from-straightforward relationships between systems design and learning outcomes. Rumble (1989) questions the seductive notion of openness and points to the illiberal political agendas implicit in some seemingly open schemes.

The current preoccupation in the developed world with quality assurance and quality audit in relation to ODL (see Calder, 1994; Henderikx, 1992) stresses the need to monitor success in terms of the starting bases of the learner. However, diversity amongst learners is acknowledged as making quality assessments of education more difficult (Brennan *et al.*, 1994). If quality assessments monitor the degree of 'value added' to learners in overcoming barriers, both of access and of lacking previous qualifications, by using support built into programmes, then equality of opportunity is an aspect of quality enhancement. The problem is that terms such as 'value added' and 'cost-effective' are often used about higher education without taking into account that definitions of 'value', 'effectiveness' and even 'equality' are contested, especially in a heterogeneous culture. Equal opportunities monitoring and quality assurance methodology can also, if implemented in insensitive ways, produce a 'compliance culture', *'whereby external requirements are met in a minimal and conformist way without connection to the reality of the educational process'* (Brennan *et al.*, 1994, p. 11), rather than a change to the philosophies and practices of educators.

This chapter addresses the broad issue of the 'equalising' capacity of support systems in ODL as part of equal opportunities policies. Such policies with their attendant codes and guidelines for good practice are now widespread in traditional educational institutions in Europe and English-speaking cultures. The translation of these policies and practices into ODL systems poses questions about how they are adapted and contextualised. Given the emancipatory intentions of ODL as a whole and the specific design of many schemes to dismantle barriers and to equalise successful participation, the incorporation of equal opportunities strategies has implications for the close monitoring of both student and staff experiences. Equal opportunities, with its emphasis on targets and monitoring, reinforces the requirement to develop the critique of the relative openness of ODL for its many stakeholders.

What do we understand by equal opportunities?

The concept of equal opportunities (EO) is itself problematic and much of the literature is descriptive rather than analytic, resulting in a range of different understandings, assumptions and policy being implemented. As Farish *et al.* point out in their study on EO in practice in UK colleges and universities, EO:

> *can be applied to a wide variety of contexts within educational institutions: for instance, to staff issues, curriculum, pedagogy, assessment, access and recruitment, priorities in funding, staff-student relations, the general work environment and so on.* (Farish et al., 1995)

In the OU UK, it has been seen as integrating curriculum, student access and support and staff issues, and treating these as interrelated in often complex ways. In other sectors, the emphasis has been primarily on staff issues, sometimes narrowly focused on particular groups.

We can, however, look at a range of different concepts. We have to start with the legal background, which, of course, varies from country to country, but is the starting point for many organisations obliged to stay on the right side of the law. In the UK, it is unlawful to discriminate against anyone on the grounds of race, sex or marital status in the fields of employment or provision of services. However, although important, it is often observed in the breach. In countries such as the US or Northern Ireland within the UK, legislation is more firmly tied into implementation practice, requiring organisations, at least on paper, to do formal audits and meet compliance conditions where federal funding is concerned. The law tends to address certain groups: women, black and ethnic minority groups in predominantly white populations, older people, disabled people. Although legislation is important as a framework, there are other powerful issues in play. The concept of 'natural justice', of equality based on ethical concerns for equity, although a slippery one, would be seen by many in ODL as the mainspring of much of their work.

The 'liberal' concept of EO focuses on the concept of fair procedures, which supposedly guarantee that each individual, regardless of race, gender, age, disability (or other factors), will be able to compete on an equal basis for social or educational rewards, based on that individual's qualities and performance. This has been characterised as the 'level playing field' (Jewson and Mason,

131

1986). This approach involves institutions in removing barriers, in, for example, having an open entry policy.

Young (1989) describes the policies flowing from this liberal model as tending to be procedural, as they proscribe certain forms of behaviour seen as discriminatory and insist on conformity to universally-applied codes of conduct, for example in the area of selection and recruitment of staff or dealing with harassment. This model has been reinforced by its links with perceived good management practice, linking anti-discriminatory measures with attendant legal penalties for non-compliance with good management practice. So, for example, the UK's Committee of Vice Chancellors and Principals has issued a body of guidance which draws on UK legal imperatives but stresses that adherence to the guidance is more a matter of good sense and that benefits will accrue to the organisation.

The 'radical' model of equal opportunities looks at redressing previous disadvantage, and is concerned with the outcome rather than the rules of the game: *'the fairness of distribution of rewards rather than the procedures'* (Jewson and Mason, 1986). It is explicit in targeting particular groups and can be seen or described as 'positive action'. It tends to lack an organisational dimension, by focusing on assimilation rather than structural organisational change.

Most feminist work, and the recent work on cultural and ethnic diversity, opposes the assimilation model and celebrates diversity or difference (Kandola and Fullerton, 1994), arguing that organisations should promote a range of strategies to support and encourage all their organisational stakeholders: in university terms, primarily students and staff, but also including funding agencies.

Where EO projects or policies have been adopted in ODL institutions, it is rarely obvious which of the above models is the basis. Sometimes the model held by institutional planners is different from that practised by those involved in student support, or those who most publicly espouse EO.

The development of accepted EO policies has always been fraught with argument and debate, often heated. The 1990s has witnessed a public opinion and in some cases policy backlash against particular aspects of EO, especially those concerned with what is seen as 'positive discrimination'; for example, in the US, some of the legislation on affirmative action is being challenged successfully in the courts, undercutting affirmative action programmes in universities. This may be the product of a compliance culture, discussed earlier, where members of an institution carry out policies to which they have little commitment and which are demolished as soon as an opportunity arises. It is encouraged by an environment of scarce resources and where short-term outcomes (such as higher student success rates) are required. It can also be seen as the victim of confusion about the aims of different EO models.

The range of groups covered under the umbrella term equal opportunities is also variable according to institutional and national concerns. Women are usually the main group perceived as disadvantaged; in addition, the other groups may include minority ethnic groups, disabled people, older people, those belonging to particular religions or castes, gays and lesbians, those belonging to particular political or union groups, those from less advantaged socio-economic backgrounds and people living in geographically remote areas.

What is the range of EO practice in ODL?

Searching international databases for information about the policies and practices which address equal opportunities in ODL institutions globally is rather like looking for the proverbial needle in a haystack. Where equality is discussed in the literature, this is through discrete projects rather than a discussion of total institutional policy. These projects, often driven by those involved in student support, tend to be based on EO models which respect diversity and operate an interaction with a disadvantaged group, rather than the assimilation of it. A review of projects which deal with gender, disability and ethnic diversity indicates the key role of student support systems.

Gender

Gender, both as an aspect of inequality and of difference, is, since the 1980s, the most extensively theorised of all the factors of educational inequality in any sector of education. (Prior to the 1980s both theoretical and practical attention was focused on class inequality.) Although ODL theory and practice has taken up gender issues somewhat late (see Kirkup, Chapter 10 of this volume), these are now being discussed both in developed and developing countries, and in any EO literature review 'gender' will produce the longest list of entries.

ODL gender literature has always attempted to be international and include the perspectives of different societies (Faith, 1988). However, Kanwar argues in the introduction to a recent collection which analyses the particular situation of women in ODL in India:

> While research by women in the First World was grounded in sophisticated theory, papers by Third World women were primarily descriptive and voiced basic concerns such as the struggle for instituting Women's Studies, convincing policy makers of the need for implementing women-related initiatives and the continuing struggle for equality. (Kanwar and Jagannathan, 1995, p. 2)

In some of the poorest countries in the world in the 1980s almost 25 per cent of girls and women were receiving no formal education.

Countries which often look to ODL to address a general issue of educational provision rarely design specific ODL programmes for women. India, although not one of the poorest countries, belongs to the developing world with respect to educational provision and provides an interesting case study. In India, as in many developing countries, an educated female workforce is seen as essential to economic development. The Indian government targeted the education of women and girls in its 1986 National Policy on Education and the associated Programme of Action (Sesharatnam, 1995):

> *Education will be used as an agent of basic change in the status of woman. In order to neutralise the accumulated distortions of the past, there will be a well-conceived edge in favour of women. The National Education System will play a positive, interventionist role in the empowerment of women. It will foster the development of new values through the redesigned curricula, textbooks, training and orientation of teachers, decision-makers and administrators and the active involvement of educational institutions.* (quoted in Sesharatnam, 1995, p. 21)

Although some ODL institutions, such as the Indira Gandhi University, have a Women's Unit, authors in the Kanwar and Jagannathan (1995) collection argue that the participation and drop-out rates of women in ODL in general in India suggest that the government policy has not yet produced programmes and student support networks which are overcoming gender inequality with any speed. Ramakrishna (1995) suggests that student support and counselling services are not yet responsive enough to the needs of women students. It will be interesting to see whether face-to-face women's universities, which are now developing into dual mode ODL institutions (for example the Shrimati Nathibai Damodor Thackersay (SNDT) Women's University in Bombay, or even the Mount Saint Vincent University in Canada), can design their ODL around women's needs as they did their face-to-face provision. Can an education system which granted women a separate sphere with gender-specific support programmes continue to do so under pressure to assimilate to a mixed-sex mass education system, usually implicit in a liberal democratic model?

Disability

One group of students who have been able to take advantage of ODL, who have been unable to engage in education in any other way, are students with physical disabilities. Those whose disabilities give them limited mobility, such as spinal injuries (Meacham and Wilkin, 1990), can simply use ODL to study at home. Others, whose disabilities involve communication, hearing, vision or speech, can often get materials in alternative media and submit assessments using alternative media. The OU UK has been the largest single provider of adult education for adults with disabilities in the UK. This has been because resources have been provided to support such students; for example, text materials are available at no extra cost on audio cassette for students with visual disabilities, as well as materials in large print and in electronic form so that they can be speech synthesised (Vincent, 1983). More recently, developments in electronic publishing and compact disc technologies have been exploited to give further choice of media for students whose disabilities preclude the use of books. It often seems that the technologies of ODL, especially the most recent electronic technologies, provide students with disabilities with what they need to study, and this often distracts attention from the 'people-based' support systems which such students need and on which technology solutions are built.

Minority ethnic groups

Some of the most interesting projects, which use an interactional model of equality rather than an assimilationist one, are those designed for aboriginal or native peoples. In both Canada and Australia ODL was identified as being the most appropriate educational system for people living in traditional rural communities. However, in both countries, aboriginal students had a high drop-out rate from the kind of ODL provided to the majority population (Grant, 1991; Goulet and Spronk, 1988). ODL educators found it was necessary both to revise and rewrite the curriculum to incorporate aboriginal values and belief systems; for example, in a land management course at Charles Sturt University (De Lacy and Birckhead, 1991), and small business and community management courses at Athabasca University (Goulet and Spronk, 1988). They also recognised that these students had different interaction and cognitive styles (Roberts *et al.*, 1990), and put a higher value on community and peer support networks, as well as the involvement of community elders. All these projects acknowledge the importance of drawing tutors from the local communities. Students did not value the European model of independent students working in relative isolation at an individual pace. Grant (1991) reported that aboriginal students at the Catholic University of New South Wales felt that their local tutor was the most important element in supporting their continued participation in their ODL studies.

Refugee education has developed similar strategies. Sometimes refugees want the kind of education they would have received in their country of origin because they are hoping to return, whilst at the same time they need practical education which will allow them and their community to survive in the meantime (Dodds and Mbango, 1990). Again, the model must be one of involvement and interaction with the refugee community.

What is often not clear from the published accounts of EO projects is how far they are supported by an institutional framework, or have developed as part of one; or how far they are single initiatives dependent on the energy and resources of a small part of the institution. There is even less literature on institutional EO policy in the ODL literature than on EO projects. There is a danger that small, unsupported projects, although very successful because of the personal commitment of staff and students, have short lives because they cannot easily draw on other institutional resources. Institutional policies, although sometimes criticised for their perceived bureaucratic nature, can, when developed through the involvement of large numbers of staff and students, provide the almost invisible scaffolding for a number of interacting EO initiatives.

Institutional policy: An example of the OU UK

One institutional policy which the authors are very familiar with (Kirkup and Taylor, 1994) is that of their own institution: the OU UK. It is a significant example of a large-scale policy which attempts to cover all aspects of the institution (see Fig. 9.1). Fig. 9.1 has 'student support' indicated as one discrete area. However, in the way that we have been talking more widely about student support issues in this chapter, many of the other cells—for example residential schools, enquiry services and preparatory material—would also be part of our wider concept of student support.

All policies need clear aims and principles. Those of the OU UK were developed in collaboration with large sections of the staff and student body:

Aim
The Open University aims to create the conditions whereby students and staff are treated solely on the basis of their merits, abilities and potential, regardless of gender, colour, ethnic or national origin, age, socio-economic background, disability, religious or political beliefs, family circumstances, sexual orientation or other irrelevant distinction.

Principles
1. Discrimination, direct or indirect, based on a person's gender, colour, ethnic or national origin, age, socio-economic background, disability, religious or political beliefs, family circumstances, sexual orientation or any other irrelevant distinction, is unjust and immoral.
2. In addition to being unjust, such forms of discrimination represent a waste of human resources and a denial of opportunity for individual self-fulfilment.
3. Notwithstanding its significant contribution to the widening of educational opportunity, the University acknowledges that, as a community, it still reflects patterns of inequality that are widespread in society at large. It is therefore determined through programmes of legally acceptable positive action to increase the level of participation as students, staff and clients of those groups that are currently under-represented.

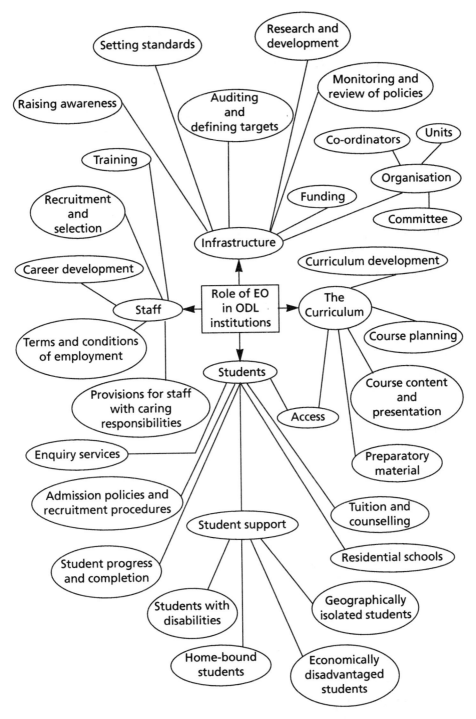

Figure 9.1 The role of equal opportunities in an ODL institution

4. A successful Equal Opportunities policy requires the active support of the University community. The University therefore intends to seek the commitment and involvement of all sections of staff and students in the implementation of this policy.

5. The University intends to encourage good practice in equal opportunities with those external organisations with whom it works. (Open University, undated)

Policy must be backed by action and this policy was developed alongside an action plan, carried out with the support of a small Equal Opportunities Unit, which functioned to promote and co-ordinate initiatives rather than carry them out itself. The action plan covered staffing, student and curriculum issues, supporting targeted projects as well as developing an institution-wide monitoring system which individual units, as well as the senior management bodies of the University, use to measure progress towards the overall aim.

A number of successful individual projects include the production of a code of practice on dealing with harassment of any kind, which applies to all staff and students and which necessitates the training of staff in handling incidents and complaints. Although harassment is more frequent in face-to-face situations such as residential schools, it can also occur in any situation in which there is communication, as shown by recent concerns in some institutions about harassment via electronic communication. A booklet of guidance on the use of non-discriminatory language and imagery has been circulated to all staff, and caused considerable internal discussion. The regular production of staff and student monitoring data has had an impact on all parts of the University, and has fed very directly into quality assessment procedures. For example, in 1995 when the courses in the field of social policy were assessed for teaching quality by a panel of external assessors, the University was able to supply data which illustrated the success of women students and students with low prior educational qualifications on these courses. This was interpreted as a measure of 'value added' and contributed to the award of 'excellent' for the teaching quality of those courses.

Student support has a specific role within the OU UK's comprehensive institutional EO policy. As discussed in the introduction, student support is relatively standardised in so far as it is built into course materials (for example, pre-start self-assessment tests, guidance on writing skills). Much more flexible is the considerable support provided by the University's 7500 tutorial and counselling staff, with the capacity to individualise the students' learning experiences. This group of part-time staff, and full-time staff in Regional Centres who manage and support them, relate to the overall EO policy in major ways: in developing access and retention strategies to turn student-related objectives into practice; and as a huge corps of staff to be recruited and managed according to fair selection guidelines and trained in EO practices. The following section looks in detail at the first of these: the extent to which support staff contribute to access and equality of outcomes. The second area, however, also merits comment.

It is in asking *who are* the tutors, counsellors, managers and course teams in an open learning organisation that EO policies for staff, students and curricula interrelate. In the OU UK considerable effort has gone into fair selection training, so that—with some residual resistance—by 1996 all recruiters will be trained in making the process more equitable and rigorous. There is also progress on generic EO training for all staff, although this is far from being one hundred per cent. Much slower though has been the process of widening the staff profile to include under-represented groups. For example, the view that OU UK tutors and counsellors (and course writers and managers) should be drawn partly from the groups we wish to serve as students remains a controversial one, despite reassurances that all staff recruited should also meet all essential academic and other job criteria. Nevertheless, in 1996 a code will operate whereby any disabled applicant for a tutorial and counselling post who meets the person specification will be offered an interview. The rationale here is that being a good equal opportunities employer also affects the nature and quality of support available to students. The experiences, histories and identities of the staff, individually and compositely, relate directly to our public 'face', our networks, our capacity for empathy and our relationships with students.

Student support: An equalising dimension?

Support systems are usually conceptualised as that range of resources—human, technical and administrative—available to learners, which are complementary to centrally-produced, possibly multi-media, materials. Within the expanding family of ODL, support systems probably vary more widely than do packages of materials in their sophistication, resourcing, accessibility and quality. Support could be described in terms of the wide range of activities potentially available to students and that range of features through which these services might be offered:

Activities

- marketing and publicity
- pre-entry guidance
- induction and preparation

- development of learning skills

- academic guidance/mediation of course materials

- assessment

- coping with administrative, personal and affective issues

- profile planning

- careers education and guidance.

Features

- home/workplace study

- study centres/exam centres

- tutors

- counsellors

- mentors

- audio-visual and broadcast media

- electronic media

- printed materials

- peer support groups

- community networks

- IT centres, libraries, laboratories.

Tait (1995) discusses how the elements of a support system might be planned in response to a preliminary audit of target groups and their likely needs, within the inevitable constraints of cost, human and technical resources. This raises quite sharply a major issue for equality. Whereas materials packages are, by virtue of being mass produced, relatively standardised, the elements of any support system from the most basic to the most elaborate will be more accessible to some learners than to others. Scheme providers have to make decisions about how to deploy elements of support. Do they aim for a baseline of common services to support the majority of students? How far do they extend and modify these to support weak, 'at risk', or disadvantaged students? What proportion of resources should be allocated to 'equalising' the learning opportunities of particular students so that they can perform to the best of their abilities? How far should support be organised to meet the specific needs of each individual student and how far should it be aimed at generic groups who have experienced relative exclusion from higher education? A brief consideration of materials and support from the perspective of differently situated learners will elaborate these issues.

A standard package of materials, delivered to the student's home, would require adaptation into other formats (Braille, tape, large print etc.) for visually-impaired or hearing-impaired students. There might also be access issues relating to computers needed to run learning programs, given the way in which gender and class are known to affect access to technology. But the differentials in access to the wide range of support elements, previously noted, would undoubtedly be greater. Self-evidently, attendance at study centres and resource centres is affected by timing, transport, money and the accessibility of the premises. Similarly, various support technologies may depend to a greater or lesser extent on the student's ability to buy into them or be granted financial assistance; her/his physical capacity to make use of them; and, less apparently, her/his facility and confidence in using them. Providing equal access to these resources for all potential learners is problematic, since this population could include, say, working parents, unemployed people, shift workers, those with mental health problems, prisoners, wheelchair users, elderly people, those on low incomes, those in remote locations, those from minority cultures, or those whose families do not support their ambition to study.

Designing support always involves some level of rationing and compromise. In many ODL systems some level of support is designed particularly to counteract disadvantage and to help identified groups to make academic progress. With finite resources, there is often a balance to be struck in the level and deployment of support services to various student groups. If extra satellite study centres are opened, there may be fewer computers for loan. If workshops are put on for students with specific learning difficulties (for example dyslexia), there may be less scope for career development sessions.

In large-scale distance systems, whether these follow the old-style industrial model or the newer service model (Sewart, 1993), the cluster of support activities often serves to individualise the process for the learner. Personal support, even if mediated by letter, telephone or computer, is vital in humanising the institution and in helping the student to 'bond' with it. A sense of personal contact and community comes not only from academic assessment and feedback but equally from help to the student in managing the administrative process, developing learning skills and surmounting obstacles thrown up by the complexity of adult lives.

Personal support in many systems includes both tuition and counselling. This is true in the OU UK, with its tutor-counsellors supporting students on entry courses and its specialist tutors elsewhere. In many systems, tutors are concerned mainly with academic progress, often on a specific course, and

141

counsellors/advisers with the student's broader development. In one formulation (Simpson, 1994) tutoring is concerned with a student's micro-progress on a course and counselling with her/his macro-progress throughout study. The two functions may or may not be combined in one role.

Counselling is of particular relevance to equality of opportunity. It can extend from problem-centred interactions to more developmental activities focused on the student's educational, vocational and personal growth through study (Brindley and Fage, 1992). Both versions can contribute significantly to equality of opportunity and outcome. Problem-centred counselling helps individual students to overcome blocks as and when they arise (arranging emergency telephone tuition for a sick student, requesting appropriate exam facilities for disabled or remote students); developmental counselling, with individuals or with groups, is aimed at increasing the student's independence and ability to manage the learning process (group sessions on assertiveness, planning a degree profile or writing a curriculum vitae). Again, resources are always rationed and realism often dictates a concentration on short-term problem solving rather than on long-term broad development.

In relatively sophisticated and well-resourced systems, support often works in these ways, individualising learning in a mass system and making a fixed curriculum accessible. The OU UK, for example, has large parts of its curriculum available to prisoners (Worth, 1994), to disabled people (Vincent, 1983), and to those in remote areas (Robinson, 1993). However there are dangers for equality in always conceptualising ODL within the binary model of production and delivery. This suggests the curriculum as a 'given' package and support as those secondary elements which allow students to access it. In such a model, women, and those from minority ethnic groups, may not recognise their experiences, learning styles, assumptions and forms of knowledge in a curriculum produced by dominant groups from within a dominant culture. The research on how ODL materials can position learners and structure their response is relevant here (Edwards, 1994; Harris, 1995). Modularisation increases students' choice over subject topics, but not necessarily over learning styles, assessment methods, range of case studies, discourse and pace of study. Models of independent learning in which students select many more elements of their own learning programme, as at Empire State College, SUNY (Granger, 1990), challenge the linear version of production and delivery dominant in ODL.

A more systemic model, which takes student support as a process rather than as a series of second order activities, may indicate more radical ways of equalising opportunity. This process includes both human and technological elements and pays attention to all aspects of knowledge production. Questions then arise about how the profiles of student groups relate to those of tutors, counsellors, course writers, managers, examiners etc. Our learning experiences are affected, qualitatively, by recognising some of ourselves in the (broadly defined) curriculum. Women tutoring non-traditional subjects (for example Swarbrick, 1986), disabled, gay, and ethnic minority writers and counsellors may develop a more inclusive curriculum and will, almost certainly, model success for students lacking in confidence. This is not to suggest a rigid 'matching' of student and staff profiles by gender, ethnicity, class or any other dimension. It does, though, suggest sensitive consideration of the collective and individual identities of staff, especially those writing courses and those tutoring and counselling students, in terms of human diversity. For these reasons, equal opportunities in ODL should be comprehensively defined to include issues relating to students, staff and the curriculum.

Conclusion

In this chapter we have ranged widely over the issue of the role of student support in equal opportunities policy and practice and the role of EO policy on student support. We have in the main raised issues rather than solved them. In the absence of a rich literature it appears to us that ODL institutions need to come to terms with EO philosophies and produce policies which make explicit the kind of philosophy they espouse. Without this, student support systems, and staff, can have no systematic overview of what the institution is trying to achieve, nor any clear view of how the institution perceives them. If a policy is in place, but without staff or students having any chance to debate or develop it—perhaps it exists as nothing other than compliance with national legislation—then it is likely to produce a 'compliance culture' rather than a 'committed' one. Certainly within the OU UK it is clear that a well constructed and funded EO policy has influenced activity considerably over the last five years. It has also at many levels provoked a healthy critique of 'openness'. All these factors argue for more international debate in the ODL community. We hope this chapter is simply the first of many contributions to such debate.

REFERENCES

Brennan, J., El Khawas, E. & Shah, T. (1994) *Peer review and assessment of higher education quality: An international perspective*, Quality Support Centre Higher Education Report No. 3, Open University.

Brindley, J. & Fage, J. (1992) Counselling in open learning: Two institutions face the future, *Open Learning*, **7** (3), pp. 12–19.

Calder, J. (1994) *Programme evaluation and quality: A comprehensive guide to setting up an evaluation system* (London, Kogan Page).

Daniel, J. (1995) Preface. In Lockwood, F. (Ed.) *Open and distance learning today* (London and New York, Routledge).

De Lacy, T. & Birckhead, J. (1991) An external Aboriginal Ranger Education program. In Atkinson, R., McBeath, C. & Meacham, D. (Eds.) *Quality in distance education ASPESA Forum 91*, Australian and South Pacific External Studies Association, Lismore Heights NSW 2480, Australia, pp. 125–131.

Dodds, T. & Mbango, J. (1990) Refugees, Zambia. In Koul, B.N. & Jenkins, J. (Eds.) *Distance education: A spectrum of case studies* (London, Kogan Page), pp. 236–242.

Edwards, R. (1994) From a distance? Globalisation, space-time compression and distance education, *Open Learning*, 9 (3), pp. 9–17.

Faith, K. (Ed.) (1988) *Toward new horizons for women in distance education: International perspectives* (London and New York, Routledge).

Farish, M., McPake, J., Powney, J. & Weiner, G. (1995) *Equal opportunities in colleges and universities* (Buckingham, SRHE and Open University Press).

Goulet, J.-G. & Spronk, B. (1988) Partnership with aboriginal peoples: Some implications for distance educators. In Sewart, D. & Daniel, J.S. (Eds.) *Developing distance education*. Papers submitted to 14th World Conference in Oslo, August 1988 (International Council for Distance Education, Oslo), pp. 218–221.

Granger, D. (1990) Open and individualised distance learning at Empire State College, *Open Learning*, 5 (1), pp. 24–30.

Grant, M. (1991) A community-based approach to distance aboriginal education in NSW. In Atkinson, R., McBeath, C. & Meacham, D. (Eds.) *Quality in distance education ASPESA Forum 91*, Australian and South Pacific External Studies Association, Lismore Heights NSW 2480, Australia, pp. 183–192.

Harris, D. (1987) *Openness and closure in distance education* (London, The Falmer Press).

Harris, D. (1995) Still seeking the audience? In Lockwood, F. (Ed.) *Open and distance learning today* (London and New York, Routledge).

Henderikx, P. (1992) Management and promotion of quality in distance education, *Open Learning*, 7 (3), pp. 34–41.

Jewson, N. & Mason, D. (1986) The theory and practice of equal opportunities policies: Liberal and radical approaches, *Sociological Review*, **34**, pp. 307–34.

Kandola, R. & Fullerton, J. (1994) *Managing the mosaic: Diversity in action* (London, IPM).

Kanwar Asha, S. & Jagannathan, N. (Eds.) (1995) *Speaking for ourselves: Women and distance education in India* (New Delhi, Manohar).

Kirkup, G. & Taylor, L. (1994) Gender and power: A case study from the UK OU. In Thorpe, M. & Grugeon, D. (Eds.) *Open learning in the mainstream* (Harlow, Longman).

Laurillard, D. (1993) *Rethinking university teaching* (London and New York, Routledge).

Lewis, R. & Spencer, D. (1986) *What is open learning?* Open Learning Guides, no. 4 (Council for Educational Technology).

Meacham, D. & Wilkin, C. (1990) Distance education as rehabilitation, Australia and South Pacific External Studies Association No. 9, November 1990.

Open University (undated) *Open and equal*. Internal document.

Ramakrishna C.P. (1995) Reaching out: The role of counselling. In Kanwar Asha, S. & Jagannathan, N. (Eds.) (1995) *Speaking for ourselves: Women and distance education in India* (New Delhi, Manohar).

Roberts, J.M., Burge, E.J. & White, R.B. (1990) Distance education for minority groups: Issues confronting a delivery agency. In Croft, M., Migridge, I., Daniel, J.S. & Hershfield A. (Eds.) *Distance education: Development and access* (Fondo Editorial Universidad Nacional Abierta, Venezuela, International Council for Distance Education), pp. 43–46.

Robinson, B. (1993) Telephone teaching and audio-conferencing at the Open University. In Harry, K., John, M. & Keegan, D. (Eds.) *Distance education: New perspectives* (London and New York, Routledge).

Rumble, G. (1989) Open learning, 'Distance learning', and the misuse of language, *Open Learning*, 4 (2), pp. 28–36.

Sesharatnam C. (1995) Women in Indian educational policies and programmes. In Kanwar Asha, S. & Jagannathan, N. (Eds.) (1995) *Speaking for ourselves: Women and distance education in India* (New Delhi, Manohar).

Sewart, D. (1993) Student support systems in distance education, *Open Learning*, 8 (3), pp. 3–12.

Simpson, O. (1994) Private communication.

Swarbrick, A. (1986) Women in technology: A feminist model of learner support in the Open University, *International Council for Distance Education Bulletin*, Vol. 12.

Tait, A. (1995) Student support in open and distance learning. In Lockwood, F. (Ed.) *Open and distance learning today* (London and New York, Routledge).

Tiffin, A. & Rajasingham, L. (1995) *In search of the virtual classroom in an information society* (London and New York, Routledge).

Vincent, T. (1983) Home computing for the visually handicapped, *Teaching at a Distance* (23), pp. 24–29.

Worth, V. (1994) The same difference: Tutoring for the Open University in prison, *Open Learning*, 9 (1), pp. 34–41.

Young, K. (1989) The space between words: Local Authorities and the concept of Equal Opportunities. In Jenkins, R. & Salamos, J. (Eds.) *Racism and equal opportunity policies in the 1980s* (Cambridge, Cambridge University Press).

10
The importance of gender

Gill Kirkup

Gender: a culturally-shaped group of attributes and behaviours given to the female or male. (Humm, 1989)

I would rather be a cyborg than a goddess. (Haraway, 1991)

Introduction

In the 1980s a title such as mine would lead an audience to presume that I would be making an argument for recognising that gender difference is at least as significant a determinant of educational inequality as race and class difference; and that any democratic education system should recognise the particular needs of women students and staff. On a very pragmatic level I believe this still to be true and it informs much of my own activity as a distance educator. However, since the mid-1980s, both feminism and educational theory have been involved in coming to grips with some radical critiques of epistemology, which have made us re-examine the foundations of our thinking about what gender is, and *why* it is. All these critiques presume that gendering is a much more significant activity than simply the social persona of human beings. Gender is analysed as one of the foundational cultural categories of our intellectual world, providing an implicit framework on which aspects of our world are placed, almost arbitrarily, in dominant and subordinate oppositional categories.

These debates interest me for two main reasons. As an educator of women I need a model of the learner which helps me decide the significance of a student's gender in my day-to-day practice. As an educator working in open and distance learning (ODL) I need a model of the educational role of the new information and communication technologies (ICTs) which takes seriously the social and cultural significance of gender.

146

In this chapter[1] I tell a kind of chronological story summarising a number of different theoretical understandings of gender and illustrate how these have influenced our understanding of women learners, particularly in ODL, although it may be that some of the most recent post-modernist theories have caused confusion, at least as much as they have provided insight. I will examine in particular Donna Haraway's concept of 'cyborg', which is proving more popular now than when it was first published in 1985 because it has such a strong resonance with much media theory about ICTs, and in particular theories about the social (and with that the educational) impact of the Internet. If ICTs are a radically different educational media from any we have previously known, or even, with respect to the Internet, a new *place* ('cyberspace') where education happens, we need to know whether gender has any reality there.

Gender: The simple story

The category 'women' has existed for as long as history; the category 'gender' applied to human beings is a much more recent historical development. As all first-year Women's Studies students learn, sex is a biological category, a problematic area perhaps for biologists and medicine, but not the focus of attention for feminist theory. At its simplest, 'gender' is defined as what society makes of sex (see Humm's 1989 definition above), and may in some circumstances not correspond with an individual's biological category. It is the existence of the concept of gender (rather than simply classifying men and women as different sexes) which makes it possible to raise questions about the social organisations which depend on gender; the power inequalities which seem to follow automatically from it, and the way our behaviour and social roles are circumscribed by it. Not least *by* and *in* education.

Gender was co-opted by feminist theory, from its original home in psychology, to explain the structural inequalities of men and women and the ideologies justifying these inequalities. It proved such a powerful explanatory theory that by the 1980s it was being used to explain the way knowledge (Harding, 1991; Fox Keller, 1986), and inanimate aspects of the material world such as technology (Cockburn and Furst Dilic, 1994; Wajcman, 1991) and physical space (Matrix, 1984) were 'gendered'. Gender identity was seen no longer as something simply ascribed or even coherent (Hollway, 1984), but the attribute of a more fluid subjectivity and a strategy for political action (Pratt, 1988). These increasingly complex reconceptions of gender have to be taken

---

[1]This chapter was first presented as a paper at the conference, Putting the student first: Learner-centred approaches in open and distance learning, Churchill College, Cambridge, UK, 3–5 July, 1995.

into account when designing educational policies or activities to be student-centred, in particular for women, but for people of any gender.

In at the beginning: Women and ODL

ODL, and its forerunner correspondence education, has provided historically, for many women, perhaps their only chance to learn when other educational institutions were not open to them. One hundred and fifty years ago it was still acceptable to argue that girls and women did not have the physical and intellectual capacity to benefit from the same education as their male peers, despite the successful demonstration by many that, given half a chance, they certainly could. In 1840 when Isaac Pitman first offered what is now considered to be perhaps the first 'modern' distance learning course (in shorthand writing), it was, at least, open to women. Then, no women in Europe or the USA had access to university education and many had no schooling at all. Many women used non-traditional modes of learning where they were available. For example, Anna Ticknor created the very successful Society to Encourage Studies at Home in 1873, which provided distance education to adult women of all classes in the East Coast of the USA. This organisation provided instruction for up to 10 000 women and flourished for 24 years. It was praised in journals such as the *New York Tribune* and influenced the development of US correspondence education for both genders (Watkins, 1991).

In those early days women were also often the mediators of ODL for others. In rural areas of North America they were involved as the unpaid supervisors and tutors of their own children. Faith (1988), for example, describes how her grandparents—Canadian prairie homesteaders—used 'home study' as a significant part of the education of their twelve children. She quotes Bolton's discussion of this aspect of women's work in the private domain of their own homes:

> *One side effect of correspondence education which appears to have been less widely publicised than it deserved was its reliance on the labour of wives and mothers as supervisors and teachers. The new democracies have always tended to regard the transmission of culture as an interest for women. It was taken for granted that as the men of the household would be fully occupied with their farm duties, the children's mother would accept the responsibility of organising the receipt and dispatch of correspondence materials, overseeing the students to ensure that they got on with their assignments diligently and regularly, and in general fitting in the role of surrogate monitors with the thousand and one tasks of a busy pioneer wife.* (Bolton, 1986, pp. 17–18, quoted in Faith, 1988)

In some countries where women are still, in 1995, seen as belonging to the private sphere of the home and family, distance education offers them perhaps their only educational opportunity.

Gender in twentieth-century education

The twentieth century has seen the increased participation of women as students and staff in all sectors of education and in most countries. It has been argued that this increased participation contributed to the development of Second Wave feminism.[2] Part of the 'problem with no name' articulated by Friedan in the early 1960s (Friedan, 1963) was the mismatch between the ideology of meritocratic education and women's experience of life and work. Highly educated women suffered the greatest dissonance between their expectations and their lives, and some of them turned their considerable intellectual skills to developing and publishing new feminist theory.

Since the 1960s there has been considerable analysis of the 'gendering' of every sector of education. First, inequalities of access and provision for girls and boys were highlighted, then the exclusion of women from some fields of education and at higher levels. The primary focus of this analysis has been on the education systems of industrialised countries, but there is a recognition that although these inequalities can be seen empirically in almost every country in the world, the nature of them may differ between societies. This leads to different forms of action being appropriate in different countries; for example, the kind of education that women want the right to in developing countries is not the same as the changed curriculum that many feminists are arguing for in English-language education.

A critique has developed of what has been called 'liberal' gender equality theory, which is based on a liberal model of equal citizenship rights and benefits for men and women. In this liberal model, male values and activities are often implicitly seen as worthy and of high status, and the aim of educational gender equality is for women to have equal access to these same activities in order to achieve full citizenship, while the nature of that citizenship (i.e. that it might be constructed round the activities and needs of men) goes unquestioned. This kind of liberal theory, it is argued, contains an implicit model of women as *deficient*, because the only explanation it can give for why women *choose* not to study some subjects or to pursue the same career paths as men is that there is something wrong with women which has to be addressed via remedial initiatives.

---

[2]A distinction is made between First Wave feminism which is associated with the suffrage movements of the late nineteenth and early twentieth centuries, and Second Wave feminism which was born as the Women's Liberation Movement of the 1960s and now encompasses a range of politics and ideologies.

More radical views of gender equality have been developed which argue from a Marxist or Freirian perspective (Weiler, 1995), sometimes also called standpoint theory (Harding, 1989), that women, as the subordinate group in an unequal gender/class system, see the world in privileged and perhaps epistemologically more 'truthful' ways than the dominant group (men). Women are likely to have different values and different skills from the dominant group, and these are exhibited in different educational aims and the achievement of different educational outcomes. There is also a moral dimension to this argument: that the values and skills of the dominant group are about *domination*, and therefore *not* the ones that should be encouraged in an egalitarian democracy. These kinds of perspectives also support the role of education as 'consciousness-raising' for subordinate groups, so that any education based on them not only privileges students' personal experience, but is designed to contain activities which require *groups* of students to articulate personal experience.

This perspective has provided the rationale for a number of books which have explored the experience, in particular of adult women, in education. These are books which take as given the importance of experience above theory and are structured around personal narratives and interviews. For example, Thompson's book about women in adult and continuing education, *Learning liberation* (1983); Pascall and Cox's book, *Women returning to higher education* (1993); and Griffin's book, *Changing our lives: Doing Women's Studies* (1994). It is also this perspective which underlies many courses in which adult students, in particular, create personal biographies in the process of their study.

Some academics working from this perspective have argued that many of the activities and values that have previously been considered as low status and 'female' should be incorporated into a 'transformed' curriculum in order to produce an 'inclusive vision of human experience based on difference and diversity, not sameness and generalisation' (Schuster and van Dyne, 1984). For them, education is still the major agent of social transformation. However, others have been criticised for using personal experience and consciousness raising only as a tool for individual personal change, effectively depoliticising the activity. Another danger of this kind of activity is that an uncritical or even anti-intellectual attitude is adopted towards personal experience: that it is the 'truth' and that it is unchangeable.

Radical transformation or essentialism

A defence of the validity of women's experience, and an argument that women do live in a different intellectual world, came in the early 1980s with Gilligan's book, *In a different voice* (1982). This is a book about the moral development of women; it builds on a particular branch of psychoanalytic theory: object relations theory, in which women are seen as developing *different* ways of thinking and experiencing the world from men, rather than what had traditionally been seen as *less mature* ways:

> The wish (of men) to be alone at the top and the consequent fear that others will get too close: the wish (of women) to be at the centre of connection and the consequent fear of being too far out on the edge. These disparate fears of being stranded and being caught give rise to different portrayals of achievement and affiliation, leading to different modes of action and different ways of assessing the consequences of choice. (Gilligan, 1982, p. 62)

This connected way of being for women comes, it is argued, out of a life in which one's relationships with others and the well-being of others are a crucial part of personal development. It is a positive way of being rather than an immature state on the road to 'separation' or 'independence', which is how it was previously described. Belenky *et al.* (1986) applied Gilligan's theoretical framework to understanding women's intellectual development and critiqued Perry's (1970) model of stages of intellectual development. They describe women as 'connected knowers' who, when they reach the highest stages of intellectual development, *equivalent to* but not the *same as* those described by Perry, continue to exhibit a strong sense of relatedness to others: something lacking in men at the same stage.

These theories have proved very useful in understanding in particular why women are alienated from some areas of science (Fox Keller, 1986) and certain kinds of computer use (Turkle and Papert, 1990), and why men and women seem to have different styles of communication (Tannen, 1990). However, they have been criticised as falling into the trap of 'essentialism'.

For many gender theorists, the strength of the concept 'gender' is that it describes the identity, roles and behaviour of men and women as socially constructed and therefore open to reconstruction and change. Gender theory has argued that the dualisms male/female are falsely dichotomous, and that they have been at the foundation of Western rationalist thought, along with a range of other similar false dualisms: nature/culture, rational/emotional, public/private, and many others (Fox Keller, 1986). Many theorists argued that to claim that women have particular female gender attributes due either to their biological functions, for example childbirth, or their psychological development, e.g. their relationship with their mothers, is to fall into the trap of seeing gender as something essential and therefore unchangeable. This would mean that men and women really are, in essence, different in ways that cannot be modified either by individual will or by social reorganisation. Gender is then a universal foundational category, and women have a unique female nature. An automatic next step for some feminists is to say that since dualisms are never equal, this female nature is superior, or perhaps historically more useful to a twenty-first-century world, than traditional masculinity.

Those who have happily embraced this essentialist position include Mary Daly (1978; 1984), the theologian and poet; Susan Griffin (1978; 1982) and many others who would call themselves 'ecofeminists'; as well as some French psychoanalytic feminists such as Luce Irigaray (Whitford, 1992). It is the theoretical foundation for many politically active groups and is at least implicit in some branches of women's education. But it has also been criticised for trying to impose a universal interest among all women in a global context in which *differences* of race, class, age and location are arguably more significant than commonality.

There is of course the opposite development. From within a heterogeneous body of theory called feminist post-modernism has come the questioning of whether there is any material foundation to any of our linguistic categories, including the category 'gender'. Along with this comes a certain relativism with respect to epistemology.

Post-modernism puts forward a strong form of the 'different not universal' argument: that 'reality' is different for each individual since it is determined by that particular individual's social and historical location. There can be no meaningful universal categories; a universal category is simply the imposition of the perspective of a dominant group:

> That is, only to the extent that one person or group can dominate the whole will reality appear to be governed by one set of rules or be constituted by one privileged set of social relations.
> (Flax, 1990, p. 49)

Therefore the universal category 'woman' cannot mean the same to all people put into it. It can only be universal because it is defined in the interests of a dominant group (crudely identified as white, middle-class, able-bodied women). Its existence means that the perspectives and voices of others called 'women' are being silenced.

Gender theorists have looked for theories of gender difference and inequality that are, in complex ways, integrated with other systems of difference and inequality (the most usual ones discussed being race and class) in order to throw light on their entwined operation. However, most feel that abandoning 'gender' as an analytical concept, and with it the category 'woman', as having no universal application, both denies what has been achieved by using them and undermines any grounds for mass social or political action by or for women.

However, the problem remains: how to break though the constraints imposed by a world of dualism, without falling into the trap of complete relativism?

As long as gender is the axis along which our world is subject to division, women will have more of an incentive to count past two—or even perhaps between one and two—than most men will, even though they may still have trouble doing so. That extra incentive derives from the particular costs they bear in a world limited to either unitarity or duality [that is either having to be like men or different from them]. (Fox Keller, 1986, p. 51)

Attempts to leap over this duality have been few. The particular one that I will return to later is that of Donna Haraway (1985; 1991) who suggests that if we are willing to stop thinking in dualist terms about the natural and manmade; living organisms and machines; and see ourselves as beings in symbiosis with machines—as cyborgs—we can achieve social and individual liberation from gender duality. If this is true, then ODL as it increasingly uses ICTs could have a key role in supporting this relationship. First, I want to review the way writers and researchers in ODL have used gender theory.

Working on gender in ODL

It has taken ODL some time to build on the work of gender theorists, even on similar work in other areas of education. Elizabeth Burge and Karlene Faith (Faith, 1988) were the first to edit and publish an international collection of essays about gender issues in ODL. Until then the sum total of published articles in *Teaching at a Distance* and *Distance Education*, which took gender as a substantive issue for ODL, was six (Burge, 1988). The Faith collection reviewed the participation of women in ODL in a variety of developed and developing countries, demonstrating that gender equality had not been achieved with respect to access, performance, or curriculum provision in most countries. It gave examples of initiatives to improve access for women, some of which were based on a liberal equality model, others on more radical views, including some which made a critique of the curriculum as gendered. Some authors were beginning to argue that the particular intellectual strengths of women as well as their learning needs were not yet recognised.

Since then there has been a steady, but small, flow of publications containing research findings and theoretical discussion about the nature of gender issues in ODL. In 1993 the University of Umea in Sweden brought together a small number of people with a specialist interest in women's education in ODL, at the first conference dedicated to gender and ODL: Feminist pedagogy and women-friendly perspectives in distance education (Women's Studies Centre of Umea, 1993). An issue of *Open Praxis* in 1994 (*Open Praxis*, 1994, Vol. 1) gave space to reviewing the situation for women staff and students in the years since the publication of the Faith book (see for example Taylor and Kirkup, 1994). Of the other authors who have written in the area, Von Prümmer and Burge are perhaps the most prolific. Von Prümmer writes about women in ODL in Germany (Von Prümmer, 1993a; 1993b; Von Prümmer and Rossie, 1990a; 1990b). Burge uses Gilligan (1982) and Belenky *et al.* (1986) to theorise the learning needs of women students and especially their relationship to computer-mediated communication (Burge, 1988; 1990; 1993; Burge and Lenskyi, 1990). In 1994 Patricia Lunneborg published the first 'experiential' collection of life histories of women studying at the OU UK: *OU women: undoing educational obstacles* (1994). Most recently, Kanwar and Jagannathan have edited a collection of essays about the particular situation of women in distance education in India: *Speaking for ourselves* (Kanwar and Jagannathan, 1995).

Before the Faith book there had been a commonly accepted view that ODL is a type of education that is particularly suited to women (for example see McIntosh *et al.*, 1976). The historical material previously discussed suggests that this view was reasonably founded in the knowledge that adult women have many more restrictions on their time and mobility than do adult men, as well as less access to disposable income, which made ODL the most practical option for post-school education. However, there is often an implicit presumption that, apart from these material factors, women are the same as men with respect to their motivations to study and their intellectual styles, as well as their domestic circumstances.

A gender analysis of the power relations within families has demonstrated the very different experiences men and women have of that same institution. Women's lives are also changing. In industrialised countries 'full-time housewives' are now a minority of women distance education students. A survey at the Fernuniversität found nearly half the women students were in full-time paid work compared with three-quarters of the men (Von Prümmer and Rossie, 1990a). At the OU UK, similarly, only 20 per cent of women undergraduate students are full-time housewives; of the rest the majority classify themselves as in full-time work. Most of our women students are very busy, at least as busy as their partners, if not more so. A national UK survey on leisure estimated that full-time working women had 3.3 hours of free time on weekdays, compared with 4.5 hours for men; and 10.3 hours at weekends compared with 12.1 hours for men (*Social Trends*, 1992).

Unequal power relations in a family can produce an absence of support for women students:

> Many women distance education students report an increase in the demands their partners and children make on them, while men often mention being relieved of household and childcare duties, being given uninterrupted time and space for studying, and having other active help from their partners such as the typing of term papers and assignments or the locating of literature. It seems that women do not have the same right as men to pursue their education, especially when this could interfere with their role as mothers and wives.

One of the problems our women students report time and again is the phenomenon that they themselves start setting higher standards in their domestic and mothering roles. They feel they 'owe' it to their families, their friends and relatives, or their neighbours to be even better mothers and partners and to have even cleaner homes in compensation for 'being allowed' to pursue their own interests and in an attempt to make up for the consequent 'neglect' of their domestic responsibilities. Male students do not report this type of conflict of interest in their private lives, although they might regret the necessity to cut back on the time spent with their families. (Von Prümmer, 1993a, p. 15)

In the 1980s there was a great deal of debate about independent learning in ODL (Gaskell and Mills, 1989). It sometimes appeared that the ideal type of ODL student is one who gets a degree in the minimum of time and makes the minimum of demands on an institution for support: the 'turbo-student' (Von Prümmer, 1993b). This returns us to a model in which women are less likely to approximate to the ideal: a deficit model of women students. Although arguments can be made that women have special needs for personal contact with tutorial staff or support networks, they are seen as psychologically dependent, that is more 'needy' than men, rather than as individuals who have communication and affiliation skills which are valuable and need to be exercised in particular ways.

Christine Von Prümmer and I carried out a large-scale survey of students at the OU UK and the Fernuniversität (Kirkup and Von Prümmer, 1990). We argued from our empirical data that we could identify differences in the preferred learning styles of men and women which made them respond differently to different ODL methods. In both institutions women were more likely to be frequent attenders at study centres, despite having more obstacles to getting there such as less access to transport and more domestic responsibility. Women valued the range of services provided at study centres more highly than men, in particular the opportunity to meet other students. Women were more likely than men to involve others, e.g. family and friends, in their learning. Most significantly, although roughly the same proportions of men and women reported feeling isolated, this was a problem for 24 per cent of the men, compared with 40 per cent of the women. We based our analysis on Gilligan (1982) to argue that this discomfort with isolation was not necessarily associated with negative personal circumstances, but emerges from a desire for connection with others.

Using this same model, we have begun to look at the different attitudes that men and women students have towards the new (and old) ODL technologies that we are all experimenting with—if not fully committed to—in our various institutions (Kirkup and Von Prümmer, 1994; Von Prümmer, 1995). The model we have used is certainly not post-modernist and is open to criticism that it could be interpreted as essentialist. The question is whether it is supported by empirical data, and whether it can provide any help in deciding future strategies for both women and men using ICTs in ODL.

At this point I want to introduce the work of Donna Haraway.

Cyborgs: A new model of ODL student?

Donna Haraway was originally a biologist and primatologist at Yale and Johns Hopkins universities, who moved into the history and philosophy of ideas. She analysed the ways that primatology has served to reinforce for human beings our superior role in a culture/nature dualism, in which animals are 'nature' (Haraway, 1989). This has always been a problematic dualism for women because of the historical association of women with nature and body, and man with culture and rationalism. This nature/culture dualism, she argues, cannot be defended on the empirical evidence of primatology; it has to be seen as a justificatory theoretical narrative. And what it justifies is a world view which gives human beings the right to behave in certain ways towards creatures categorised as 'non-human', and to categorise some human beings as less than fully human. She then argues that if the human/animal dualism proves to be only a justificatory fiction, best abandoned, so perhaps are human/machine dualisms.

In her essay called 'A manifesto for cyborgs' (1985) (later one of the main chapters in her book *Simians, cyborgs and women: The reinvention of nature*, 1991) Haraway argues that our increasingly symbiotic relationship with machines, through things like medical technology and the intellectual applications of computers, means that a strict conceptual separation between people and machines becomes unproductive:

> It is not clear who makes and who is made in the relation between humans and machine. It is not clear what is mind and what body in machines that resolve into coding practices. In so far as we know ourselves in both formal discourse (for example, biology) and in daily practice (for example, the homework economy of the integrated circuit), we find ourselves to be cyborgs, hybrids, mosaics, chimeras. Biological organisms have become biotic systems, communication devices like others. (Haraway, 1991, pp. 177–178)

She describes the situation of women in ways which appear to be very oppressive:

> The actual situation of women is their integration/exploitation into a world system of production/reproduction and communication called the informatics of domination. The home, workplace, market, public arena, the body itself—all can be dispersed and interfaced in nearly infinite, polymorphous ways with large consequences for women and others. The

cyborg is a kind of disassembled and reassembled, post-modern collective and personal self. (Haraway, 1991, p. 163)

She nonetheless argues that embracing the cyborg metaphor will provide women with liberation from the old nature/culture, mind/body, male/female gendered dualisms. Her notion of 'cyborg' has been enthusiastically adopted by many women working with ICTs in the visual arts and in cultural studies. At least one significant feminist conference in 1995, Desire by design (University of Westminster), had both artists and theoreticians using Haraway's work to suggest that women could now play a full and different role with respect to ICTs than any previous technology. Not surprisingly, people working from a more established social constructivist perspective remain to be convinced. For them ICTs have acquired the gendering of the society which has constructed them and of technologies which have predated them, which makes them (ICTs) a rather dubious candidate for the catalyst to demolish gender inequality.

Empirical evidence of the gendering of ICTs in education

So far research on ICTs in ODL has been depressing in its confirmation that technologies exhibit gender. An early analysis of the personal computer (PC) industry has shown how, in the UK at least, PCs were designed and marketed for a *male* leisure industry (Haddon, 1988). Computers in schools have become the domain of boys, and fewer girls study the subject in the UK and US examination systems (Kirkup, 1992).

Access to PCs is much less for adult women ODL students whenever this has been measured, and the quality of access when it exists is lower than that of men students (Kirkwood and Kirkup, 1991; Taylor, 1992; Kirkup, 1993; Jones *et al.*, 1993; Kirkup and Von Prümmer, 1994). The material reality of access is of inequality for women. For women who do get involved with using a PC to study with the OU UK, there seems to be quite different motivation and interest from that of their male colleagues. Baines interviewed a number of OU UK women students who were using a PC as a tool on an introductory technology course. She reported that:

Women's initial interest in PCs was almost invariably related to the specific and significant events in their personal lives, principally changes at work or children's needs. The strong but unfocused desire to be involved in a modern technology which men report was not described to me by any woman. However, although women rarely seem to embark upon computing as a personal hobby as men do, it does not seem to follow that their use and enjoyment is puritanically restricted to the practical. Despite their busy lives, some of my female interviewees admitted to sheer pleasure in computing. However, for the women I spoke to,

> *male hobbyist computing was irrelevant rather than excluding or threatening.* (Baines, 1991, p. 11)

Baines' work again demonstrates that it is important not to have a simple deficit model of women with respect to ICTs, but to examine more subtly the different ways men and women relate to them. Can computers be incorporated into ODL systems and taught about in a more 'women-friendly' fashion? This is another area where the work of Gilligan has provided insights. For example, Turkle and Papert (1990) have argued that the domination of the computing profession by men has led to a privileging of particular styles of thinking which are not the styles preferred by women. Turkle bases her argument on empirical work with young people and children:

> *Several intellectual perspectives suggest that women would feel more comfortable with a relational, interactive and connected approach to objects, and men with a more distanced stance, planning, commanding, and imposing principles on them. Indeed we have found that many women do have a preference for attachment and relationship with computers and computational objects as a means of access to formal systems.* (Turkle and Papert, 1990, p. 150)

Unfortunately, Turkle watched women students drop out of computing programmes, not because they were not learning how to program or to carry out assignments, but because they were constantly being told that their preferred styles of working and programming where not the 'proper' ones. Their style was not the style of the (masculine) computer culture.

Potentially probably the most important ICT development in ODL is the use of computer communication. Simplistically it has been assumed by some that the gender inequalities that happen in face-to-face interactions would be lessened when actors were not visible to each other. (Such an idea contains very simplistic notions about gender.) Unfortunately, the operation of gender in language seems to be more subtle than this. Tannen (1990) argues that men and women have different speech patterns. Men favour expository 'report' talk; women exploratory 'rapport' talk. When men and women engage in conversation these different styles lead to misunderstandings and sometimes to the silencing of women. It may be that the style that participants of computer-mediated communication are forced to adopt to engage in dialogue—a style which is different in many ways from verbal communication—may already be privileging this expository style. Work is only beginning to be done on analysing the discourse of this kind of communication, but Taylor *et al.* (1993) have demonstrated that not only can women become silenced in this medium, they can be pursued and frightened.

The Internet: The final frontier for gender

The expansion of computer communication and information networks through the sound and graphics capacity of the Internet has been enthusiastically heralded as the most important new ODL medium, with the potential to bring global information sources as well as communication into the homes of all students. It could be the basis for Haraway's 'post-modern collective and personal self', but is that basis equal for both men and women?

Eva Pascoe, the founder of Cyberia, the first Internet café in London, found that despite all attempts to publicise the café as being specially geared to women, in the first month only 4 per cent of users were women; the rest were young male computer hobbyists (Pascoe, 1995). She has attempted to overcome this by having times when the café is dedicated to women's training sessions and by encouraging content to be put onto the Internet through World Wide Web that might appeal particularly to women's needs. However, surveys by Cyberia suggest that less than 10 per cent of users accessing Cyberia from machines in their homes are women, whereas the number rises to nearly 50 per cent of users on public access machines in libraries, universities etc. Surveys from other Internet providers all show the same pattern. Compuserve in 1994 recorded women as only 20 per cent of users (Pamintuan, 1994). The first survey of Word Wide Web users by Pitkow and Recker in 1994 (quoted in Anthony, 1994), got 4000 responses. The typical respondent was male, was aged between 20 and 30, knew six or more programming languages and had been a computer user for more than six years. Rather than being a global village (argued Anthony, *ibid.*), the Internet is a global male, middle-class, white suburb.

Once on the Internet the communication differences begin:

> In studies of Internet discussion groups, researchers have found that men contribute consistently more than women. In fact when women contribute more than 30 per cent of the conversation, they are perceived by the on-line community to be 'dominating' the discussion ... even in feminist forums, where women are ostensibly most interested and expert men consistently dominate the conversation ... In a study of the newsgroup alt'feminism ... men contributed 74 per cent of the postings, women 17 per cent and 9 per cent were of unidentifiable gender. (Wylie, 1995, p. 4)

Cockburn used to argue, about technologies prior to ICTs, that men found it easier to confuse the boundary between themselves and the machines they worked or played with. She noted that small boys often became in their imaginations the machines they were playing with and the popularity of 'transformer toys', where humanoid creature turned into wheeled machine, was one example of this. There are similar gender differences in the way that men and women incorporate a computer into their lives.

A survey by Logitech of PC users (Reddy, 1992) found that, although both men and women saw computers as more like work companions than simply tools, men had and wanted a more anthropomorphic relationship with their machines. They were keener to communicate with them via speech and handwriting, bypassing the keyboard. Twice as many men as women had personalised their computers with messages and displays and were more likely to give them names and credit them with personalities. It appears that at present men are keener to see themselves as cyborgs than women. Perhaps this is to the disadvantage of women who will never get the full benefit of the symbiosis, but this depends on how you understand gender.

One of the most worrying aspects of the Internet for both feminists and educators is that it does not embody the kinds of values that educational institutions do. Kramarae and Kramer (1995) raise the interesting issue of whether the Internet is a medium or a place (i.e. cyberspace). If it is a place, is it a public or private place? The answers determine the way legislation can have an impact on it and the content of communications that happen there. At the same time as education has developed strong institutional policies to restrict pornography and sexual harassment, these have become a particular problem on the Internet (Canon, 1995). A World Wide Web site called 'Babes on the Web' is a clear example of this. Women who participate in the Web, by putting up information about themselves, and a picture or graphic, are likely (*unknown to them and without their permission*) to have that information and the picture copied by a man called Taup and pasted into a kind of electronic catalogue of women. Taup then rates each one according to how desirable he finds her. This catalogue is then publicised on the Web and can be reached by using search words such as 'women', 'gender', 'babe', even through listings of the most popular sites. Not only is this behaviour offensive, it has led to the women receiving obscene messages from strange men who, finding them in this catalogue, have presumed that they were looking for sexual partners. This has silenced many women who may now 'lurk' on the Internet without wanting to risk declaring information about themselves. Along with a variety of other dubious services, messages and graphics, the atmosphere of much of the Internet is very gendered in a form of masculinity that is rarely on display in other public arenas. Women students will be expected to navigate their way through to find those educational and information services they need as students. It is equivalent to a university library filling its reception, through which women students must pass, with pornographic magazines and adverts for dating agencies. The atmosphere at present appears more reminiscent of the masculinity of some university departments of the 1960s than the 1990s. It also bodes ill for the possibilities of self-determination for any woman 'cyborg'.

Conclusion

I have tried to summarise the different perspectives developed by feminists and others on gender theory and show how these have been used by educators in ODL to focus on the needs of women students in particular. The range of perspectives is wider and more sophisticated than my representation makes it. I have also tried to suggest the present unresolved tensions between post-modernist gender theory and standpoint theory. I have presented a very simple version of Haraway's metaphor of the 'cyborg', since it is seen by many as a new way of avoiding the trap of gender dualism. Unfortunately, I have not found empirical evidence in the present gendering of ICTs to support the liberatory potential claimed for the identity 'cyborg'. It does, however, raise questions about the liberatory potential of ICTs for women ODL students in particular.

Given the choice, I'd rather be a goddess!

REFERENCES

Anthony, D. (1994) Wasps on the Web, *The Guardian*, Thursday 9 June, p. 10.

Baines, S. (1991) Personal computing, gender and distance education. Paper given at the International Federation of Information Processors (IFIP) Conference, Helsinki, June 1991.

Belenky, M.F., Clichy, B.M., Golberger, N.R. & Tarule, J.M. (1986) *Women's ways of knowing: The development of self, voice and mind* (New York, Basic).

Bolton, G. (1986) The opportunities of distance. In *Flexible designs for learning*. Report of the Thirteenth World Conference of the International Council for Distance Education, Melbourne, La Trobe University, quoted in Faith, 1988.

Burge, E. (1988) Foreword to Faith, K., *op. cit.*

Burge, E.J. (1990) Women as learners: Issues for visual and virtual reality classrooms, *The Canadian Journal for the Study of Adult Education*, 4 (2), pp. 1–24.

Burge, E.J. (1993) Connectiveness and responsiveness. In Women's Studies Centre of Umea, *op. cit.*

Burge, E. & Lenskyi, H. (1990) Women studying in distance education: Issues and principles, *Journal of Distance Education*, 5 (1) pp. 20–37.

Canon, M. (1995) Life in the big city (Internet concerns), *MacUser*, 7 (5), p. 17.

Cockburn, C. & Furst Dilic, R. (Eds.) (1994) *Bringing technology home* (Buckingam, Open University Press).

Daly, M. (1978) *Gyn/ecology: The metaethics of radical feminism* (Boston, MA, Beacon Press).

Daly, M. (1984) *Pure lust: Elemental feminist philosophy* (Boston, MA, Beacon Press).

Faith, K. (Ed.) (1988) *Toward new horizons for women in distance education: International perspectives* (London and New York, Routledge).

Flax, J. (1990) Postmodernism and gender relations in feminist theory. In Nicholson, L.J. (Ed.) *Feminism/postmodernism* (London, Routledge).

Fox Keller, E. (1986) How gender matters, or, why it's so hard for us to count past two. From Harding, J. (Ed.) *Perspectives on gender and science* (Brighton, Falmer Press). Reprinted in Kirkup, G. & Smith Keller, L. (Eds.) (1992) *Inventing women* (Cambridge, UK, Polity Press).

Friedan, B. (1963) *The feminine mystique* (New York, W. W. Norton).

Gaskell, A. & Mills, R. (1989) Interaction and independence in distance education: What's been said and what's been done?, *Open Learning*, **4** (2), pp. 51–52.

Gilligan, C. (1982) *In a different voice: Psychological theory and women's development* (Cambridge, MA, Harvard University Press).

Griffin, G. (Ed.) (1994) *Changing our lives: Doing Women's Studies* (London, Boulder Colorado, Pluto Press).

Griffin, S. (1978) *Women and nature: The roaring inside her* (New York, Harper and Row).

Griffin, S. (1982) *Made from this earth* (London, The Women's Press).

Haddon, L. (1988) The home computer: The making of a consumer electronic, *Science as Culture*, (2), pp. 7–51.

Haraway, D. (1985) A manifesto for cyborgs: Science, technology, and socialist feminism in the 1980s, *Socialist Review*, **15** (80), pp. 65–107.

Haraway, D. (1989) *Primate visions* (London and New York, Routledge).

Haraway, D. (1991) *Simians, cyborgs and women: The reinvention of nature* (London, Free Assocation Books).

Harding, S. (1989) How the women's movement benefits science, *Women's Studies International Forum*, **12** (3), pp. 271–283.

Harding, S. (1991) *Whose science? Whose knowledge?* (Milton Keynes, Open University Press).

Hollway, W. (1984) Gender difference and the production of subjectivity. In Henriques, J., Hollway, W., Urwin, C., Venn, C. & Walkerdine, V. *Changing the subject: Psychology, social regulation and subjectivity* (London, Methuen).

Humm, M. (1989) *The dictionary of feminist theory* (Hemel Hempstead, Harvester Wheatsheaf).

Jones, A., Kirkup, G. & Kirkwood, A. (1993) *Personal computers for distance education* (London, Paul Chapman).

Kanwar Asha, S. & Jagannathan, N. (Eds.) (1995) *Speaking for ourselves: Women in distance education in India* (New Delhi, Manohar).

Kirkup, G. (1988) Sowing seeds: Initiatives for improving the representation of women. In Faith, K. (Ed.) *Toward new horizons for women in distance education: International perspectives* (London, Routledge).

Kirkup, G. (1992) The social construction of computers: The gendering of machines to think with. In Kirkup, G. & Keller, L.S. (Eds.) *Inventing Women: Women in science and technology* (Polity Press).

Kirkup, G. (1993) Equal opportunities and computing at the Open University. In Tait, A. (Ed.) *Key issues in open learning* (Harlow, Longman).

Kirkup, G. & Jones, A. (1995) New technologies for Open Learning: The superhighway to the learning society. In Raggatt, P., Edwards, R. & Small, N. *The learning society—challenges and trends* (Routledge).

Kirkup, G. & Von Prümmer, C. (1990) Support and connectedness: The needs of women distance education students, *Journal of Distance Education*, **5** (2), pp. 9–31.

Kirkup, G. & Von Prümmer, C. (1994) How can distance education address the particular needs of European women? Paper given at EADTU workshop on University Level Distance Education in Europe, 2–3 December 1994, Hagen.

Kirkup, G. *et al.* (1995) Diversity, openness and domestic information and communication technologies. In Sewart, D. (Ed.) *One world, many voices.* Proceedings of the 17th World Conference for Distance Education, 26–30 June 1995, Birmingham, UK.

Kirkwood, A. & Kirkup, G. (1991) Access to computing for home-based students, *Studies in Higher Education*, **16** (2), pp. 199–208.

Kramarae, C. & Kramer, J. (1995) Net gains, net losses, *Women's Review of Books*, **12** (5).

Lunneborg, P.W (1994) *OU women: Undoing educational obstacles* (London, Cassell).

McIntosh, N.E. with Calder, J.A. & Swift, B. (1976) *A degree of difference* (Guildford, Society for Research in Higher Education).

Matrix (Eds.) (1984) *Making space: Women and the man-made environment* (London, Pluto Press).

Open Praxis. The bulletin of the International Council for Distance Education, 1994, Vol. 1.

Pamintuan, A. (1994) Can women's magazines change cyberspace?, *Interactive Content*, **1** (8), p. 4.

Pascall, G. & Cox, R. (1993) *Women returning to higher education* (Buckingham, Society for Research in Higher Education and Open University Press).

Pascoe, E. (1995) Life in cyberspace. Unpublished public lecture at Destination Cyberspace workshop, Science Museum, 21 June 1995, London.

Perry, W.G. (1970) *Forms of intellectual and ethical development in the college years: A scheme* (New York, Holt, Rinehart and Winston).

Pratt, M.B. (1988) Indentity: skin blood heart. In Bulkin, E., Pratt, M.B. & Smith, B. *Yours in struggle: Three feminist perspectives on anti-semitism and racism* (Ithaca, NY, Firebrand Books).

Reddy, S. (1992) Study finds that men and women relate differently to PCs (Logitech's study of how men and women relate to PCs), *Computer Shopper*, **12** (9), p. 80.

Schuster, M. & Van Dyne, S. (1984) Placing women in the liberal arts: Stages of curriculum transformation, *Harvard Educational Review*, **54** (4).

Social Trends (1992) Social Trends 22 CSO (HMSO).

Swarbrick, A. (1986) Women in technology: A feminist model of learner support in the Open University, *International Council for Distance Education Bulletin*, Vol. 12.

Tannen, D. (1990) *You just don't understand: Women and men in conversation* (New York, Ballantine Books).

Taylor, H., Kramarae, C. & Ebben, M. (1993) *Women, information technology and scholarship* (University of Illinois).

Taylor, J. (1992) *Access to new technologies survey 1991: Access to microcomputing equipment for study purposes.* Internal report of the Programme on Learner Use of Media PLUM, paper no. 21, obtainable from IET, Open University, Walton Hall, Milton Keynes, UK.

Taylor, L. & Kirkup, G. (1994) From the local to the global: Wanting to see women's participation and progress at the OU UK in a wider context, *Praxis*, Spring 1994, Vol. 1, pp. 12–15.

Thompson, J. (1983) *Learning liberation: Women's response to men's education* (London and Sydney, Croom Helm).

Turkle, S. & Papert, S. (1990) Epistemological pluralism: Styles and voices within the computer culture, *Signs: Journal of Women in Culture and Society*, **16** (1), pp. 128–157.

Von Prümmer, C. (1993a) Women-friendly perspectives in distance education. Keynote address in Feminist Pedagogy and Women-Friendly Perspectives in Distance Education. Papers presented at International WIN Working Conference, 10–13 June 1983, Umea, Sweden. Available from the Women's Studies Centre of Umea, Report No. 4.

Von Prümmer, C. (1993b) Women in distance education: A researcher's view. Paper given to the Nordic Research Conference, Umea, Sweden, June 1993.

Von Prümmer, C. (1995) Communication preferences and practice: Not always a good fit for German distance students. In Seward, D. (Ed.) *One world, many voices.* Proceedings of the 17th World Conference for Distance Education, 26–30 June 1995, Birmingham, UK.

Von Prümmer, C. & Rossie, U. (1990a) Value of study centres and support services. Internal report from the Zentrum fur Fernstudienentwicklung/ZFE Dec.

Von Prümmer, C. & Rossie, U. (1990b) Enrolment patterns and course choice of women and men studying at the West German Fernuniversität in the eighties. Internal report from the Zentrum für Fernstudienentwicklung/ZFE Dec.

Wajcman, J. (1991) *Feminism confronts technology* (Cambridge, Polity Press).

Watkins, B.L. (1991) A quite radical idea: The invention and elaboration of collegiate correspondence study. In Watkins, B.L. & Wright, S.J. (Eds.) *The foundations of American Distance education* (Dubuque, Iowa, Kendall Hunt).

Weiler, K. (1995) Freire and a feminist pedagogy of difference. In Holland, J., Blair, M. & Sheldon, S. *Debates and issues in feminist research and pedagogy* (Clevedon, Philadelphia and Adelaide, Multilingual Matters).

Whitford, M. (1992) *The Irigaray reader* (Oxford, Blackwell).

Women's Studies Centre of Umea (1993) Feminist Pedagogy and Women-Friendly Perspectives in distance Education. Papers presented at the International WIN Working Conference, 10–13 June 1993, Umea, Sweden.

Wylie, M. (1995) No place for women: Internet is a flawed model for the infobahn, *Digital Media,* **4** (8), p. 3.

11

Supporting older learners in open and distance learning

Barbara Bilston

Older learners in distance education

This chapter will look at the emergence of people over 60 years old as a group of learners within the open and distance learning setting, together with their needs and potential achievements as a discrete group within the general student body. It will go on to consider whether the educational needs of older learners differ significantly from those of younger people, and how far educational methods in teaching them have been influenced by stereotyping and expectations about their abilities. The chapter concludes with some consideration of how teaching might address these needs to enhance the potential of older learners for improved functioning and greater personal satisfaction.

Older learners form a small but increasingly significant group of the learning population. In 1992 it was estimated that about three-quarters-of-a-million third-agers enrol annually in some kind of formal education, and a similar figure receive some kind of organised training (Schuller and Bostyn, 1992). These developments are significant, first, because they suggest need and demand, both present and potential, and second, because they question the whole basis of the design of education programmes for older people. Open and distance learning is a particularly suitable educational medium for this group because it removes many of the obvious access problems.

Life expectancy has risen steadily through the twentieth century, and by the year 2000 it is estimated that 20 per cent of the total population will be over 60 (Central Statistical Office, 1982; 1983). They form a generation which has benefited from advances in medical science, improved public health, hospital and state welfare systems. For many, their quality of life at home and at work has risen well above that of their own parents, and they see their adult children

165

and grandchildren taking full advantage of even better educational, training and social opportunities than they managed for themselves.

Thus education for older people has to be seen in the wider context of how education is perceived in contemporary society. Social change in the second part of the twentieth century offers the possibility of education as a leisure activity as distinct from preparation for a job. Significantly, education, other than for formal or functional purposes, has scarcely featured as a legitimate personal objective for older people in their lifetime. Yet economic, techno-logical and demographic changes mean that, for some people, paid employment ends in their fifties and, for many of these, the third age can last almost as long as their working years. As Kelly (1992) points out, the main goal of social policy for the general population for much of this century has been to raise the standard of living and improve the quality of life, and yet little thought has been given to how this extended third age could be spent.

Throughout the 1980s and 1990s, older people as a group have increased their participation in education and training, but as Schuller and Bostyn (1992) point out, it remains fragmentary. All the research which has taken place suggests that social class and educational background play an important part in access to educational opportunities, strongly favouring those with higher educational qualifications, and thus men rather than women. One-third of BA graduates and 46 per cent of Open University Honours graduates over the age of 60 are drawn from the professions, compared with one in ten who were clerical and office workers, and only 5 per cent from the skilled and semi-skilled manual occupations (Kelly, 1992).

Retirement—voluntary or involuntary—can take place at any age from about 50 to 65 or over, and many of those who retire from full-time work are in good physical and mental health, with many years of active life in view. Some have held responsible technical or professional jobs, others have management expertise, and all have acquired life experience. Yet their place in society is largely determined by social expectations of a generation of older people and the widely held notion of a demographic time bomb. Older people are regarded as a steadily increasing burden on a steadily decreasing working generation. Little distinction seems to exist in the popular mind between the young-old and the old-old. Cultural expectations of age anticipate the steady attrition of physical and intellectual powers, and steadily increasing demand on the already overburdened medical and social services.

These stereotypes are gradually beginning to change both in this country and in Europe. They have been challenged by much of the research which has been carried out over the past fifteen years. Not all older people are a drain on scarce resources and, in fact, many make a significant contribution to social and economic life. A study of students over the age of 50 in four European countries (Clennell *et al.*, 1993) surveyed 1853 people in Britain, France, Germany and

Belgium. The objective was to establish whether or not there was a link between current learning activities and their quality of life. Their responses give clear evidence of active social and civic responsibility in the broad categories of helping the sick and disabled, the elderly, prisoners, women with problems, refugees and the educationally deprived, to mention just a few. In Britain the high level of participation in voluntary activities was particularly noticeable. Over half (54 per cent) said they had administrative, secretarial or committee skills to offer the voluntary sector, and nearly two-thirds (59 per cent) mentioned three or more different kinds of activity, of which domestic activity was only one: nearly half (46 per cent) were engaged in voluntary work outside the home. A collection of reports from the same four countries on the training opportunities for over-50s has given a picture of older people actively engaged in voluntary work for which they are required to follow programmes of training (Clennell et al., 1995).

Older learners do not appear to make demands for specialist or age-related support. This is the more striking since it is evident that this is an age group which includes many who are too old to have enjoyed the benefits of improved educational opportunities in the second half of the century. Clennell et al. (1984) considered the educational support needs of nearly 3000 students of over 60 currently studying with the Open University. The OU's distance learning mode of delivery is augmented by some face-to-face tutorials, day and summer schools, and some individual student-tutor contact. Responses showed that the over-60s made rather better use of tutors, counsellors and summer school staff than students under 60, except where there were transport or other logistical difficulties. Fewer of them dropped out of their courses and their overall performance was strikingly similar to that of younger students. The picture which emerged was of older learners, nearing retirement, or already retired, who were taking on difficult courses and persisting with them. The report concluded that to make special provision for over-60s within the student body was not appropriate, though full- and part-time staff and other students should be made more alert to some of the particular concerns of older people. Another survey of older students in four European countries (Clennell et al., 1990) reached the same conclusion, based on evidence from 4461 students who were studying in a range of institutions in France, Belgium, Germany and the United Kingdom.

Who are the older learners?

Today's older learners come from the generation which was at school either between the wars or during the Second World War, when educational opportunities were limited by social and financial considerations. Some of these, particularly the older women, missed out on higher education in their youth because they were victims of cultural beliefs about the value of educating girls. The war disrupted the aspirations of others and prevented them achieving their ambitions. A number have seen their children graduate and this has roused a mixture of pride and mild envy: the feeling, as one respondent put it, of *'wanting to be able to hold my own at the table when the family gets together'*. Others have continued a lifelong habit of study, or have studied to get qualifications for their job. In the distance learning institutions (such as London University Extra-Mural Department, the National Extension College and Wolsey Hall) two-thirds (63 per cent) of the students already had certificates or degrees. In this country, people over 60 with the ambition to study for a degree by distance learning can do so through the Open University. As Midwinter pointed out (1989), more than 90 per cent of the older students in the UK taking higher level courses were studying with the OU and, despite the lapse of a decade, it is unlikely that this has changed.

Why are they wanting to learn now?

The principal reasons given by older people for wanting to study are remarkably consistent. *'To make up for lost opportunities'*, *'to keep my mind active'*, *'to develop as a person'* are responses which show just how strong is the quest for personal fulfilment once the days of dedicated wage earning are over. *'Wanted to widen my horizons'*, *'my father said educating girls was a waste of time and money'*, *'the war made it impossible for me'*: all suggest that education in retirement is perceived as a personal benefit to make up for earlier deprivation or misfortune or perhaps as a reward for earlier self-denial. Coming just behind such reasons are others concerned with developing new interests and meeting new friends to enhance their lives (Clennell *et al.*, 1984).

Schuller and Bostyn (1992) detect a strongly rising demand for learning amongst older people, for several distinct but related reasons. One is what they describe as an inbuilt momentum towards third-age education from a generation which has enjoyed increasing levels of initial education. As succeeding generations of children enjoy better educational opportunities, they approach their own third age with higher expectations, making higher demands on an educational system which, being unaware of their presence, has not surprisingly failed to provide for their needs. One of the weaknesses of our understanding of the needs of older learners in open and distance education is that we have no information about those who drop out, or indeed have been deterred from entering the system in the first place.

Stereotypes about older adults and their ability and willingness to learn are gradually being eroded but they have drawn from two very powerful sources. First, educationalists and psychologists have traditionally been sceptical about the capacity of older people to take in new information. Memory tends to decline with increasing age, and studies which concentrate on the deficits of cognitive ageing confirm the impression of decreasing cognitive ability. Since the 1970s, studies have relied less on the efficiency of quick and detailed recall and have considered instead some of the ways in which adults select, store and use existing knowledge (Labouvie-Vief and Blanchard-Fields, 1982). In practical terms this suggests that, although memory function changes from middle life onwards, what is lost in active recall is compensated for by a more efficient use of retrieved knowledge and wider knowledge sources (Johnson, 1995). Second, powerful political pressures in some countries have increased resistance to educating older people, and these values have been incorporated into the thinking of older people themselves, who hesitate to claim opportunities which they fear might lead to the educational deprivation of younger people. Even where external students are admitted to undergraduate lectures, for example in some European universities, they have traditionally not been assimilated into the undergraduate group, with consequent tensions, although there are signs that this is changing and in some places inter-generational studies are beginning to appear.

The University of the Third Age (U3A) movement which began at Toulouse in 1973 has done much to establish the importance of education for people over 60. In some places, initially in France, U3As were attached to existing universities through departments of extra-mural studies, thus giving many older people access to higher education for the first time in their lives. In Britain, the U3A movement has developed differently, with fewer institutional links with existing universities and much greater reliance on self-help.

How far do their needs differ from those of other students?

Students over 60 are distinguished from younger students largely because they are not preparing themselves for a future career; relatively few are working for vocational qualifications. They may be taking advantage of open and distance learning to acquire new skills to enable them to function in a new or unfamiliar setting, such as in the field of voluntary work, or they may have chosen to study for a degree. Thus their learning can be both instrumental and expressive: it enables them to acquire skills for work, for their general interest, or for a chosen leisure pursuit, and at the same time it offers them opportunities for personal fulfilment.

Unlike most younger students, many older students have to contend with external distractions. They may have to contend with caring for other family members (their own partners, parents or grandchildren); their own health may be failing; or they may have to cope with financial problems.

Finance is a critical factor for students of all ages, but it is particularly relevant here to note the importance of pension income. Older people who receive an occupational pension are at a considerable advantage over those who are dependent solely on the state pension. Higher education is expensive and, even in the LEA sector, discounted fees for over 60s are by no means the norm. It is impossible to estimate how many older people are discouraged from studying for financial reasons. Kelly (1992) noted that the level of fees in the Open University is a deterrent for older people, as it is in other institutions. The availability of financial assistance has declined steadily in real terms over the past decade and little information is available about concessionary fee systems.

There is a strong link between the level of initial education and participation in learning activities later on in life, but it is not overwhelming. Kelly (1992) showed that although four in ten respondents had gone from school into higher education, a similar proportion had left school at 16 with no educational qualifications at all. There is, however, a link between those who enjoyed their school days and those who continue to enjoy learning in retirement. Their attitude towards learning in later life appears to be a reflection of positive educational experience in their youth. Clennell *et al.* (1984) noted that the Open University students over 60 made up a group of educational enthusiasts, most of whom had enjoyed school and had continued to learn on and off for the rest of their lives.

Motivation is a critical factor in all forms of higher education but nowhere more so than in open and distance education where students are isolated: getting a degree was a powerful goal in itself for many older students in the Open University (Clennell *et al.*, 1984; 1987). Nevertheless, their academic qualifications are low (Kelly, 1992) and this in itself has a knock-on effect on their confidence. The use of the Approaches to Study Inventory was used with older students in the Open University and in Europe (Clennell *et al.*, 1987; 1990). The Inventory contains 64 statements about approaches to academic work and was applied to students in a wide range of institutions studying different classes, including both leisure subjects and degree-level work. The findings of the Inventory suggest not only that all the older learners appear to have satisfactory approaches to study but that their approach is very similar to that of students of all ages. These findings were repeated in the European survey (Clennell *et al.*, 1990) and it was significant that both surveys stressed the immense satisfaction which the older learners clearly got from their studies, the amount of effort they put into them, and the value which they appeared to gain as a result.

Tutorial support for older learners in open and distance education

Little or no time is spent on training teachers in open and distance learning for work with older students, and yet in teaching this age group the tutorial role is clearly critical and deserves further attention (Bilston, 1989). Some older learners seemed to feel they are not always taken seriously by younger tutors for reasons which, rightly or wrongly, they believe are age-related (Clennell *et al.*, 1987). For some, the critical written comments tutors put on their work makes them anxious. Women often have lower educational qualifications than men (Kelly, 1992) leading to lower self-esteem and greater self-doubt. Without close peer support, the isolated distance learner is at a disadvantage. There is thus an obvious need to make open and distance education more supportive and user-friendly for students of all ages, particularly perhaps for older women.

Older learners are as heterogeneous a group as younger learners, and yet it is noticeable that many older learners do not identify themselves as 'students' at all; that is a term which they themselves seem to associate with instrumental learning earlier in life. Nor do they identify themselves as a separate group, and since many colleges do not record applicants' ages, information is hard to come by. Although some colleges do still offer concessionary fees, even this information is incomplete, since some pensioners do not opt to pay the concessionary rates even where these are offered.

Some of the principal areas in which tutorial support is of critical importance are listed below.

Memory

Memorising is a cognitive skill. Many older learners are concerned about their memory and the common stereotype of older people is that they are forgetful. Clennell *et al.* (1984) found that to older Open University students memory was a cause for concern, but it was difficult to assess the extent to which learning difficulties and study problems generally can be attributed to failing memory. There was a striking contrast between the 47 per cent of students over 60 who expected to have trouble with their memory and the 26 per cent who did have problems. Nevertheless, it is important for tutors to recognise that the *fear* of memory problems is in itself enough to put some older students at a disadvantage. Kelly (1992) noted that it was impossible to ascertain the accuracy of *perceptions* of memory loss. It was not clear how far older students were describing the pathological effects of ageing on themselves, or simply the difficulties that many students encounter. It may be that they lumped them together and simply attributed them to memory loss because of the prevalence of stereotypes which associate old age and forgetfulness. What may be more significant is how older learners attempt to counteract the effects of failing memory. Little is known about the remedial techniques which older people adopt, but some individual learners (Clennell *et al.*, 1984; Kelly, 1992) mentioned retraining their memory as a skill to be acquired, rather than as an inherent biological problem. For certain others, memory loss was less significant than developing analytical skills, which could actually be enhanced by intellectual maturity and life experience. A student over 60 remarked:

> *what I lose in a less efficient memory for learning lists of facts I gain on a greater breadth of reading and experience ... incidentally, I recovered from a paralysing stroke five years ago, and had to learn to write again from scratch.*

Since, in the 1985 report by Clennell *et al.*, students found memory loss less of a problem than they anticipated, it is possible that some older people devise successful strategies to overcome it. Studies in the United States have suggested that a number of factors temper the effects of memory loss and reasoning power. Of these, the ones which concern us here are familiarity with the material being studied, and having more time allowed for learning. A more optimistic view suggests that as people grow older they develop compensatory strategies, making up for what they have lost in abstract reasoning power by selective use of relevant life experience.

Study skills and examinations

Studies which invite older learners to describe their study habits suggest that many appear to be struggling with study skills which are either inadequate or inappropriate for work at this level. Some have retained faulty habits from schooldays, such as revising for examinations by reading all their notes and trying to memorise chunks of material from them. Clennell *et al.* (1987) found that the single most important study aid mentioned was the learner's own written notes. A few used highlighters to emphasise key sections in written course materials as memory aids, but in general there is an impression that older students tend to rely heavily on traditional methods of memorising.

Nowhere is this approach more of a disadvantage than in examinations.

Kelly (1992) mentions the examination as the single most intimidating aspect of Open University study. Clennell *et al.* (1984) found that while older students do much better than the under-60s in the middle range of continuous assessment scores, examinations are a serious hurdle. Although most of them get through, the experience is a difficult one, and the question of how far examinations are a reliable test of ability for older learners is one for further investigation and debate. Where exam scores count for 50 per cent of the final result, the examination can dominate the course. Plenty of anecdotal evidence exists which suggests that the same students over 60 who gain above average scores in continuous assessment get below average scores in examinations. Said one older student:

> *My professional work obviously gave me study training, but writing exam papers with a set time is quite taxing since one has no set approach to topics and a slower memory retention than when younger.*

When asked about their revision techniques, just over six out of ten older Open University students (Clennell *et al.*, 1987) listed the following as their most important:

- going through their own notes thoroughly (22%)
- working through specimen exam papers (16%)
- memorising key facts and concepts (10%)
- going through assignments and tutors' comments (9%)
- increasing study time (8%).

This suggests that many of them adopt a very general strategy, with four out of ten relying on going through their notes and re-reading all the course material to get them through. Only one in four appeared to be taking a more selective approach. Certainly there is scope for many older students to be helped by tutors to develop a more cost-effective time routine.

It is thus conceivable that older learners taking courses which are formally examined may be at a double disadvantage. On the one hand, the examination system imposes a discipline which demands sustained mental and physical effort for a concentrated period of time, whilst at the same time students may lack the very revision skills which are demanded by the system. The implications for tutors of older learners in open and distance education are important. More effective ways of maximising memory by teaching examination technique could shift the balance of advantage in the students' favour.

Pace of study

The pace of study varies: degree-level work is demanding, and distance learning, with the submission of regular assignments and an examination, imposes strict demands. Older learners worry about their ability to keep pace with a course, and yet in practice they keep up effectively. Some three-quarters of students in Open University and distance education were either on schedule or only a little behind (Clennell *et al.*, 1987). Forty-two per cent worried about continuous assessment and exams, yet only just over a quarter (27 per cent) found that they had a problem. Between 40 per cent and 60 per cent of those who fall behind believe in simply working harder to catch up. A few said they could re-schedule their work, but many were reticent and seemed to have no clear idea of how to solve the problem. Older students drive themselves hard, perhaps to compensate for what they perceive as their reduced cognitive capacity. The same report notes that two-thirds of distance education students, and 85 per cent of OU students, study from four to seven days a week, the majority putting in between two and six hours a day. Between 40 and 50 per cent reported that they could maintain concentrated study for one to two hours, and one in four said they were in the habit of studying continuously for up to three hours.

A striking finding was that older learners seem surprisingly reluctant to ask for help when in difficulties, and virtually none of them considered asking for tutorial help as a strategy. It is possible they have a very traditional concept of the tutor-student relationship which discourages them from seeking help in this kind of dilemma. Self-reliance is a quality which tends to be greatly valued in this age group, or they may see their tutor merely as a kind of academic referee. Interactive styles of learning are new to some, and although some may find them liberating, others can be made to feel uneasy when tutors are challenged by other students or when there does not seem to be a 'right' answer.

Conclusions

Older learners are a small but significant group of the total learning population. Their experiences of education have been different from those of younger people and many of them have been, and still are, lifelong learners. Studies in Europe have shown that there are striking similarities across national boundaries.

Patterns of educational provision make no concession to older learners. It is very clear, however, that the roles of tutors and counsellors are of critical importance in helping them to identify key skills and develop learning strategies which are suited to their experience and learning needs. This is particularly true of open and distance settings where students lack close peer support.

As a consequence of demographic trends, older people are likely to become a growing sector of the educational market. Spread as they are through all educational institutions, they should be identified as a significant group of consumers of educational services. There is no evidence, however, that they define themselves as a priority group: instead, they seem simply to regard themselves as independent and isolated learners in a system designed primarily for younger people. Without complaint, they struggle to compete on equal terms.

Their attitudes serve to underline the need for more conscious attempts to accommodate them. There is nothing to suggest that large-scale provision of special institutions or courses for elderly people is desirable. Educational provision could nevertheless be substantially improved by imaginative and flexible tutoring, and in the development of more refined and efficient methods of examination preparation.

Older learners are people who have busy lives in which learning is but one activity amongst many. They do not in any sense retire from active life in society. Social and demographic change has meant that although 'productive' work is decreasing, there is an increasing amount of 'social' activity which will not be done unless people volunteer to do it. Associated with this is the importance of the right to a pension which gives people a degree of freedom of choice in what they want to do, which may not have been there when they had to work for a living.

A small but important group of people choose to study for a degree. For this group the rewards of higher education can bring intense satisfaction. As one student wrote:

> When . . . I received official notification I had a First Class Honours degree, I spent the whole day walking on clouds . . . My success enhanced the realisation that after my retirement, when my career is over, my husband has died, my family all living away from home, then there is still a future, so much to learn and to do and so many new openings available. I shall not use my degree in any practical sense. It will not result in increased income or status. But the studies involved in obtaining it have made me a new person, more mature in outlook and more confident in approach to others, also more ready to realise how little I actually know and to listen to the opinions of others. (quoted in Kelly, 1992)

REFERENCES

Bilston, B. (1989) Teaching the older learner, *Adults Learning*, **1** (1).

Central Statistical Office London (1982; 1983) *Social Trends 12 and 13* (HMSO).

Clennell, S. (Ed.), Bilston, B., Butterworth, W., Cutress, N., Gethins, M., Kelly, P., Morrison, V., Palmer-Jones, F., Ryan, S., Varney, P., Watts, W. & Wyld, C. (1984) *Older students in the Open University* (Open University Regional Academic Services).

Clennell, S. (Ed.), Bilston, B., Butterworth, W., Cutress, N., Kelly, P., Lawless, C., Morrison, V., Proctor, P., Varney, P., Wareham, C. & Watts, G. (1987) *Older students in adult education* (Open University Regional Academic Services).

Clennell, S. (Ed.), Bilston, B., Butterworth, W., Cutress, N., Kelly, P., Lawless, C., Morrison, V., Palmer, F., Proctor, P., Thompson, J., Varney, P., Wareham, C. & Watts, G. (1990) *Older students in Europe* (Open University Regional Academic Services).

Clennell, S. (Ed.), Bilston, B., Kelly, P., Proctor, P., Thompson, J., Varney, P. & Watts, G. (1993) *Older students and employability* (Open University Regional Academic Services).

Clennell, S. (Ed.), Bilston, B., Kelly, P., Proctor, P., Thompson, J., Varney, P. & Watts, G. (1995) *Training opportunities for older adults* (Open University Regional Academic Service & School of Health and Social Welfare).

Johnson, M. (1995) Lessons from the Open University: Third age learning, *Educational Gerontology*, **21** pp. 415–427.

Kelly, P. (1989) Supporting and developing adult learning: Older students in adult education, *Adults Learning*, **1** (1).

Kelly, P. (1992) *Living and learning: Older Open University graduates*, Open University Older Students Research Group.

Labouvie-Vief, G. & Blanchard-Fields, F. (1982) Cognitive ageing and psychological growth, *Ageing and Society*, **2** (2).

Midwinter, E. (1989) Review of older students in adult education, *Open Learning*, **4** (1).

Schuller, T. & Bostyn, A.M. (1992) *Learning: Education, training and information in the third age*. Research paper no. 3 (Carnegie UK Trust).

12

Supporting learners in prison

Vincent Worth

Make no mistake, education does change people. More should be done to encourage people to pursue educational ventures. (Open University prison-student)

In reviewing the provision of degree-level work for learners in prison and the kinds of support that can contribute to their educational aspirations and achievement, this chapter focuses on the Open University (OU) distance education programme. This programme makes available a distinctive curricular package and a delivery system that can transcend institutional as well as geographical boundaries. Many of the principles and practices that the chapter reflects on or recommends are relevant, however, to a much wider area of provision of open and distance education which is directed towards the intellectual progress of incarcerated students.

Background

Before the OU opened, it was possible for a few, exceptional students to follow an external degree programme. Most other institutions of higher education had formal entry requirements and few prisoners possessed these. By contrast, the OU was founded on an open entry policy and the modular, independent learning system that the OU offered promised to extend the possibility of degree study in prison to a considerably wider audience. In 1972, the year after courses were first made available to the country at large, an Open University-Home Office Scheme was initiated in four prisons (Tunstall, 1974). Since then, the Scheme has expanded so that a large number of prisons can now offer Open University programmes of degree-level study to inmates approved by their prison education departments.

The government departments responsible for prisons, the Home Office in England and Wales and the Scottish and Northern Ireland Offices, fund the provision of courses through prison education departments which, since 1993, have been 'privatised' and managed by local colleges and other providers. The Scheme imposes a number of conditions. Students' programmes are limited to no more than 400 study hours per year. Tutorial contact time conforms to a (Home Office funded) pattern of ten hours for a foundation (Level One) course of 400 study hours; and for higher level work, six hours of contact time is assigned to 400 study hours, and four hours to 200 study hours courses. Certain courses which may be considered to pose a security risk are excluded from the Scheme; those, for example, whose components include chemical materials or require access to a modem.

The Open University Prison Scheme clearly represents an application of an equal access policy that has characterised the OU ethos since its inception. The programme seems especially appropriate for students in prison. It enables those for whom other opportunities to participate in higher education are closed. Of particular importance is the programme's ability to facilitate the studies of those who may be transferred and relocated several times during their sentence, since it uses the same learning materials and follows much the same pattern of teaching as that provided for OU students in the outside world. The principal, formal difference lies in the reduced hours of tutorial contact compared with those available to other students (although it has to be noted that not all outside students wish or are able to take advantage of face-to-face tutorial provision, and that the prison tutorial 'class' may sometimes be a single student!).

At the level of personal goals, OU studies can fulfil purposes, some of which the inmate may share with those outside; for example, for vocational advancement, as an interesting and challenging pastime, or for personal development. An OU programme may additionally meet the particular goals of people in custody: a means of reasserting some control over an otherwise closely monitored and controlled way of life and, because courses require full immersion in their subject matter, a way of distancing oneself and mentally escaping from the prison regime (Laycock and Griffiths, 1980; Davis, 1991).

In such a destructive and depressing environment as prison, education is one of the few constructive outlets open to prisoners, giving them a chance to play a productive role in society and enabling them to see life with a different perspective from the one imposed by the culture of the institution. (OU student)

Difficulties of studying in prison

If we want to use the opportunities and means of supporting students' learning in prison to the full, we need to understand something of the kinds of difficulties and challenges they may face. Some of these may be similar to those encountered outside, but in prison they are often experienced more *intensely*. If we assume that learning is a social as much as an individual activity, then the inmate-student can experience a heightened sense of isolation, where no other students in the same course may be accessible or where there are no other OU students in the wing or prison at all. Associated with this condition may be a feeling of remoteness from the tutor or counsellor, who perhaps cannot be contacted easily or quickly, especially during evenings and weekends when students, both inside and out, can find that most help is needed. Students sometimes become aware of an anti-intellectual culture that treats academic study with suspicion (McVicar, 1978) and may generate hostility on the part both of other inmates, for some of whom education belongs to the social world of 'them', and of some officers to whom the educated inmate may seem a status-threat.

As well as these kinds of interpersonal problems, the student faces other difficulties relating very specifically to the prison environment and management (Fitzgerald and Sim, 1982). For example, the image of the prisoner with 'all the time in the world' is quite misplaced: time constraints—most inmates are expected to work—affect those inside as much as their outside counterparts. Appeal processes can make heavy demands on both time and emotional resources. Students are likely to experience great difficulty in finding a quiet area in which to study: prisons can be very noisy most of the time. And students are especially vulnerable to the life-crises that their continuing links with the outside world bring, like family disruption and break-up, or financial problems, over which they have little control but which often demand heavy emotional investment. In a situation of stress, in which academic studies may lose their meaning and their rationale, dropping out can sometimes offer one way of relieving what otherwise seem unbearable pressures. The kind of academic support that most students benefit from may, therefore, have a special value for students who are also prison inmates.

> *Studying in prison has its hazards as can well be appreciated. The conditions under which we work are really not that conducive to the type of serious studying that is required of us. We need to go through the daily routine with some relaxation, some unwinding. But also, we are worrying about the predicament we are in and the problems that have arisen meantime at home, and with our individual family members. All this means we are totally unmotivated for some considerable number of days.* (OU student)

Supporting the student: a model

The student career can be located at the meeting point of a number of personal and institutional factors which are common to all OU students, in varying

179

degrees of significance and meaning, and whose exploration here may be particularly helpful in understanding the situation of those pursuing their studies in a prison setting. A simple, conceptual model constructed around these factors may help us to identify where support can be made available or enhanced, directly or indirectly, which will help students study effectively and enjoyably and facilitate their progress towards achieving their academic goals (see Fig. 12.1).

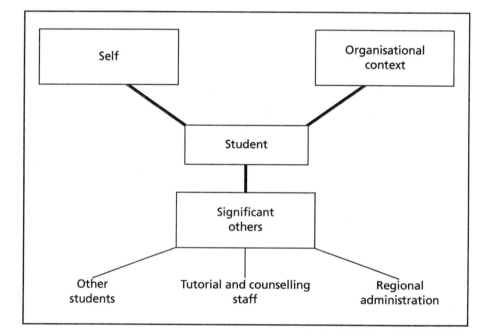

Figure 12.1 Model of student learning career

Self

This category includes all those elements that constitute the person who presents her/himself as an aspiring student to the prison education department and whom an OU staff member will meet at some point. The identity of that person is constructed from a range of social and psychological characteristics: gender, class, ethnicity, family background, and the intellectual and emotional strengths and weaknesses that have emerged during development, including the experience of the criminal justice system.

An important component of identity is the earlier educational career of the applicant and its outcomes in terms of self-esteem and motivation. Like his/her outside counterparts, the beginner has realistically to match these with the 'openness' that the OU proclaims and try to understand how he/she can achieve his/her own goals within the kinds of programmes that the University offers. Although printed information geared to the needs of newcomers is readily available, most applicants may still have little idea of what degree studies entail. At an early meeting, one of the first supportive tasks for an OU staff member is to try to depict the basic features and requirements of (Open) university study in a way that is clear, realistic and encouraging.

Motivation has to be developed in somewhat different circumstances and a probably different timeframe to those outside prison. First, students have to be serving medium- to long-term sentences since the application/enrolment period takes some time and, to attract Home Office funding, a course has to be undertaken and completed inside the prison. This probably entails a period of a year or more during which time the inmate has to 'discover' the OU, develop motivation and construct an incipient student identity (Worth, 1994, p. 38). That process may be similar to the development of motivation for outside students, although the inmate is additionally involved, at the same time as developing motivation, in presenting a self which is evaluated by persons who make decisions about 'appropriateness' for OU studies. Developing an authentic student identity involves, then, processes quite different from other existential features of inmate life in that the OU student has to take responsibility for his/her studies in a climate in which almost all decisions are made for the inmate by someone else, by an authority.

What you are going in for is specifically related to people's choosing for themselves, learning to make decisions, coming to conclusions, and thinking about things, and yet all this is taking place in an environment where these are the one thing they cannot do. (OU tutor)

The support that can be given in this area of the 'Self' is of two broad kinds:

1. Inmates are frequently studied, observed, analysed and assessed. As a consequence, they are probably more sensitive to and perhaps more defensive about their first encounter with OU staff than are students outside. Since the first meeting may significantly shape subsequent relations and temper the quality of later support, it should hinge on the OU staff member's showing respect for the student and the student's aspirations by being perceived to take these seriously and 'normalising' them. This can be furthered by helping the student to see him/herself as one of a larger body of similar-minded adults. The adult-student role is, to some extent, a 'deviant' one in society at large and may perhaps, in the anti-intellectual culture previously referred to, be a target for ridicule. The staff member's approach can do much to establish a solid base on which a strong, authentic student identity can be built: an approach that suggests respect, a non-judgemental friendliness, combined with conveying a

sense of the seriousness of the work the student is taking on. It may help to know, when the student has family members, whether they support the student's endeavours so that he/she is aware of the tutor's interest in the personal background of the 'whole' person.

2. The other type of support more specifically involves preparation for study, perhaps built around, should resources allow, a short series of tutorials but, at the least, a meeting directed towards helping and encouraging students to take a *systematic* approach to the task of preparation. It has to be kept in mind that potential inmate-students may not have as much access as new students outside to OU tutorial and counselling staff who can help them in a personal way to prepare for studies. Nevertheless, clear guidance concerning the kinds of activities that can be undertaken should be presented to students. Such an agenda of activities may follow three main strands:

- **The subject matter of the course in question:** First-level Open University courses include a pre-course preparatory pack around which activities can be based. Other available reading can be recommended.

- **Study skills:** This is probably the most important aspect of preparation and may involve, for example, practice in reading for meaning and in note-making in Arts and Social Sciences and maths work for the Mathematics (and Science and Technology, in so far as inmates are permitted to study these) courses. One of the central principles to be explained, as the context for justifying and stressing these kinds of skills, is that OU learning and teaching are based primarily on the written rather than the spoken word. *The good study guide* (Northedge, 1990) can very helpfully be recommended both as a starting point and as a continuing, reflective commentary on preparatory activities undertaken.

- **Contextual features:** Some attention needs to be given to the possibly constraining effects of the culture of the prison and official, managerial routines, but above all to *time* and the need to structure study time in an effective, realistic way that acknowledges all these constraints on inmates' lives. Trying to construct an initial study timetable may both indicate how much time is required and enable the issue of the learning quality of that time to be explored.

It is assumed that supportive guidance of this kind is framed, as far as possible, by an atmosphere of enthusiastic anticipation. Preparation centres on the notion of the independent, but not isolated, learner, with its implications developed further in an introductory tutorial where this is possible.

Organisational context

There are two elements in the institutional context of the prison that affect the inmate as student and the learning support that can be expected: the prison regime—its management personnel and style—on the one side, and the education department on the other. The prison regime may take an apparently favourable approach to education as part of an assumed rehabilitative programme (and as part of the control apparatus). One report, for example, (Home Office, 1977) comments on OU studies which:

> have been of value in taxing the wits [of inmates] and must have contributed to stability in their establishments.

Education, as a routine inmate activity, is mediated by the officers who represent the prison culture on a day-to-day basis and administer physical access and movements in liaison with the education department. Prison staff can contribute very positively or otherwise to students' commitment and progress, but not normally in a way that may be apparent to OU staff. An increasing number of prison officers are OU graduates or students and their often unpublicised support for inmate students can be a very valuable resource, although not, of course, one that can be officially acknowledged or integrated into the work of OU staff or the education department.

The work of the education department in supporting student learning is obviously crucial in a number of ways. Inmates can obtain information, advice and encouragement in their first approaches towards OU student-hood, along with a realistic appraisal of their prospects, based on the often extensive experience that staff can call upon. Staff can advise interested inmates about how they should proceed; for example, whether the applicant should try to develop language or mathematical skills before attempting an OU course. Education departments are officially assigned the task of 'sifting' student applications, although final approval has to take account of available resources as well as readiness to study at degree level. The department tries to create a learning climate by providing appropriate tutorial space, helping to induct and taking care of visiting tutorial and counselling staff, and enthusing students. Education department staff can fulfil many of the functions of the outside counsellor by acting in a facilitating, enabling and progress-monitoring role. OU staff try to maintain as close, friendly and co-operative relations with the department as possible because members of that department can provide invaluable, supportive backup on an almost day-to-day basis.

Significant others

As well as administrative and other help that students can receive from their sponsoring education department, the central figures in supporting and helping students meet the challenge of their courses are, of course, OU tutors and counsellors and, where such are present, other OU students; the whole educational undertaking facilitated by regional administrative support.

Other students

Students can play a most important part in supporting the progress of their fellows and in helping to overcome academic isolation. We are all aware that a good deal of learning in a conventional university setting takes place informally, outside the lecture or tutorial room. In a similar way, inmate students may be able to help one another, even if studying different courses, by sharing the problems (and perhaps joys) that OU work may entail. This kind of informal self-help may take place during association or even other times and can be encouraged to the extent perhaps of giving students on the same course a shared task to try to work on, a question that remains unresolved or undiscussed from a tutorial: some way of breaking down the barriers separating education from 'real life'.

Where there is more than one student taking a particular course then the tutorials associated with that course probably become much more effective learning occasions than the one-to-one tutorial that can, although not invariably nor necessarily, prove stressful for the student and very demanding for the tutor until a tutorial routine becomes established. This possible difficulty may suggest that when students are advised about choosing the course to begin their studies, or which to take when they continue in the following year, the benefits of group study could well be pointed out. It has also to be borne in mind, however, that an apparently coherent group centred on the same course may quite quickly break up because of transfers and similar reasons. Nevertheless, students should be encouraged to be aware of and take account of any fellow students who may prove important resources in their learning progress. Some tutors have tried to bring in members of their outside tutorial group to give inmates experience of other students and of other perspectives. Where this has been possible, it has worked well, but arrangements, including security clearance, can involve considerable additional work.

> Sometimes I feel very positive and then there's times I really stop and question myself. Can I really do this? Will I be able to understand what the material is putting across? But then I hear of ones who have done it, who had the same doubts yet managed it. (OU student)

Open University tutorial and counselling staff

The OU tutorial and counselling staff are clearly those primarily involved in supporting students' learning, within the broad administrative framework provided by the education department. They are normally experienced in the sense of having successfully tutored outside prison for at least the previous year, and currently tutor the same course outside and in prison. They can thus bring an understanding of problems that their outside students encounter in studying the course, additional learning materials that they may have developed and general news of the course and the faculty. Some staff are appointed as (academic) counsellors, either in that role only or combined with their tutorial role. Their work is to help students with study skills and learning difficulties as well as degree-programme planning, including choice of courses for the following year.

Briefing new prison OU staff is usually more effectively undertaken in a group setting where experienced and new staff can meet, where the formal aspects of working in prisons can be reviewed in the context of the experiential knowledge and expertise that continuing tutors and counsellors can deploy. Such occasions may be difficult to organise, however, because the fluid nature of inmate student numbers may mean that staff members may be appointed after the briefing meeting, and because the funds to pay for staff to attend briefing meetings may be limited. Briefing may, therefore, be done on a one-to-one basis out of necessity and, in any case, staff require specific briefing relating to the prison to which they have been assigned.

An OU publication, *Tutoring and counselling students in prison* (Ashley, 1994), meets many of the briefing needs of new staff by introducing them to the historical and organisational aspects of the OU Prison Scheme, to thoughts and suggestions about teaching and counselling, and about security in prison. The central, larger part of the booklet addresses many of the issues and activities that tutors and counsellors are likely to be concerned with, which they can read as part of their preparation for prison work but which also enables them reflectively to evaluate their continuing work with students, whether class-tutoring, counselling or marking their assignments.

When tutors take on prison work, they have to assume a somewhat different supportive role as class tutor. They have to change from their 'normal' mode of teaching which centres on the group, where learning can be managed and supported through the medium of various group-based activities, to a probably less familiar and more directly personal, intimate and intensive style in prison, with long time gaps between meetings during which indirect and often delayed communication only is possible. As outsiders, tutors may become aware of a diminished status and of their dependence on the good will of custodial staff. Their patience may be frequently tested by the delays that security measures entail.

It is not easy, therefore, to slide into a role whose strength in effectively supporting students' learning may seem to depend on the absence of the stresses and strains associated with unfamiliarity and unpredictability. (One small way of reducing unpredictability for both the tutor and students is to construct a tutorial visit timetable early in the year, with any subsequent changes notified to or by the education department.) The tutor role makes many demands, especially in the one-to-one relationship where the tutor has to try to develop the student's interpersonal skills so that he/she is aware of a responsibility in the relationship without, at the same time, feeling excessively burdened. This kind of relationship has to be cultivated on the basis of the respect shown the student, as previously discussed, on responding to the perceived needs of the student and helping the student to articulate these, and in trying to achieve a subtle balance between taking a leading role in course-based discussion and helping the student to set and develop the agenda. The tutor may be tempted to feel that prison teaching, in the absence of student peers and set in spatial constraints and time limitations, is somehow 'deficient'. The moods and responses of the student may seem less predictable than those of outside counterparts, partly because behavioural norms and assumptions differ between the two. Prison tutors have to employ, then, a much greater degree of sensitive flexibility in their class-teaching work.

It became apparent that the one-to-one tutorial can be intensive and mentally draining. This needed care. It was important to avoid overstressing the student through direct questioning and to make sometimes lengthy comments to direct his responses and challenge his viewpoints. This he recognised when he stated that the tutorial was something of a 'culture shock', given his daily routine and the limited opportunities he had for academic debate. (OU tutor)

Correspondence teaching, which is at the heart of OU teaching and learning, is normally handled similarly for both inmates and outside students. Critical comments on the work of inmate-students may have to be framed with particular care, however, since students' self-esteem, probably diminished by their status in any case, may be especially vulnerable to written criticism which can be mulled over and reinterpreted into a perhaps cumulatively negative message. It is in the area of assignments that the supportive relationship may be challenged and stretched almost to breaking point, since inmate-students cannot easily contact their tutor. If a student has an urgent need to communicate with the tutor, a message at second hand can be sent via the education office or by means of a letter, both entailing some inevitable delay, by which time the issue or problem may have 'cooled out'. It may be that assignments should include a section where students can state briefly any (exceptional) problems they encountered in completing the work. Part of the students' supportive training in this respect should be devoted to trying to get them to note specific problems clearly so that they may be addressed at the next tutorial. Perhaps making students aware that some of their counterparts outside face a similar situation in accessing their tutor may help to reduce any negative feelings.

When tutors were asked about how their work in prison differs from their teaching outside (Worth, 1994), in terms of the support they could provide for their students, they stressed particularly the lack of direct contact with students in between tutorial sessions and the probably negative effect this had on learning progress, especially of the student who was already beginning to slide. However, they were also able to speak of the very important role that the counsellor could play in mediating the relationship positively (Purcell, 1988), for example, in trying to make an agreement, on behalf of the tutor, concerning the completion of late assignments, and generally helping to restore confidence and a sense of progress in spite of stumbles along the way. More than one counsellor stressed the importance of helping students to assess and appreciate their progress *from* the beginning of their course, as well as their progress towards its successful outcome, and to take some consolation from that, if such consolation were needed.

Outsiders sometimes ask whether the student's criminal background affects the pedagogic relationship. Tutors do not attach much importance to this background and do not seek information about it because it seems to bear no relationship to the kind of teaching or counselling support they can give to their students. OU studies may, in any case, represent a way of preparing for life beyond prison, so that part of the supporting function of the OU staff member can be to help the student 'to dissociate study from the circumstances of imprisonment' (Ashley, 1994, p. 15).

I do not initially approach people outside with questions of what dark secrets are in their lives. I try to find a basis for the relationship that relates to the here and now. (OU tutor)

Staff development

The Open University has always seen the professional development of its tutorial and counselling staff as of primary importance in ensuring and enhancing the quality of the learning programme it offers. This development is furthered through printed materials but especially through the work of regional academic staff, who monitor correspondence tuition, visit study centre tutorials, and arrange meetings and workshops devoted to particular issues. OU tutorial and counselling staff working in prisons are closed off from some of the continuing aspects of staff development in that, although their correspondence work may be monitored, no particular attention is paid or needs to be paid to the location of the student whose marked assignment is reviewed. Similarly, class tutorials or counselling sessions in prison do not lend themselves to visits by senior regional staff who might, in other circumstances, be able to provide a different and perhaps helpful perspective on tutorial relationships, students' learning and counselling strategies as they are observed. One or more sessions during the year may, therefore, be arranged for developmental purposes, in addition to the more casual, occasional conversations between prison tutors and regional staff about specific administrative matters or the progress of particular students.

The primary purpose of such a session is to provide the opportunity for staff to exchange views on their prison work and to compare practice, thereby overcoming to some extent the professional isolation that parallels students' separation from their academic peers. Staff may represent different faculties so that the programme has to concern itself with matters of a general nature: pedagogy, or relations with the education department, for example. The following brief summary of an evening meeting that took place typifies the kind of session that can be arranged.

6.30–7.15 p.m. Refreshments. To facilitate informal staff interaction, perhaps between those tutoring the courses of the same faculty.

7.15–9.00 p.m. Discussion initiated by some extracts from the *Tutoring and counselling students in prison* booklet, chosen as trigger topics as much as for their own intrinsic interest. Staff had been asked to read through the extracts before the meeting. Among the ideas aired and discussed during the evening meeting were:

- What allowance should one make for late submission of assignments?

- How much time should be allowed for social 'chat' as against academic 'discussion'? In what ways can these two kinds of interaction be constructively linked?

- How do we interpret and handle students' complaints about prison staff?

- What is a good prison tutorial? How do we know?

These kinds of topics illustrate how invaluable a meeting of this kind can be: it may address topics that range widely across teaching and counselling, that may be specific to prisons, or whose general relevance to supporting students crosses inside-outside boundaries. But whatever tutors wish to discuss is relevant to them and almost certainly to others present. The meeting may be the only occasion during the year when these kinds of issues can be raised and discussed, when ideas and real instances can be shared and later used to inform good tutorial and counselling practice.

Regional administrative support

As well as its central headquarters at Milton Keynes, the Open University in Britain is organised into thirteen regions, each of which centres on a regional office whose personnel include academic as well as administrative and secretarial staff. Regional office administrative services constitute an essential part of the supportive framework within which students' careers can progress. Regional staff in the areas of admissions, student services and tutor services try to maintain an up-to-date information flow and to respond to need, so that senior counsellors with oversight of the Prison Scheme can be kept fully informed and can take appropriate action, whether planning admissions advice, for example, or arranging counsellor and tutor appointments. Regional staff can contribute significantly to student support in the sense of minimising learning 'gaps' when students are transferred in or out, by ensuring that new information about movements is acted upon as soon as possible, and by taking steps to inform the new, host region. It probably goes without saying that a good deal of the effectiveness of regional support depends on good working relations between academic and regional office staff, with the latter kept fully informed about policy and administrative changes.

Conclusion

By constructing a conceptual model of how we might understand the background and motivation of the inmate-learner, and the environment of learning and the work of OU staff, this chapter has tried to set out some of the principles and practices that inform the provision of distance education by the Open University for its students in prison. Many of the ideas discussed can be applied to programmes other than the specific degree-level work of the Open University. It has to be noted that attrition rates for inmate-students probably exceed those of outside students for the kinds of reasons associated with the difficulties of studying, both personal and institutional, previously discussed. And there are other kinds of costs. For those staff who are directly involved, whether making a counselling visit or giving a tutorial, occasions almost certainly occur when other aspects of their OU work may seem more attractive: prison work can entail considerable self-sacrifice, especially the time taken in travel and the frequent need to wait until entry or exit arrangements are completed. Yet, in supporting the educational careers of inmates through distance education, there are many compensations, not least in seeing progress and intellectual, as well as emotional, development among those who, from other viewpoints, may have seemed least likely to succeed.

Tutors who have been worried about coming in have remarked to me that they found the enthusiasm and interest of the student makes it all very worthwhile. (OU tutor-counsellor)

REFERENCES

Ashley, C. (1994) *Tutoring and counselling students in prison* (Open University Regional Academic Services).

Davis, M. (1991) *The Open University in a closed environment: A student survey*. Unpublished paper.

Fitzgerald, M. & Sim, J. (1982) *British prisons* (Oxford, Blackwell).

Home Office (1977) *Prisons and the prisoner* (London, HMSO).

Laycock, G. & Griffiths, M. (1980) Degrees of imprisonment, *Prison Service Journal*, (43) January 1980.

McVicar, J. (1978) Life as an OU student, *Times Higher Education Supplement*, 22 September 1978.

Northedge, A. (1990) *The good study guide* (Milton Keynes, Open University).

Purcell, D. (1988) Counselling Open University students in prison in Ireland, *Open Learning*, 3 (2).

Tunstall, J. (Ed.) (1974) *The Open University opens* (London, RKP).

Worth, V. (1994) The same difference: Tutoring for the Open University in prison, *Open Learning*, 9 (1).

Part 4

Quality, evaluation and student progress

13

Quality assurance and assessment in distance learning

Tim O'Shea, Sandra Bearman and Anne Downes

Introduction

Quality assurance and assessment processes are becoming a feature of higher education systems around the world. The adoption of formal quality assurance procedures can be related partly to the industrial 'quality movement' and partly to a concern with the emergence of new fields of study such as educational technology and higher education policy, directly concerned with how universities support learning. There is great variation in the extent to which assessment processes are externally imposed on higher education by the state in different countries. However, the pattern of change is very clear and individual countries can easily be placed on a quality assessment 'learning curve' which has the United Kingdom, Australia and New Zealand further on, and France and Germany at the start of the trajectory. The move to quality assessment comes from external political demands that higher education be accountable to its funders for delivering services that meet agreed standards. The principal driver for these new procedures and policies is the desire to ensure that standards are maintained as the world moves to systems of mass higher education which are 'efficient', in the sense that the expenditure per student drops while the participation rate increases. As distance education is at the forefront of the movement to greater access to higher education, quality assurance and assessment are key topics for this book.

Role of audit and assessment

So if, as we have seen, external quality assurance and assessment processes now play an increasingly important role in the internal life of higher education institutions, what are the implications of this for enhancing the quality of student support in an open and distance learning system? Will external processes, which are mainly driven by a conventional university model and conducted by assessors and auditors drawn from conventional institutions, be the force for quality enhancement in an open and distance learning system that they set out to be? In this section, we will look at the role and development of external audit and assessment in the UK and comment on its application to and implications for an open and distance teaching institution.

The statutory framework provided by the Further and Higher Education Act 1992 requires the Higher Education Funding Councils to ensure that provision is made for assessing the quality of education in institutions for whose activities they provide financial support. The Higher Education Funding Council for England's (HEFCE) stated purposes in assessing the quality of education have been to ensure the quality of funded provision, to encourage improvements and to inform funding.

A system of academic quality audits had been instituted in 1991, conducted by the Academic Audit Unit of the Committee of Vice Chancellors and Principals (CVCP), and subsequently the Higher Education Quality Council (HEQC). Audit *'is a procedure for scrutinising the way in which institutions of higher education manage the quality of their educational provision'* (HEQC, 1994) and has two main aims:

- to provide accountability for the quality of their educational provision
- to provide the opportunity for development and improvement made available through sector-wide publication of institutional practices.

Audit and assessment, although developed in parallel by different agencies, with one accountable to institutions and the other to government, actually had very similar aims relating to accountability and development.

Components of audit and assessment

The Funding Councils for England, Scotland and Wales adopted a broad comparability of approach to assessment. The Department of Education, Northern Ireland, sub-contracted assessment to the HEFCE, and assessment in

Northern Ireland accordingly followed the practice in England. All developed a method based on a subject or discipline area, an institutional self-assessment in the subject, and a judgement as to the quality of provision in the subject area which involved assessment by a peer group. England and Wales adopted three assessment categories: Excellent, Satisfactory and Unsatisfactory; Scotland added a fourth of Highly Satisfactory. Judgements and the reasons for them were made publicly available through published assessment reports. Due to the scale of provision in England, HEFCE originally adopted an approach which did not necessarily involve an assessment visit, but this was changed following a review of the methodology by the Council and representations by institutions.

The HEFCE review saw other developments in the assessment method. The fundamentals of the method were to remain the same, i.e. assessment against the subject provider's aims and objectives; assessment of the student learning experience and achievement; and a combination of internal and external processes: a self-assessment prepared by the subject provider and an assessment visit by external assessors. The main developments were as follows: universal rather than selective visiting; the establishment of a graded profile based on a core set of aspects of higher education provision; and an overall judgement only at the threshold level. The Council would continue to publish an assessment report for each visit. The graded profile is now created by applying a four-point numerical assessment scale, in ascending order of merit, to the core aspects of provision. All the profile elements are of equal weight. A profile with all elements graded 2 or better is considered to be 'quality approved'. Any provision which is graded 1 for any element is subject to reassessment within one year; and if, after reassessment, the profile still contains one or more elements graded 1, the education is recorded as 'unsatisfactory quality' and funding is withdrawn in whole or in part.

Audit, on the other hand, takes place at the institutional level, is operated by means of analysis of existing rather than specially produced institutional documentation, both prior to and during a visit to the institution, involves no overall judgement as to the quality of provision, and is not linked with funding. Audit reports comment only on the quality assurance mechanisms and structures.

Development of a single system

Given the similarities between stated purposes, the amount of work that audits and assessment involve for institutions, and the completion of the first complete round of audits in December 1996 and a round of assessments in

September 1996, it was not surprising that the Secretary of State for Education at the end of 1994 requested HEFCE to bring forward proposals for combining audit and assessment activities: proposals which would preferably have the support of representative bodies in higher education. She also set out her own requirements for a system of quality assurance in higher education: requirements which would need to be addressed as well as the existing statutory and developmental purposes.

HEFCE's report *Developing quality assurance in partnership with the institutions of higher education* was published, as were comments and proposals from sector representative bodies in England, Scotland and Wales. All commented on the need for a single agency to manage the integrated process of quality assurance, and made proposals on the properties of the process itself. 1996/97 will therefore see the introduction of a new, national, single system of quality assurance, which at some stage in the near future will be managed by a single agency.

Both HEFCE and HEQC look for evolution of structure and process in external quality assurance. Whether the new arrangements will continue to achieve the purposes of accountability and development remains to be seen, but it is timely to look at the achievements of audit and assessment to date and examine, within the context of support for the open and distance learner, whether such external scrutiny has brought about the enhancements to quality that it purports to deliver.

Impact of audit and assessment

Although staff may be appreciative of the accountability provided by external audit and assessment processes (and accountability is also, in practice, providing an indication of status), the real payoff for the time and effort involved must be the improvements which follow from insights gained, either through the self-evaluation process or through comments made by auditors/assessors. Because of the level at which it is carried out and because assessment is based on the process of self-evaluation, it could be argued that improvements in the quality of support to learners have been more evident through assessment than audit. In addition, the process of peer review has meant that large numbers of senior academics have now been trained in assessment processes and visited and scrutinised a number of other institutions teaching their specialist subject area. This is bound to have implications for the exchange of good practice within and between higher education (HE) institutions in a way that has hitherto not existed and on a far larger and more complex scale than the external examiner system. Again, because this development is at the practitioner level, improvements in quality of all aspects of student support should be a direct consequence.

Some aspects of quality assurance do need to be considered at an institutional level, for example when issues raised apply to the institution as a whole, and it would be absurd to wait for all subjects to be assessed before making changes across the institution. By the end of 1996, however, all institutions will have been through the audit process at institutional level, and through that learning process, coupled with experience of assessment, they will have become more sophisticated in their ability to develop rigorous and robust processes of self-evaluation and to scrutinise their own quality assurance processes. Evolution of the process is, therefore, likely to make such external scrutiny at the institutional level, in the main, unnecessary, although periodic external checks may be necessary to maintain accountability.

Problems of application in open and distance learning and implications for support of the open and distance learner

Whatever the external assurance process, it must be flexible enough to allow individual institutions to represent their provision in a way that is meaningful for them, and respect diversity of mission. Neither the Funding Councils nor representative bodies would disagree with this in theory. In practice, though, open and distance teaching organisations have faced fundamental problems with the processes of audit and assessment. These arise mainly because, to be effective, the processes rely on the validity of the judgements made by the assessors, the vast majority of whom are drawn from a conventional HE background. They also work to a method devised for application to a conventional institution and are guided by a handbook (HEFCE, 1995) and training provided for assessment of a conventional institution. However, the assessors are crucial to the process. If those who are assessed do not have faith in the quality of the judgements, doubt is cast over the whole process and the opportunities provided for enhancements will inevitably be diminished.

In a conventional institution, the quality of teaching can be judged largely by sitting in on face-to-face teaching sessions. Open and distance teaching can be said to have three main components:

- teaching and learning materials which combine the presentation of the academic subject matter with structured patterns of learning

- correspondence tuition, by marking and providing feedback on assignments

■ tutor and counsellor support, both face-to-face (including formal tutorials) and other telephone, computer conference and correspondence contacts, by which groups of individuals are offered support in the course of their studies.

Therefore, the biggest obstacle that assessors have to overcome in assessing an open and distance teaching institution is knowing and recognising the teaching to be assessed.

In addition, one of the initial criticisms to be made of the first round of HEFCE assessments was that assessors were applying a 'gold standard' when judging the quality of provision. It is probably not surprising that assessors appeared to be comparing the standard of teaching that they saw at one institution with what they saw at another, or with practice at their own institution. If such comparisons were being drawn, despite the guidance and training to the contrary provided by HEFCE, how would an open and distance teaching institution fare in such judgements?

'Teaching' had to be appropriately recognised before it could be judged; face-to-face support sessions had to be considered in the context of their non-obligatory nature; and open entry foundation-year students could not be compared with traditional university entrants. When compounded by a completely open choice modular structure, such as that offered by the Open University, then, in any comparison with a single subject honours degree, and with assessment taking place at the subject level, the open and distance teaching institution could be considered to be starting with a handicap under the external assessment system.

During early assessments at the Open University, assessors had to be continually reminded of the nature of the student intake, the role of face-to-face sessions, the importance of seeing course materials as fully-integrated teaching and learning materials rather than textbooks, and correspondence tuition as a crucial teaching and learning, as well as an assessment, tool. Once the nature of these problems became apparent, the institution was better able to prepare for assessment visits, and a string of 'Satisfactory' gradings was followed by a run of 'Excellents'.

The original assessment methodology placed far more emphasis on assessing the quality of teaching. As part of the development of the process, the focus is switching to assessing the student learning experience and achievement: this should make it easier for assessors to be truly mission-sensitive when scrutinising the quality of educational provision. Improvements in the quality of the judging should lead to better assessments and hence increased opportunity for improving support for learners through external assurance procedures.

Aspects of quality provision in distance education

The rich diversity of a large academic institution can lead to different approaches, priorities, and views of how quality is best achieved. A wide range of interpretations of quality assurance can result in unnecessary duplication for staff, and an incongruous mix of service levels and published quality assurance processes for students who are involved with a number of academic and service departments. Quality assurance is therefore best supported by an institutional framework and structures which provide clear guidance but are facilitative, reward quality and serve the dissemination of good practice. It is important for an institution to set its own quality agenda which meshes the requirements of external scrutiny with internal review processes, to maintain a focus on quality issues, and to address future development and the enhancement of quality as an ongoing process. Some institutions, including the Open University, have decided to achieve this by the establishment of a Pro-Vice-Chancellor or other senior post which includes a specific remit for ensuring the overall integrity and effectiveness of the university's policies and procedures for quality assurance.

Whether this or a mainstream approach is chosen, there are additional complexities in setting up quality assurance processes for open and distance education as distinct from face-to-face teaching. These arise from the scale of the operation, multi-media teaching, often a less structured learning programme, a self-selection approach, the diversity of the student body, and the range of units and staff who are responsible for the delivery of the institution's 'products'. It is important that the entire chain, from course planning, design, production and delivery, to student choice of course, study, assessment and award, is consistent within a set of clearly expressed aims, objectives and principles, owned by the institution as a whole, and clearly communicated to students.

Enhancement of quality in distance education has often led to increased diversity of provision. Open and distance education offers the opportunities to meet student demands, by tailoring course materials, delivery methods or assessment methods to the needs of particular groups, and offering a more flexible learning programme to individual students. It is therefore essential that quality assurance is embedded in the framework within which the institution's core activities are carried out. These core activities might usefully be grouped into the three broad areas of academic content, tuition and learning experience, and assessment.

The following paragraphs highlight some of the quality assurance processes employed by the Open University to assure quality in these areas, and explain why they are seen as being important.

Quality of academic content

We are focusing here on the quality of support to the learner, and will not therefore dwell too long on processes for the assurance of quality in the production of course materials. However, the integration of these materials into a coherent package, which acknowledges the expected progress rate of the student, and provides checkpoints and encourages reflection on the learning which is taking place, is key to a supported learning environment. Distance education teaching materials must lead the student from a clear statement of aims and objectives, through a learning process, to assessment or self-evaluation (in the case of non-assessed materials) of the effectiveness of the process. They must be presented in such a way that the expectations of the students are clear, and the students are able to judge whether they have fully understood the content or need to seek further help. They must also be of an appropriate level and relate well to any prerequisites or assumed prerequisite knowledge. One of the essential functions of an Open University Course Team is to make sure that they are clear about how the delivery process of the course as a whole will support the materials.

Quality of tuition and learning experience

In order to ensure that the delivery process is well-integrated with the structure and content of the course materials, the course development process must be informed by feedback from, and preferably participation by, those responsible for the appointment and development of the tutorial staff who will teach the material.

Open University students are allocated to a specialist tutor who normally lives in their area. These tutors are appointed, trained and supervised by full-time members of the University's academic units, based in Regional Centres. The function of these Staff Tutors is to provide a link between the academic unit and the region, and, just as important, a link between the processes of course development and course delivery. They are frequently involved in course writing, and are in a strong position to resolve problems, pass back information to their colleagues about the student experience on the course, and ensure that the tuition provided is in accordance with the tutorial strategy determined by the Course Team.

Tutors are often full-time academics at other institutions, and will normally have experience of teaching adults and an appropriate range of skills. They must, for instance, be ready to support students, in accordance with the ethos of the Open University, with a commitment to equal opportunities. The tutor's role is to interpret the materials and guide the student through the learning process and, as such, the tutor is the mainstay of the support service offered to the student. It is therefore essential that the University can assess the effectiveness of the service provided by the tutor and can supplement briefing materials or provide further guidance if necessary.

Correspondence tuition, with extensive written feedback on written assignments (tutor-marked assignments), is the chief means by which Open University tutors support students. The assignments are also part of the assessment strategy and contribute to the final course grade, and so the quality assurance mechanisms for this teaching method are described in the following section.

Tutors also provide academic support by individual contact and by optional face-to-face tutorials, which are intended to direct the student towards more independent learning. The overall tutorial strategy for each course, including the number of hours of face-to-face tuition intended, is determined by the Course Team, but the Staff Tutor has considerable discretion in the interpretation of this strategy into a tutorial programme which best meets the needs of the course in the regional context. Staff Tutors visit tutorials, particularly during the tutor's probationary period, to assess the quality of the tuition being provided, and to receive overall feedback from the students on the course.

Quality of assessment

The Open University uses a range of assessment methods, including the tutor-marked assignments (TMAs) previously described, usually with an end-of-course examination. In some cases, the examination is replaced by a project, and Course Teams also have the option of setting computer-marked assignments (CMAs). The distribution of the assignments is an intrinsic part of the course design, and the assignments themselves are carefully designed to test whether the student has understood the teaching material. Tutors are provided with a detailed marking scheme, which indicates how the scripts should be marked, and suggests points on which feedback should be given. The feedback is intended to be constructive, comprehensive and clear. The quality of tutor-assignment-marking is monitored, usually by Staff Tutors or members of the central academic staff. A sample of scripts is extracted for the monitor, who reviews the grade awarded by the tutor, and the quality of the feedback given, and provides feedback to the tutor through the Staff Tutor. The process places a heavy demand on resources, but without it, the University would have no way of assuring the quality of the assignment-marking process, identifying needs for staff development, or measuring the effectiveness of the assignment.

There is a further need to ensure that allowance is made for tutors who are more, or less, severe in their marking than others. Monitoring and the availability of management information on the range of grades awarded enables examination and assessment boards to identify severe and lenient markers, and to operate a standardisation procedure, if necessary. Since examination script marking is also carried out by a large body of staff, a similar sampling process is employed to ensure that students are awarded a fair grade in relation to the rest of the student cohort.

This level of sophistication demands a major investment in infrastructure, and in the technology used to handle, record and process large quantities of data quickly, since both the return of assignments to students and the ratification and release of examination and overall course results are time-crucial. Failure to comply with published standards and schedules in these areas would in itself represent an unacceptable reduction in quality of service.

Applying feedback to quality enhancement

We have already seen that a large distance teaching operation requires quality assurance processes which are well understood, widely owned and adequately resourced within the institution. However, the quality of the material and the strategy for delivery of the learning experience may be sound, but the quality of the experience as perceived by the student will depend upon the institution knowing its student body, understanding the processes which are actually taking place, and taking these factors into account when planning courses or services.

In Chapter 14 of this book, Judith Fage and Rosemary Mayes examine the reasons for monitoring learners' progress, and how this is carried out in an open learning or distance teaching system. Here, we look at processes which might provide feedback on progress to the institution, but might also encourage learners to reflect upon their own progress, identify choices and needs which occur as their learning develops, and demand the support they need. The shift of control over the students' learning experience from the institution to the students signals that one of the main aims of distance learning, to foster independent learners, is being achieved. We are therefore seeking to assure that students receive tuition and advice in such a way that they will achieve increasing autonomy over the organisation, motivation and direction of their studies.

A modular structure allows increased choice and flexibility of pace and workload, and the students are encouraged to feel that they have embarked on an individual, and maybe unique, learning programme. However, open entry and credit transfer between institutions increasingly require students to be well-informed about their own level of ability and requirements at the start of a course of study, and so it is important that these skills are embedded in courses which are likely to be chosen at entry. Course choice represents a key point in the learning process.

Expectations are raised by seeking feedback from staff and students, and it is essential that there are mechanisms in place for the analysis and review of feedback within the policy and practice development structures. Quality enhancement requires a clear identification of an issue, realistic assessment of current quality, a target for improvement of the service, and a route by which this target is to be achieved. In the provision of support services, this process is often blurred by other change factors, which remove the opportunity to compare like with like, and contribute to a tendency to move forward without full regard to feedback.

Response to increased choice: A case study

In 1994, the Open University allowed a limited number of students, who had already successfully completed at least half a year of full-time study at higher education level or equivalent, to bypass the foundation course normally required on entry to its undergraduate programme, and to enter at a higher level. Although it is too soon to draw any conclusions from the progress of students who chose this option, the University learned a number of interesting lessons from this experiment:

1 Although the aims, objectives, level and content of the five foundation courses were widely understood by advisory staff, those for higher level courses were not always as well expressed, and queries raised by applicants identified some differences in understanding between front-line staff and those who had been involved in course design and development.

2 Many students, who could have bypassed the foundation course quickly, recognised the benefits of a broad introductory course and an enhanced level of support for their first experience of distance learning, and chose the foundation course route when they had more information. (Although there is no reliable data on this, anecdotal evidence from staff involved in the University's advisory service for applicants suggests that 20 to 30 per cent of applicants for post-foundation study eventually chose the foundation course route.)

3 Many students had no way of knowing whether or not they were ready to enter undergraduate studies at post-foundation level, because the outcome of previous study had demonstrated their knowledge base but not their level of competency.

Further analysis of the cohort of students who entered at higher level will provide useful insight into the information students need to make the right choices for their own development.

Encouraging feedback

At all stages of provision in distance education, we need to be able to check whether the course, associated services, and outcomes, meet the needs of the learner, and we need to teach our students to be able to feed back this information in a meaningful way. One way of doing so, which accords with a quality assurance approach, is to be explicit about the mission, aims and objectives of the institution, the aims and expected outcomes of each course, and the institution's standards and expected level of service; and make sure that all staff, students and customers are aware of these, and are encouraged to respond on the value they attach to those standards, and on how far they perceive them as being met. It is the level of energy and effort applied to this process, throughout the institution, which determines whether quality is enhanced as a result.

Each activity or process should include a mechanism for the learner and the staff involved in assisting with the learning to feed back on their experience. This is not easy to achieve, without creating a heavy burden for students and staff alike, and so it is important that the process of feedback is approached creatively, and in ways which are open but not intrusive. These include:

- **Publications**, which inform the learner what to expect from the institution, and what is expected of them, so that their expectations match the stated level of provision, and they are able to feed back on the basis of criteria which are commonly understood: a Student Charter, a formal complaints system, standards which are stated explicitly by courses and service areas.

- **Formative assessment**, which includes detailed and constructive feedback on the learner's performance.

- **Structured feedback**, in the form of surveys on courses and services.

- **Representation**, or a formal route of some sort by which the feelings of the student body can be shared and conveyed to policy-makers.

We can also use management information on enquiry, applicant and student numbers and profiles, retention rates, progress rates, success rates and course choices to test the effectiveness of the institution's provision, and also its communications.

Conclusions

If we compare distance teaching universities with conventional universities, it seems clear that, in many ways, the former are better suited than the latter to operate systems of quality assurance and assessment. Also, as universities are increasingly obliged to participate in external quality assessment and audit processes in order to secure state funding, the significant question is how best to augment internal systems of quality enhancement in order to meet the external functions. The two key processes are the use of feedback for quality enhancement and the induction and development of staff to meet quality enhancement goals. In many ways, these processes are complementary, as an effective staff development programme must be based on two-way communication between the designers and the deliverers of the distance learning materials. In a large distance teaching institution, feedback and staff development are complex processes and, even at the level of an individual course, may involve thousands of students and hundreds of staff working over a number of years. As we argue elsewhere (O'Shea and Downes, in draft), computer and communication technologies play a critical role in supporting the management of feedback and development processes.

Finally, quality assurance and assessment represents an additional major task for distance teaching institutions. Our experience is that there are benefits for students and for the institution in addressing this task proactively; that it is possible to integrate much of the work necessary to meet external requirements with the internal course planning and quality enhancement activity; and that it is possible for distance teaching institutions to display and refine their special strengths by a vigorous approach to quality assurance and assessment.

REFERENCES

Higher Education Funding Council for England (1995) *Assessors' handbook*, April 1995–September 1996.

Higher Education Quality Council (1994) *Learning from audit.*

O'Shea, T. & Downes, A. The synergy between IT and QA in distance education (in draft).

ACKNOWLEDGEMENTS

We wish to thank colleagues in the OU Institute of Educational Technology and Quality Support Centre, and other members of the Quality Assurance team, whose work has contributed to our thinking.

14

Monitoring learners' progress

Judith Fage and Rosemary Mayes

Knowing how students, at all levels and in all kinds of educational contexts, progress through their studies has always been important. Schools, colleges and universities have built up a battery of strategies, mostly involving various forms of testing, to assess levels of competence and knowledge. These strategies range from the very formal, such as final examinations for degrees, to the small and informal, for example, reading to the teacher each week in primary school classrooms. This chapter looks at a range of student progress monitoring strategies used in open and distance education, and at the structural changes in the educational environment which are affecting learner monitoring, and considers some of the developments in this field, notably through the use of new technology.

First, however, it is important to state that although many of the same methods may be used for both, monitoring of learners' progress is a different concept from measurement of achievement. The latter has a public focus and is an end product in itself: it certifies the student's achievement to the world at large. The monitoring of learner progress is developmental and implies continuity: it uses the result of assessment as an indicator of progress, a stage on a journey. Within this framework, student progress monitoring can be approached from two angles, although both are directed towards the same broad objectives. These might be defined as the 'internal' and the 'external' perspectives.

Progress can be identified from the 'internal' perspective of the learning process itself: has the student 'learned' as expected from the previous study experience, so as to be ready, in terms of skills, competences and knowledge, to move forward to the next stage or level of study? This is primarily a concern for the curriculum itself: for its structure and delivery. Testing has an important part to play; in open learning, and in particular adult learning, this is ideally built in to the course components. There are many examples of successful embedded assessment of progress: computer assisted learning (CAL) offers one such approach. For instance, North Island College in British Columbia developed a classic CAL system in the late 1980s for a geographically-dispersed community college:

> Each unit (of work) contains two to seven CAL lessons. Each lesson consists of instruction, practice and test. Access to instruction and practice are optional, but a lesson is considered to be completed only when the test is completed with 100% mastery. Any completed units or lessons can be specifically accessed, but it is not possible to access a unit or lesson if the prerequisite has not been completed. (Cowper et al., 1987)

Contrasting examples use both summative and formative assessment, the latter being a widely used approach in dealing with project work in which a proposal is formulated which is assessed and commented on by a tutor before the student moves on to the next stage; it is also a useful way of diagnosing student needs. For example, an evaluation of preparatory materials for new Open University UK students suggested that:

> a relatively simple, speedily-marked diagnostic quiz ... which formed the basis for further preparation if need be ... was a model which achieved a good take-up and which tutor-counsellors found useful. (Fage and Johnson, 1993)

Self-diagnosis and self-assessment are also frequently-used tools, ranging from a series of activities in a workbook intended to help students assess their understanding of the reading or work they have completed and thus, too, their readiness to move on to the next, to self-diagnostic tests which identify, for example, linguistic or mathematical preparedness for a particular course of study.

This 'internal' perspective is thus highly learner-focused, concerned with individual learners' needs and development through a curriculum. The more 'external' perspective, although capable of being both student-focused and institution-focused, is nevertheless an institutional device for tracking and monitoring the progress of students through the use of a range of progress indicators. These indicators may incorporate some of the previous strategies, but will exclude the informal, private methods, especially any self-assessment, and will extend to take an overview approach, capable of identifying trends and patterns. To clarify the distinction: summative assignments may act as an internal means of monitoring progress through the tutor's and thence, through feedback, the student's identification of learning progress and needs; and as an external means through the institution's interpretation of the visible outcome of the assessment. In the main, this chapter will be concerned with the institutional monitoring process and the ways in which open and distance learning organisations can keep a track of the stages reached by their students along their educational journey.

Why monitor learners' progress?

This is the kind of question which is deceptively simple in construction and begs a response which may be equally simplistic in terms of being 'a good thing' and, therefore, worth doing irrespective of any resource or other cost-related implications. It is important at this point to recognise that the intrinsic worth of monitoring progress lies not in the activity itself but in the reasons for it, as perceived by those whose progress is being monitored and those doing the monitoring. These 'internal' and 'external' reasons may converge in crucial ways and, in particular, in relation to issues which are of common concern to both the individuals being monitored (i.e. the students) and those doing the monitoring (i.e. the institutions, including not only the directly-responsible teaching institutions but also national bodies such as, in the UK, the Higher Education Quality Council (HEQC), the Higher Education Funding Councils, and the Higher Education Statistics Agency). What follows is an attempt to identify some different reasons for monitoring student progress on the basis that they fall into these three categories: 'macro' reasons, generally supported at all levels; institutional reasons; individual reasons—this categorisation is indicative only and definitely not the final word on the subject.

Perhaps the issue in higher education about which there is most agreement currently at all levels, from the individual student up, is the need for quality assurance procedures which ensure the quality of the courses under offer, both now and over time. As the UK Higher Education Quality Council (1995a) puts it, in its paper *A single system of academic quality assurance*:

To be effective and durable, any system of academic quality assurance must:

■ *provide reassurance that the educational provision for which each institution takes responsibility meets a minimum acceptable standard*

■ *provide information about the quality and standards of the programmes and awards which institutions offer*

■ *produce lasting quality improvement through the promotion of innovation and development.*

Ensuring that information is collected on student progress at all levels (i.e. from the individual student to students as a whole at national level) and can be easily extracted and disseminated is a crucial part of putting such quality assurance mechanisms into place. Without the necessary data in accessible form, institutions of higher education cannot satisfy the requirements of both internal stakeholders (e.g. their governing bodies, students, local funders) and external stakeholders (e.g. Funding Councils, the population at large) for accountability in relation to quality assurance and control mechanisms.

Allied to the quality issue is a thirst at all levels for information, especially of the kind that can be measured and monitored. It is not the intention here to examine the serious and much-underrated dangers of information 'for the sake of it' or the pitfalls attached to undigested and indigestible masses of statistical information. On the positive side where student progress monitoring is concerned, improving collection methods and ensuring that data is accurate, accessible, clearly interpreted, and disseminated with due sensitivity to real current requirements and the varying needs of different audiences are worthy goals and crucial as inputs into the ongoing assessment of quality and standards. In other words, 'good' student progress monitoring data will reinforce the HEQC's contention that:

> to improve the quality of teaching and learning in British higher education in the interests of external and internal stakeholders alike ... requires both open recognition and genuine acceptance that the quality and standards are the responsibility of institutions, individually and collectively.

As has already been indicated, institutional reasons for monitoring student progress are very much bound up with the generally perceived need for them to provide 'quality' services and to be able to prove that quality assurance mechanisms are in place and effective over time. To a certain extent, therefore, institutions have very little choice about monitoring student progress; the imperative is imposed externally as the result of the wide range of accountabilities under which they operate. To put it very basically, the level of funding depends and will increasingly depend on institutions' abilities to maintain and improve standards and effectively prove they are doing so. This rather cynical response should be countered by an instinctive belief, difficult to prove but persuasive nevertheless, that institutions, if free from such external accountabilities, would still aim for quality and improvement of standards and monitor their students' progress as part of the quality process, because institutions of higher education comprise people, teachers and students, involved in a mutually dependent process which can only work if all parties involved are satisfied with it. It is also probably true to say that considerations related to the upholding of institutional reputation not only are the result of the increasingly competitive environment but also arise from feelings of institutional loyalty and an innate desire to promote excellence. Effective student progress monitoring is a means of testing instincts and feelings of this kind against facts.

In terms of individual requirements, progress needs to be known not just for reassurance and validation, but in order for the institution to take action if progress is not being achieved. The need for formal systems is especially acute where staff are not in daily contact with small numbers of students whose progress is visible. Students who are gaining poor scores may need to be offered remedial teaching; students who do not complete assignments should be offered counselling and, where appropriate, support; students who fail examinations would benefit from additional help with examination techniques or coping with stress; students who achieve a low grade on a Level 1 course may be advised to take another at the same level before moving on to Level 2; those who achieve high scores may be guided to consider more demanding courses. Responding to the results of monitoring at the individual level is an important aspect of the teaching process, and tutors, advisers and counsellors all have a key role to play here.

At a wider level, student progress monitoring can provide valuable feedback regarding the curriculum, the teaching, the behaviour of student cohorts, and a range of educational services. In the OU UK, there are several opportunities for this. Regional Student Services have used information on, for example, early student drop-out, to improve their support for student preparation, with encouraging results. Management Information has been used to track the progress of groups of students, for example, visually-impaired students taking science courses, or all students on a new, innovative type of course. Dissatisfaction with retention levels on the Mathematics Foundation course has led to a different approach in the production of a new suite of 'entry' courses. Student difficulties in moving from Level 1 to Level 2 in Social Sciences has led to the development of a small number of particularly accessible and well-supported Level 2 courses. Examination boards routinely use information from scores to identify problems with particular examination questions or markers.

Thus, institutions will wish to monitor student progress to ensure that their curricula are appropriate and that academic services or facilities established to support student learning are operating effectively. In the 'Starting points' section of the HEQC's *A quality assurance framework for guidance and learner support in higher education: the guidelines* (1995b), the following are identified as being key institutional student support activities:

- ensuring a range of services and support as an integral part of teaching and learning

- recognising that learners require effective guidance and support to achieve their full academic potential

- seeking ways to support more diverse and flexible patterns of teaching and learning

- ensuring the quality of the student experience

- attaching different degrees of importance to guidance and learner support

- having diverse arrangements for guidance and learner support, often within one institution

- maintaining interest in the quality assurance and quality enhancement of guidance and learner support arrangements

- developing responses to the Charters for Higher Education

- being willing to consider the implications of the full range of guidance and learner support activities

- recognising that staff roles and responsibilities for guidance and learner support are changing and may in turn require different kinds of support.

If institutions are to monitor the impact of the student services they provide on student progress they will, in the context of this list, need to ensure, at the very least, that the nature of such services are documented, that data about student use of such services is recorded as part of the student progress record, and that students' complaints/comments on the services are recorded as part of both the student progress and support services records. Systems, computerised or otherwise, which link student progress records with support services records and feedback on the services provided, should assist institutions to assess the appropriateness and efficacy of student support services as part of the process of monitoring student progress. Given the investment in time and resources by institutions in providing student support services which are intended to meet the needs of students and facilitate progress, it is obviously vital to ensure that these aims are being met both at the individual and collective levels and over time.

To turn to the perspective of the learners themselves, the HEQC guidelines offer a checklist of learner and potential learner expectations of higher education, as follows, where learners:

- are prepared to take responsibility for their own learning

- are faced with widening choice and recurrent decisions about learning

- are entitled to a range of guidance and learner support services

- are willing to work in partnership with staff and, where appropriate, their peers, in achieving their own learning goals

- are willing to offer regular feedback on the quality of their educational experience and of the guidance and support services available to them.

In terms of monitoring learners' progress, it is worth looking at these expectations in some more detail.

Although it is true that learners and potential learners in higher education are prepared to take responsibility for their own learning, they also expect to know what the outcome of that learning will be and that they are reaching and passing the milestones along the way to that goal. Monitoring progress is the means by which the compact between learners, who take on responsibility for their learning, and the institutions, who provide the services to enable that learning to take place, is tested and fine tuned as necessary. The individual choices involved in taking responsibility for one's own learning are numerous and complex, ranging from choice of course and institution to adapting one's lifestyle to take on resultant workloads. Such choices need to be accompanied by the reassurance that the individual learner is coping with the course of study and that progress is being made against agreed indicators.

The phenomena of widening choice for learners and the need to take recurrent decisions about learning also provide potent reasons for monitoring student progress. The implication of widening choice is increasingly movement between institutions of higher education, as learners 'pick and mix' between the offerings of various providers to put together the study profile that best fits their needs. In such a situation, it is vital for both learners and institutions that progress is monitored for each course of study and from course to course. Learners need a record of progress and achievements on previous courses to inform future choices about further learning and to ease access. Institutions also require this information for admission of new learners and to produce management information about learner categories. The existing credit accumulation and transfer systems ensure that many previous achievements can be transferred between institutions, but progress monitoring data tends, currently, to remain the property of the institution running the particular course. As the mobility of learners between institutions continues to grow, the need for transferable progress monitoring data will also increase.

Guidance and support services are an essential aspect of the learner's expectation of the institution, as are the standard of such services which the individual learner 'has a right to'. It is increasingly recognised, especially in relation to open and distance learning, that requirements for such services vary drastically between individual learners and between groups of learners. Again, in relation to open and distance learning, some services might be regarded as core, e.g. all learners need an allocated tutor to mark assignments and give individual feedback, and others as specific to certain individuals or groups, e.g. teaching accommodation with wheelchair access, or special tuition for a student having problems with a particular aspect of a course. It is important for the individual learner, therefore, that progress monitoring includes data about the use made of guidance and support services and that this data is included in the interpretation of monitoring information, to assess not only the impact of the services on the individual's progress but also the services themselves. This should enable institutions not only to monitor the effect of specific services on individuals and groups of learners but also to inform future policy decisions about service provision.

The increasing emphasis on learners setting their own learning goals has already been referred to. An additional dimension to learner choice is provided, however, by the concept of a working partnership between learner and teacher, and between learners, to achieve learning goals. This expectation is firmly based on the notion of the importance of individual learning needs and the requirement for flexibility in the teaching/learning relationship to facilitate them. The learner is seen as a very active partner in this relationship and it is interesting to speculate on the effect this has on the student monitoring process. The implication is that progress monitoring is a continuous and pervasive aspect of the relationship between staff and learner or learners, as goals are continuously set, challenged and revised. Thus, progress monitoring is integral to the way the process works and woven in the fabric of the teacher/learner relationship. The needs of open and distance learning institutions in terms of progress monitoring will be considered later in this chapter but it is important to emphasise at this point that effective capture of progress monitoring data is more difficult when the progress indicators are continually shifting. From an organisational viewpoint, progress monitoring is facilitated when prior agreement is reached about what aspects are to be monitored, how and when.

Finally, there is the issue of learner feedback on the educational experience, including guidance and support services. Learners need to have confidence in the progress monitoring process and, crucially, to have seen the results of it, to be able to provide rational, informed feedback on the experience. Again, effective progress monitoring is inextricable from the other key aspects of the educational experience and it is difficult to see this experience as complete without this aspect. Perhaps it is invidious to draw analogies, but it is inconceivable, in any quality manufacturing or service industry that can be imagined, for the consumer not to have expectations about progress chasing and quality audit or to complain about deficiencies in these aspects.

The changing context of learner progression

We have already touched on some significant changes in the context in which both 'external' and 'internal' student progress monitoring take place, which have an important impact on the means required to achieve it. Most notably, the stable, monolithic curricula of the past, offering a single structure which tended to encompass the entire qualification route and effectively limit students to a single institution, are now giving way on a rapidly increasing basis to the modularised approach referred to in the previous section, in which modules, often with commonly-recognised credit values, can be taken in any order and, moreover, transferred to other institutions.

This pattern is increasingly becoming the norm, not just within nations but between them. For example, there are qualifications which can be built up within European Union institutions; and the OU UK at least recognises overseas qualifications for advanced standing and is working with the Commonwealth of Learning to examine the feasibility of establishing a database of credit ratings for modules of distance education programmes in Commonwealth institutions. In this context, the need for an effective tracking mechanism is crucial. In the UK, this was identified by the Higher Education Quality Council's major report (1994) *Choosing to change: extending access, choice and mobility in higher education*. This notes a lack of reliable statistical data to describe patterns of student behaviour and laments the fact that:

> *we have not been able to identify data which reliably records inter-institutional transfer, or internal institutional mobility, or mobility between 'off-campus' and institutional programmes.* (HEQC, 1994, para 24)

The report also comments on the rising demand for international credit transfer, within Europe, trans-Atlantic, and global; it comments that:

> *it is possible to imagine a much more expanded and electronically-integrated international system of higher education, within which credit transfer of learning achievement will play a prominent part. We may need to suspend our assumptions that international credit transfer means physical relocation if a network of provision focused on multi-media, electronic and satellite technologies is established. Developments of this kind in India and Australia suggest that progress will be more rapid than we may imagine.* (HEQC, 1994, para 317)

This is a revealing and important statement. It suggests, in accord with experience on the ground, that the clear distinctions which were deemed to have existed between 'campus' and distance learning are now becoming increasingly irrelevant. This is not a sudden occurrence: distance education institutions and departments have always used face-to-face teaching as a component, on their own or others' campuses; conventional campus colleges and universities are increasingly using open learning and teaching electronically through audio, video and computer conferencing. The technology explosion is partly responsible; but even in areas where access to technology is limited or non-existent, ways of using a combination of distance and contact methods are being developed in imaginative ways. The gap is closing.

What do students themselves need in respect of progress monitoring?

The first stage of progress monitoring may arise before students begin a new course of study. Some assessment of their readiness is important, in order to assist suitable course choice and provide appropriate advice on and help with preparation. Where students are at a distance from the assessor, a range of distance diagnostic tools may be useful. The diagnostic quiz has been mentioned earlier; information on previous educational qualifications, obtained from formal data collection, has also been shown to provide a useful predictor of need in the OU UK, but with caution; it must be used as a guide to past experience, not an assumption of future achievement.

Once students are embarked on a course of study, regular assessment is important as both an academic and a progression measure. Students themselves need to know how they are achieving; this is especially true where students do not have regular contact with a tutor. However, there is evidence from the OU UK that its tutors have carried their positive experience of marking and responding to students' assignments in the OU back into their conventional class-based institutions, as a reliable and effective way of assessing students' real academic understanding and progress. Such assessment can be both qualitative and quantitative: qualitatively in respect of students' learning process, as just described; quantitatively in respect of a score which is both an outward symbol of the qualitative result and a permanent record of a level of attainment. This score can become a device for representing student progress, and its simple numerical value can contribute to a database of progress which is capable of extensive manipulation to represent individual student progress and that of a range of groups. In that respect, the need of distance education to monitor the progress of dispersed, 'invisible' and often large numbers of students (the large distance education universities such as the OU UK, India's Indira Gandhi OU, and Sukhothai Thammathirat in Thailand are larger than most non-distance universities) has led to the development of computerised systems which are likely to become increasingly useful to other educational institutions. For example, the Commonwealth of Learning (COL) has developed a student record management system in response to demand from member institutions, especially in developing countries. Susan Phillips (1995) writes:

it is ... necessary to have systems in place to register students and monitor their progress, both within courses and within programmes of study ... COL had received a number of requests from administrators in developing countries for assistance in identifying and acquiring such a system. Many of these came from small institutions with only microcomputer capacity, or from departments in larger institutions which needed help to track students in distance education courses.

COL found that no appropriate system existed and has therefore developed its own for use by institutions in developing Commonwealth countries. In the OU UK, a major new systems development project (Corporate and Individual Records for Customers and Enquirers, or CIRCE) is underway, introduced incrementally from the beginning of 1996. The student progress monitoring facilities of CIRCE will be discussed later in this chapter.

What are the needs of open and distance learning (ODL) institutions in terms of progress monitoring?

Such needs will vary in some respects between different open and distance learning institutions, depending on the character of each institution, the preoccupations of its staff, and the emphasis placed on particular aspects of progress monitoring. They will also change over time as the demands placed on institutions by external agencies, such as funding bodies, alter. Generally, though, there are core needs which open and distance learning institutions share in relation to progress monitoring. Some of these have been identified in the Project Initiation Document for the study support area of the OU UK's new integrated computer systems development, CIRCE, as follows:

The recording, monitoring and dissemination of information relating to student progress; the recording of student progress against regulatory criteria; the recording, monitoring and notification of student involvement in study support activities and any related asseessment; the recording of contacts made with students; access to individual student records by staff to enable progress to be monitored; access to records of groups or categories of students by staff to enable patterns and trends to be identified.

This listing of progress monitoring needs recognises the fundamental importance for both the institution's 'internal' and 'external' dimensions of progress monitoring systems, which provide *quality* information on individuals, selected groups and all students; which are *flexible* in terms of access and outputs, and which are *dynamic* over time, thus allowing for inevitable change. In this section, these key attributes of progress monitoring systems will be explored to illustrate in more detail institutional needs, especially from the perspective of the Open University UK and in the light of the CIRCE development. However, it is important to note that although the OU UK reassessed these needs in preparation for a new technical base for its records, the principles it established are independent of the technology which supports them.

The importance of accurate data on student progress is probably so obvious that even mentioning it in passing may seem unnecessary. It is also self-evident that such data is important not just to open and distance learning institutions but to all other institutions of higher education. It is possible to argue, however, that reliable data on student progress is even more important to ODL institutions than to their 'conventional' counterparts, because of their differing fundamental characteristics: ODL institutions can expect to have less face-to-face contact with their students over time and must, therefore, have even more effective tracking systems for progress monitoring. Such tracking systems can only be effective if the data they contain is of high quality, in terms of accuracy and appropriateness. From the context of the study support area of the Open University's CIRCE development, some examples will serve to illustrate the key aspects of achieving quality progress monitoring data.

Consultation

A large portion of the time set aside for business analysis (that is, an analysis of the present and future activities, interactions and requirements of the institution) was devoted to, first, defining exactly what was inside the scope of the project and what was outside and, second, testing the results of this scoping exercise on existing users in the study support area of the Open University's operations. In general and practical terms, this was to ensure, from the inception of the project, that as wide an agreement as possible was obtained about what was important in current operations and needed retaining, what was unimportant or was no longer necessary and could be abandoned; and what were the problems that required addressing. In respect of student progress data in particular, all categories of staff with any interest in this area, from clerical to academic to counselling to managerial, were consulted about the scope of the project, the real requirements based on their own diverse experience, and the problems. The investment of time was considered more than worthwhile in order to ensure that the breadth of experience in this area was reflected in the analysis and, after that, in the design solutions.

Definition

After the consultative stage of business analysis, it became increasingly obvious that student progress monitoring meant different things to different people. For some, monitoring meant purely looking at assessment scores and academic results from course to course for individual students; for others, it involved this but also taking into account support services provided whilst still emphasising the individual student. Others still were much more interested in the totality of students, or at least of significant groups, and were concerned with the measurement of student progress overall against resources allocated for student support. These examples represent only a few of the positions taken but are, nevertheless, illustrative of the need for a full definition of the student progress monitoring data which is required at an early stage of producing the systems. Although each item of student progress data which is to be collected is unlikely to be specified at this stage, the broad definition represents a consensus and the basis for the detailed development.

Relevance and consistency

A consensus amongst all those involved about what quality student progress data is, and how it should be collected and disseminated, is crucial. Part of this process, and one that is often underestimated, is the need to take into account the practical implications. When student progress monitoring was being discussed during the CIRCE development, a question which was frequently asked by users and by members of the Project Team was 'What are the significant events in an individual student's contact with the University which need to be recorded in order to enable that student's progress to be monitored and for that student to be compared with other students in a selected group?' Recording every event was not realistic, necessary or desirable and had horrific implications for inputting volumes and standards. On the other hand, there had to be sufficient information recorded to satisfy the differing requirements for monitoring output (referred to in the 'Definition' section above) and this information had to be recorded in such a way that like could truly be compared with like and valid comparisons made and conclusions drawn. Efforts are still being made to define what constitutes a 'significant contact' between student and university and how to codify this to ensure consistency between student records. This has proved to be a difficult exercise, not least because of the inevitable element of individual subjectivity in defining 'significant' in this context. This very difficulty has underlined the importance of the exercise in achieving quality student progress monitoring data, however.

Although student progress monitoring data of high quality is undoubtedly the greatest need of ODL institutions, data by itself is of little use, however superior, unless it can be accessed by those who need to (and not, incidentally, by those who do not need to!) and outputs can be obtained according to a diverse range of individual requirements. Flexibility of access is required for the following main reasons:

1 So that progress monitoring data can be obtained directly by those who need it. The OU UK, for example, aims, as part of the CIRCE developments, to make such data available electronically to part-time tutorial and counselling staff working from home.

2 So that the latest monitoring data can be available at all times. One of the main problems the Open University has had to contend with over the last five years is the provision of current, up-to-date student progress monitoring data to those who need it.

3 So that consistent monitoring data can be shared by all. The Open University's new systems are based on the concept of an integrated student record which will contain all information about that student from first until last contact with the University. All users, subject to appropriate safeguards regarding confidentiality of some information, will therefore see the same data.

4 So that access rights can be suited to individual needs for data rather than vice versa. The Open University CIRCE development recognises the tension which exists between the students' rights as data subjects under the Data Protection Act and the needs of the institution, and individuals within the institution, to use such data to monitor progress. New and emerging system administration technologies make it possible to ensure a sensitivity to the data itself whilst permitting access on a 'need to know' basis.

Flexibility of output from student progress monitoring systems is required:

1 To provide a range of choice. Users will require output from student progress monitoring systems according to a wide range of selection criteria, e.g. by individual student, by course cohort, by entry qualifications, by category of study support provided, or by any mixture of these and/or a large number of other possibilities.

2 To satisfy both internal and external expectations. Internally, users would expect to be able to obtain information on individual students' progress and on groups, selected according to user-defined criteria. Some users would also wish to monitor trends, especially in the relationships between progress and resource allocation on student support services. Externally, agencies such as the Funding Councils would expect institutions to provide progress monitoring data as required.

3 **To ensure information is timely and at the right level.** This is a key performance indicator for student progress monitoring systems. Those who need the information must be able to access it, retrieve it in the form they select, and disseminate it as they decide. Considerable emphasis has been placed on this in the student progress area of the CIRCE developments, and the Project Team emphasised its importance in the Business Analysis report, as follows:

> *The emphasis on standard of services to students and cost-effectiveness will require the OU to meet high performance criteria in these respects:*
>
> ■ *the production of systems which are sufficiently flexible to cope with likely changes in the patterns of study support*
>
> ■ *efficient and accurate student progress record management*
>
> ■ *ease of access to and output from student progress records by all appropriate categories of staff.*

Closely allied to flexibility is the need for dynamic progress monitoring systems which can be adjusted to take account of change, either in the institution's internal or external environment, and the consequent require-ments of the systems. Current technological developments are ensuring that systems are no longer designed 'in stone', making post-implementation change very much easier without the investment of huge additional resources in programming. Users' expectations of themselves are changing too with the new generation of end-user database application tools. Indeed, the edges between the 'professionals' and the 'users' are becoming increasingly blurred, and this is well illustrated by the partnership approach to development used by the Open University in relation to the CIRCE developments, where users have frequently been appointed as Project Managers leading teams comprising joint numbers of users and professional computing staff. The whole issue of student progress monitoring in CIRCE has been in the hands of a group of users from differing academic and administrative backgrounds in the University, working alongside analysts and programmers. The range of experience provided by the users has been complemented by the analytical skills of the professional computer staff with the result that the solutions being proposed take proper note of the shortcomings of existing systems and also reflect the changing needs of the future. There is still a long way to go for the Open University UK in building the student progress monitoring system in CIRCE, but the foundations are strong and complete.

What next?

We have described the framework within which learner progress monitoring is and should be carried out, discussed the reasons why it is important, and given an example of a major development in this area within the OU UK. We have noted the importance to individual learners that their progress be monitored in partnership with their teachers; and that the requirements of quality audit and assessment are also demanding good information on student progress from institutions, as they are expected to be increasingly accountable. Moreover, competition requires institutions to be more focused in their marketing and advertising, and to have a good understanding of the implications, not only for recruitment but also for retention, of using particular marketing strategies. The ability to use Management Information systems to manipulate student progress data quickly and flexibly to identify trends and problems, and to set up longitudinal studies, will become increasingly important in the interests of both efficiency and quality.

In the longer term, the growing need for inter-institutional information, on a national and international basis, will require moves to common, or at least compatible, 'macro' systems for monitoring learners' progress. The global student, whether geographically or electronically mobile, is increasingly seeking to build up an educational profile which makes sense and which is universally recognised. As the HEQC's *Choosing to change* report (1994) indicates, the project to facilitate this has barely begun, and is likely to form the basis of the next stage of development in monitoring learners' progress in a world in which the differences between 'conventional' and open and distance learning are being increasingly eroded.

REFERENCES

Cowper, D., Godfrey, D., Hart, R. & Sterling, S. (1987) Teaching at a distance with CAL, *Open Learning*, 2 (1), pp. 25–30.

Fage, J. & Johnson, M. (1993) *Evaluation of the wrap-around preparatory materials 1992/3*, OU UK Regional Academic Services report.

Higher Education Quality Council (1994) *Choosing to change: extending access, choice and mobility in higher education*, report of the HEQC CAT Development Project.

Higher Education Quality Council (1995a) *A single system of academic quality assurance*.

Higher Education Quality Council (1995b) *A quality assurance framework for guidance and learner support in higher education: the guidelines*.

Phillips, S.E. (1995) The Commonwealth of Learning student record management system. In Sewart, D. (Ed.) *One world, many voices*. Proceedings of the 17th World Conference for Distance Education, 26–30 June 1995, Birmingham, UK, Vol. 2, pp. 437–440.

15

Issues of evaluation

Mary Thorpe

The aim of this chapter is to discuss the implications for evaluation of open and distance learning (ODL) created by public assessment of the quality of teaching in higher education. With the delivery of mainstream education programmes through open or distance means, institutions such as the Open University UK have had to match their teaching of and services for students against those of any other university provision in the same curriculum area. This emphasis on quality and demonstrable quality assurance systems is widespread and a more prevalent concern now than earlier emphases on the need for evaluation (Thorpe, 1993a). However, the teaching quality assessment process represents threats as well as opportunities for evaluation of learner support or indeed any other elements in the provision of ODL.

Public accountability

In public sector provision of education, across the UK, Australia, New Zealand (Campion and Guiton, 1991) and a number of European countries, quality and standards in higher education have been subject to new forms of scrutiny and regulation. Universities have not necessarily lost their control of what counts as quality but they are no longer trusted to deliver it without inspection. Evidence and not simply assertion of quality is required, and the assurance that systems are in place which can reasonably be relied on to deliver what is claimed on a regular basis.

In the UK certainly, assessment of the quality of teaching, with the results publicly available, is set to continue, whatever the changes in the organis-ational details of how such assessments are made. Two types of scrutiny are involved here. First, there is the measurement of the quality of the teaching against a number of factors, such as teaching aims and objectives, student profile and progress, resources and learning outcomes. This is usually referred to as 'quality assessment'. Quality assurance refers to the existence of systems which ensure that the quality being claimed is delivered in practice. Quality assurance systems are typically audited by peer review, often including peers external to the university. Both kinds of quality, quality assessment and quality assurance, are necessary.

Whether or not this is a positive context for evaluation is not easy to judge. Evaluation is likely to thrive where there is encouragement for self-criticism and a self-improving climate within teaching departments. We should also recognise that it will thrive if it has some prestige and is rewarded, rather than paid merely lip service. There are signs of all these elements in the quality assessment processes that have been applied to the distance education delivery of higher education in the UK. There are equally some dangers, and both require exploration.

Departments being assessed have been required to submit a self-evaluation in which some evidence of a self-critical stance is seen as a positive sign. A glowing self-report with no admission of failures or action to put things right is not to be taken at face value. It might even be seen as grounds for suspicion that everything is not as right as claimed.

Quality assessment has also created a positive climate in relation to the rewards for evaluation, which are also more evident now than before an external system was in place. Peer judgements of the quality of teaching and student support are likely to be influenced by evidence of effective evaluation and improvement. Evaluation may make a positive judgement more likely, and thus it acquires an importance which it has often lacked. That has indeed been the case so far, in that where evaluation can be shown to take place, and to feed back improvements into practice, this is recognised as a positive indication of quality in teaching and student support.

So far, so good for evaluation. Where the quality assessment and quality assurance (QAQA) emphasis is less likely to support evaluation is perhaps no less easy to see. First, there is the risk that what is encouraged is compliance rather than a genuine attempt to implement best practice. Evaluation which is only initiated because of the imminent arrival of external assessors is unlikely to survive beyond the moment of public attention. The other risk is that QAQA leads to the expansion of particular sub-sets of evaluation models which dominate attention and undermine other approaches. In some cases, feedback and surveys become the specialised roles of non-teaching staff and 'evaluation' is located quite outside the responsiblities of academic staff.

This can be dangerous because it absolves teachers of the responsibility to evaluate themselves and to strive for improvement in relation to their own objectives and standards. It is also dangerous because, in separating off evaluation of quality from those who must deliver quality, it opens up the possibility that such staff can disown findings because they have not been involved in the process by which they were produced.

How can we in distance education operate so as to make appropriate quality assurance procedures work in favour of evaluation and not so as to undermine it ? The first point would be to recognise the existence of evaluation as a field of academic study in its own right and as a diverse set of practices for action and intervention in education generally. There is, for example, several decades of evaluation literature on topics at the heart of the quality debate: accountability, control and the measurement of process and outcomes in education, to take just a few.

There has also been fierce debate within the evaluation field around issues such as ownership of data and whether goal-free or goal-directed models are most appropriate. Interestingly, UK quality assessment by the Higher Education Funding Council has developed as a goal-directed version, in the sense that providers can set their own aims and objectives as the framework against which they will be judged. Goals formulated by any other stakeholders have not been used directly in establishing the criteria against which quality judgements are to be made.

It would also be appropriate at this point to recognise that distance education has generated a considerable body of evaluation literature which builds on the academic field and extends it into issues relevant to the distance model (Woodley and Kirkwood, 1987; Thorpe, 1993b; Calder, 1994). One of the positive features of our field has been the acceptance of the need for evaluation, given the innovative nature of the methods pioneered in ODL and the access orientation of many programmes (Freeman, 1991; Thorpe, 1993b). Now that ODL is a recognised player on the world stage of education and training provision—in some senses the only hope of our meeting the very ambitious targets being set for lifelong learning—we should remind ourselves of the evaluation tradition we have initiated and use it in the quality assurance processes we put in place.

In the following section, three approaches to evaluation are outlined, each of which takes a focus on learner experience and explores it in a different way. The distinctions between each type of approach are not hard and fast but do seem to separate out important differences of ownership, methodology and use of findings.

Evaluation as ideology critique and conceptual review

Distance education has been a fertile ground for conceptual review and there is a growing confidence in developing a critique of the ideology which goes with particular developments. The differences between ideology critique and conceptual review are not clear cut. An important difference, however, is that, in the case of ideology critique, the social and historical context within which certain ideas attain dominance, or suffer a reversal, is to the fore in the analysis. Conceptual review gives much less, if any, attention to these contexts of power and social relationship, and focuses on the analysis of ideas and their relationship to other ideas, in theory and perhaps also in practice.

The main aim of ideology critique is thus to explore in whose interests certain practices are being promoted, and to compare and contrast the rhetoric with which particular actors and social groups accompany their actions and pursue their goals. The methods used may draw upon historical analysis through a discussion of particular events, but data collection and empirical evidence is not the primary issue. The emphasis is on the social and political currency of ideas, who uses them, and to whose benefit.

Classic instances of ideology critique in the ODL field are offered by Harris' well-known study of the establishment and early development of the Open University UK (Harris, 1987), and more recently, Edwards' analysis of the relationship between wider economic and social change and the promotion of open learning (Edwards, 1991).

Harris bases his study on a critique of the rhetoric and early decision-making of a single institution, challenging its claim to be open. Edwards is concerned to highlight the way in which open learning has been used as part of economic practices which reduce employment, intensify working conditions and depend on a labour force which can be used, as necessary, on a temporary basis. This Post-Fordist stage in capitalist development (he argues) has found the flexibility and acclaimed cheapness of open learning methods well suited to its needs. In Edwards' words, the basis for his interest in Post-Fordism is:

> that the 'progressive' discourse and practice of open learning has burgeoned at a time of resurgent right wing economic liberalism. Possible conflicting partners (i.e. 'progressive' open learning and right wing Post-Fordist practices) are walking hand in hand into the sunset. Why is this? (Edwards, 1991, p. 36)

The answer Edwards gives is to contest the assumption that open learning is by definition 'progressive'. Rather than see it as the innocent appropriated by Post-Fordism, he argues that it is part of a Post-Fordist construction of the meaning of late-twentieth-century economic change, and of how best to respond to such change. The Post-Fordist premise is that the highly-skilled worker should be taken as the norm, and a goal all could achieve if they take up opportunities for education and training. The likelihood that large-scale unemployment is going to be the norm for a large minority, if not the majority, is obscured by this discourse in which individuals are assumed to be responsible for their own unemployment and also for taking advantage of opportunities for reskilling and further education.

Edwards, like Harris earlier, provides an important critique of practitioner discourse, in so far as this has offered an uncritical acceptance of ODL as necessarily more open, flexible, or progressive than traditional education and training. His arguments are, in effect, prompting practitioners to reflect on the social context in which practices are promoted and funded, and to see their own discourse as inescapably operating within structures of power and inequality.

Both Harris and Edwards have prompted a series of contributions taking issue with, or supporting, their views. This is also true of Rumble's critique of the terminology of openness and the use of open learning, although his approach is closer to that of conceptual review (Rumble, 1989). On the whole, conceptual review has been a more frequent approach than ideology critique, with many contributions to the debates over concepts such as industrialisation applied to the distribution of labour in ODL teaching (Peters, 1983; 1989), independence/autonomy (Daniel and Marquis, 1979; Gaskell and Mills, 1989; Morgan, 1985), and the importance of relationship, tuition and learner support (Thorpe, 1979; Sewart, 1987).

Both ideology critique and conceptual analysis play an important role within evaluation because they offer evidence of the meanings and interpretations in use in the field, and the value systems of the users. Such material is central to evaluative reports which take into account the intentions and motives of actors in the field, as in *Evaluation as illumination* (Parlett and Hamilton, 1972). This approach to evaluation aims to go 'beyond the numbers game' (Hamilton *et al.*, 1977) and to seek to portray the broader significance of innovation and change in teaching and learning practices, particularly as these affect relationships of power in institutions.

Evans and Nation have published two collections drawing together contributions in this tradition (Evans and Nation, 1989; 1993). In each case, the publication has been harnessed to meetings and critical commentary between the contributors in order to promote a critical community around issues raised in the book. As practitioners in ODL, the contributors emphasise reflection on their direct experience of some aspect of ODL practice and policy, with the aim of stimulating debate and sharpening the terms within which policies and practice are evaluated.

This perspective sits somewhat uneasily alongside the QAQA emphasis on 'customer satisfaction' and fitness for purpose. However, it could be argued that one of the signs of a high quality institution is that it is open to challenge and that it fosters work which is critical of its own practices. It is important neither to avoid engagement with the political and social theory implications of educational practice nor to allow evaluation to be subordinated to the demands of management for smooth-running institutions. The chapter in Evans and Nation (1993) by Woodley, Taylor and Butcher, for example, demonstrates the politically-charged nature of what may seem a detail of research, such as the wording of the questions about ethnicity on the application form for applicants to the Open University (Woodley et al., 1993). This account of the introduction and monitoring of an explicit equal opportunities strategy embodies many of the contradictions, not only for the OU UK (Evans and Nation, 1993), but for ODL in general. This dilemma concerns whether or not to go along with all the opportunities for the market development of 'packaged learning', both nationally and internationally, or to persist with some of the original ODL goals of access and openness.

Evaluation as institutional research

Evaluations in the institutional research tradition stress empirical evidence and tend to be dominated by the presentation and analysis of findings. They provide a strong contrast to work which would fall into either the conceptual review or ideology critique category. On the whole, they are carried out by professional researchers and evaluators who may themselves be contracted or employed by institutions, governments or funding agencies to carry out specific projects, either on particular issues or the performance of the institution as a whole.

Evaluation in this tradition is, for example, carried out by Zentrales Institut für Fernstudienforschung (ZIFF) at the Fernuniversität, Hagen, and by the Deutsches Institut für Fernstudienforschung (DIFF) at Tübingen University. This is also a major component in the evaluation carried out by the Institute of Educational Technology (IET) at the Open University UK, although staff do have 'room' to define and pursue projects of personal interest as well as the more directly-contracted evaluations.

An example which has drawn on both institutional and personal concerns in this way is the work that has been done to evaluate progress in the achievement of equal opportunities. Von Prümmer and Kirkup, for example, have studied the different rates of take-up by women at the Fernuniversität and the OU UK, and there have been various reports which document positive action initiatives pushed by particular individuals and groups, as well as those which present statistical data on the progress of the institution towards achieving equal opportunities targets which it has set for itself (Von Prümmer and Rossie, 1988; Kirkup, 1989; Kirkup and Taylor, 1994).

Since the key feature of this work is policy or institutional review, use of the findings is an important issue, and one which demonstrates most of the difficulties which have been documented in the wider field of educational research more generally (Nisbet and Broadfoot, 1980). In the context of the OU UK, one of the factors affecting use has been the positioning of the evaluation with regard to internal politics and relationships, bearing directly upon those most able to apply the results of an evaluation. During the 1970s, for example, the evaluations of the OU UK Broadcast and Audio Visual Media Research Group were more widely applied to broadcasting than were those of the Tuition and Counselling Research Group to the teaching and counselling in regions. This was in part because OU BBC Productions staff were a more cohesive group, resident in the same location and more able to control their 'product', than was the case with regional academic staff. Academic staff resident in regions are dispersed geographically and across several faculties, with only indirect influence on the quality of teaching which each tutor-counsellor or tutor carries out. There were other factors of course, but issues of power and organisation were crucial to take-up and use of evaluation findings.

This creates one of the continuing struggles for specialist evaluators, which is the timing and communication of the results of their work in such a way as to influence decision-making and events. Sometimes external pressures force institutions to turn to their evaluators for evidence which will support senior management's claims about the institution. This can create the unusual experience for an evaluator of finding an open door for discussion of the detailed evidence about this or that feature of the institution's performance. This was the case, for example, when the Department for Education reviewed the Open University in 1991, and posed challenging questions about a whole range of issues around which much folklore had gathered, but for which hard evidence was not easy to find. The input of IET researchers, with extensive experience of survey and statistical analysis of issues such as student progress and drop-out, became essential to the response made by the University.

It is only, however, in the context of an institution where there is continuing employment for institutional evaluators that the question of *framing* issues for evaluation arises. Staff on short-term contracts are likely to be expected to evaluate issues decided elsewhere and often by groups with a vested interest in particular outcomes. Where employment is protected, evaluators then have the 'luxury' of facing the challenge of control of their own work.

The challenges are various: to what extent should evaluation be initiated by researchers themselves, rather than done purely reactively at the request of senior management? To what extent should long-term research be pursued as the best strategy for answering questions which are of broad-based relevance to institutional concerns, such as retention of students, course choice and study patterns? These issues of control are sharply focused for staff who, as evaluators, can review one, possibly two decades of the policy- and crisis-driven senior management interest in evaluation. Issues come to the top of management agendas for a variety of reasons and create pressure on evaluators to 'come up with some answers'. Some degree of protection from this pressure is needed, however, if the snapshot approach of one survey after another is to be avoided, or at least balanced, by evidence of trends over time, and in-depth understanding of processes and outcomes.

Practitioner self-evaluation

Although there may be a degree of overlap in practice between practitioner self-evaluation and other forms of evaluation, the emphasis on one's own practice as the subject for reflection, research or evaluative review, makes practitioner self-evaluation a distinct form in its own right.

The practitioner as researcher or evaluator has antecedents in the teacher as researcher model which is still alive and well, in theory at least, within the pages of the British Educational Research Association's journal (Vulliamy and Webb, 1991). In practice, however, the position is more troubled and less certain than it was when Stenhouse and his colleagues, in the late 1970s, actively developed the ideas of teachers as researchers of their own practice (Stenhouse, 1975).

The teacher/practitioner as researcher is a model which draws upon interpretative sociology for its inspiration and which seeks to demystify the research process through validating the accounts of practitioners. The importance of the contribution has been justified both in relation to practitioners and to ODL more generally (Thorpe, 1993b). Practitioners evaluate issues which would otherwise not receive the attention of specialist evaluators, and in the process of carrying out evaluation, they themselves discover more about their practice and those it affects. It carries value both as curriculum development and as staff development.

One of the claims for practitioner evaluation, therefore, is that it avoids the key problem previously identified for institutional evaluation, in that application back to practice and use of findings is direct, without the intermediary group of policy-makers and management which creates problems for the professional evaluator. The sphere within which findings and insights are used, however, may well be restricted to the practice of the individual concerned, for whom limitations of time, support staff and expertise lead into small-scale case study as the most manageable methodology.

However, in the case of the OU UK, such case studies may cover the activities of several hundred students and several dozen tutorial and counselling staff. Both Kelly and Simpson, for example, have sustained important evaluative studies over many years and contributed to knowledge of the effects of

229

particular regional and central practices and the development of new initiatives (Simpson, 1977; 1995; Kelly and Swift, 1983; Herman and Kelly, 1994).

While acting as a tutor-counsellor, Simpson collated and analysed the records of counsellors working in one of the OU's study centres, and surveyed and interviewed local students, in order to evaluate, as he put it:

> *the usual trinity of perspectives, i.e. what the Open University believes is desirable, what part-time staff do, and what students actually need.* (Simpson, 1977, p. 60)

The frequency of contacts between counsellors and their post-foundation students was monitored, and the views of both were explored. Simpson was able to throw light on two approaches to being a counsellor: the 'surgery' approach versus the 'interventionist' approach. His findings suggested that more frequent early contact was established by staff adopting an interventionist approach, and that this provided a better basis for later contact initiated by the student.

The concept of intervention was developed considerably as a result of this evaluation and its publication in a journal circulated to all tutor-counsellors and University staff at that time. The substantiation of the effects of different ways of being a counsellor enabled clarification of the role required by the University, and informed the staff monitoring and staff development carried out by regional senior counsellors.

Other studies have focused on the need to retain students and to minimise drop-out which might result from poor or uninformed practice by the Open University. During the early 1990s, Kelly and Herman surveyed all new students in the North West Region who had notifed the University that they wished to withdraw by March of their first academic year. (The academic year normally begins every February, after several months of preparatory and induction opportunities during the preceding autumn.) These students can be termed 'active decliners' (some just drop out by not responding to University correspondence) and the response rate on the questionnaire was reasonable at 58 per cent (273 returns from 473 mailed).

This study, like many on this issue, identified 'personal factors' as the single most frequent reason given by students for non-continuation: job change, house removal, illness, children and family relationships and so on. However, it identified something else too: between 40 and 50 per cent of respondents (127 of the 473 who withdrew) stated that they *did* intend to study with the OU again, and a similar percentage had yet to finally make up their minds. Only 25 stated that they did not intend to study with the OU again.

These findings also accord with a study carried out quite independently in the East Anglian Region. The Region has mailed a leaflet to all new students who withdraw, every year for the last ten years. The purpose of the leaflet is to check whether action might have been taken by the University to keep the student studying effectively. An evaluation of student replies on the issue of reasons for withdrawal confirms again that personal reasons are dominant (Gaskell and Simpson, 1995). Many respondents were also prepared to consider reapplying to the OU when circumstances allowed, and the report notes that more could be done to encourage such ex-students to return. Our orientation at the level of policy-making in the University tends to assume that 'drop-outs' are an undifferentiated mass for whom the University is of no further interest. The University has tended to show a reciprocal lack of interest which is demonstrably not necessarily in either its own or its ex-students' best interests.

The particular studies mentioned here demonstrate two features which may apply to practitioner evaluation more generally. First, the selection of issues and methods for evaluation reflects the immediate decision-making context of practitioners, for the good reason that these studies are action-oriented. The motivation for the evaluation is both to understand the students' perspective and also to generate better information for action locally. However, the second point of note is that practitioner evaluation, well organised and reported, can reveal assumptions embedded in 'the system' as a whole, and which ought to be challenged. The examples discussed here, for instance, relate to the Open University's orientation to students who drop out early in their first course but who have not necessarily rejected the idea of study with the OU in the future.

A future for both evaluation and quality assessment

This chapter previously identified some of the ways in which quality assessment might have contradictory effects on evaluation, both undermining yet in some ways stimulating certain kinds of evaluation. It would be misleading, therefore, to conclude by suggesting that the two can cohabit in simple harmony. However, in relation to my own institution, cautious optimism about the future of evaluation could be justified at the present time. In a number of ways, quality assessment has been a positive stimulus for new forms of recognition and enhancement of evaluation. It is early days to herald a new beginning, but there are positive signs and a determination to build on the best of the past.

First, there has been a clearer recognition from senior managers that a University-wide framework for quality is needed. Since 1994, a Pro-Vice-Chancellor has taken responsibility for quality, and a Quality Assurance Panel chaired by the Vice-Chancellor oversees procedures and responsibilities. This has provided a much needed legitimation for the work of specialist evaluators in the Institute of Educational Technology and for practitioner researchers in Regional Academic Services and Faculties. It also enables the integration of these different perspectives and of those from specialist groups such as the Quality Support Centre. This Centre was set up in the Open University in 1993 as one of the outcomes of the end of the binary line and the closing of the National Council for Academic Awards. It carries out consultancies and services for UK higher education and thus brings into the Open University a much-needed insight into what other HE institutions take for granted and what, by extension, they might find unusual about distance education as practised at the Open University.

Second, the OU already has a strong tradition of evaluation and a variety of forms of feedback. Quality assessment does have a firm base on which to build and there has been a stimulus effect rather than the introduction of entirely new sets of practices. The stimulus has been both to quantitative surveys and to practitioner evaluation, with some promising institutional development created around the expansion of these activities in order to embed practices and integrate people.

Staff have been appointed, both in the Institute of Educational Technology and in Regional Academic Services, to expand the content and frequency of student surveys of courses and services. This expansion is building on regional initiatives to explore how data can best be used by regions for the improvement of services and academic support provided at regional level specifically. A joint IET and Regional Academic Services group has been set up to co-ordinate this collaborative development of institutional and practitioner research in tandem. A good beginning has been made in bringing together specialist researchers with academics who provide student support at faculty and region level. We are exploring, for example, how increasing the frequency with which we survey courses can also be used to generate data on a region-by-region basis. This would enable regions to have regular (probably annual) access to indicators of student satisfaction and response, which can be tracked over time. It might also be possible for one region to compare itself with others, or to establish benchmarks for provision of services to students.

Funding has also been found for quality-related initiatives undertaken by practitioners and inspired by any aspect of teaching and learner support. Efforts are being made to foster ownership of quality issues and to support small projects and local interests.

The OU does have a model in which a specialist unit (the Institute of Educational Technology) carries the major responsiblity for quality-oriented surveys which generate student feedback. It does recognise, however, that explicit evaluation of this type is something akin to the tip of an iceberg. It rests on much implicit monitoring and review of practice by people who would not consider themselves evaluators at all. These practices need to be supported and probably to be formalised, so that we ensure that they can continue and be protected from the potentially detrimental effects of increased workloads, which are endemic to organisations in both public and private sectors at the present time.

These are, I believe, all positive signs that the OU is using the opportunity side of external QA to good effect. If I were to identify the single biggest risk, it would probably be the increased workloads to which I have just referred. Staff who no longer have time to do their jobs to their own satisfaction cannot be helped by evaluation. Unfortunately, such work pressures are increasing in my own university and doubtless in many others. Distance education is promoted as a cost-effective mode of provision, and it would indeed be unfortunate if best practice in evaluation were squeezed out in the drive to continually cut costs.

Evaluation ought to be at the heart of the public process of accountability and judging effectiveness in distance education. In the final analysis, it is the process through which we test out whether we have reached our goals and targets on access and student-centred learning, and which stimulates the kind of critical awareness which is developmental, leading to improvements in practice. It provides an important means, both for individuals and for institutions, of taking control and shaping events in response to student and staff perceptions. It provides standards of self-criticism and analysis which are in the spirit of the most enlightened approach to quality assessment. This is surely the approach most likely to deliver quality for our students' benefit in the long term.

REFERENCES

Calder, J. (1994) *Programme evaluation and quality: A comprehensive guide to setting up an evaluation system*. Open and distance learning series (London, Kogan Page).

Campion, M. & Guiton, P. (1991) Economic instrumentalism and integration in Australian External Studies, *Open Learning*, 6 (2).

Daniel, J.S. & Marquis, D. (1979) Interaction and independence: getting the mixture right, *Teaching at a Distance*, (14), pp. 29–44.

Edwards, R. (1991) The inevitable future? Post-Fordism and open learning, *Open Learning*, 6 (2).

Evans, T.D & Nation, D.E. (Eds.) (1989) *Critical reflections on distance education* (London, Falmer Press).

Evans, T.D. & Nation, D.E. (Eds.) (1993) *Reforming open and distance education: Critical reflections from practice* (London, Kogan Page).

Freeman, R. (1991) Quality assurance in learning materials production, *Open Learning*, 6 (3).

Gaskell, A. & Mills, R. (1989) Interaction and independence in distance education: What's been said and what's been done?, *Open Learning*, 4 (2), pp. 51 & 52.

Gaskell, A. & Simpson, O. (1995) *Customer defection in the OU: 'Bailing out' revisited*. The Open University East Anglian Region Projects, Research and Other Developments, no. 19, Cambridge, UK.

Hamilton, D., Macdonald, B., King, C., Jenkins, D. & Parlett, M. (Eds.) (1977) *Beyond the numbers game: A reader in educational evaluation* (Basingstoke and London, Macmillan).

Harris, D. (1987) *Openness and closure in distance education* (London, The Falmer Press).

Herman, P. & Kelly, P. (1994) *You lose some: A survey of new students who declined final registration in the North West Region.* Open University North West Region, Manchester.

Kelly, P. & Swift, B. (1983) Tuition at post-foundation level in the Open University: Student attitudes towards tuition. SRD Paper No. 253.

Kirkup, G. (1989) Equal opportunities and computing at the Open University, *Open Learning*, 4 (1).

Kirkup, G. & Taylor, L. (1994) Gender and power: A case study from the UK OU. In Thorpe, M. & Grugeon, D. (Eds.) (1994) *Open learning in the mainstream* (Harlow, Longman).

Morgan, A. (1985) What shall we do about independent learning? *International Council for Distance Education Bulletin*, 15, pp. 47–53.

Nisbet, J. & Broadfoot, P. (1980) *The impact of research on policy and practice in education* (Aberdeen University Press).

Parlett, M.R. & Hamilton, D.F. (1972) *Evaluation as illumination: A new approach to the study of innovatory programmes.* University of Edinburgh, Centre for Research in the Educational Sciences, Occasional Paper no. 9.

Peters, O. (1983) Distance education and industrial production: A comparative interpretation in outline. In Sewart, D. Keegan, D. & Holmberg, B. (Eds.) (1983) *Distance education: International perspectives* (Croom Helm/St Martin's Press), pp. 95–113.

Peters, O. (1989) The iceberg has not melted: Further reflections on the concept of industrialisation and distance teaching, *Open Learning*, 4 (3).

Rumble, G. (1989) 'Open learning', 'distance learning' and the misuse of language, *Open Learning*, 4 (2).

Sewart, D. (1987) Limitations of the learning package. In Thorpe, M. & Grugeon, D. (1987) *Open learning for adults* (Harlow, Longman).

Simpson, O. (1977) Post-foundation counselling, *Teaching at a Distance*, 9 (Milton Keynes, The Open University).

Simpson, O. (1995) *Seizing the initiative on student progress.* East Anglian Region Projects, Research and Other Developments, no. 18. Open University, East Anglian Region, Cambridge.

Stenhouse, L. (1975) *An introduction to curriculum research and development* (London, Heinemann).

Thorpe, M. (1979) When is a course not a course?, *Teaching at a Distance*, (16), pp. 13–18.

Thorpe, M. (1993a) *Evaluating open and distance learning* (2nd ed.) (Harlow, Longman).

Thorpe, M. (1993b) Quality in materials design and production. Proceedings of EDEN Conference, May 1993, Berlin.

Von Prümmer, C. & Rossie, U. (1988) Gender in distance education at the Fernuniversität, *Open Learning*, 3 (2).

Vulliamy, G. & Webb, R. (1991) Teacher research and educational change: An empirical study, *British Educational Research Journal*, 17 (3).

Woodley, A. & Kirkwood, A. (1987) *Evaluation in distance learning* (Institute of Educational Technology, Open University, Milton Keynes).

Woodley, A. Taylor, L. & Butcher, B. (1993) Critical reflections on developing an equal opportunities action plan for black and ethnic minorities. In Evans, T.D. & Nation, D.E. (Eds.), *op. cit.*

Index